PENGUIN BOOKS

EYES ON THE PRIZE

Juan Williams is a top political analyst for Fox Television and a columnist for *The Hill* newspaper in Washington, D.C. He is a regular panelist for *Fox News Sunday*. A former award-winning *Washington Post* columnist, Mr. Williams also served as the paper's White House correspondent. During ten years at NPR, he was the network's senior correspondent and also the host of NPR's nationally broadcast afternoon talk show *Talk of the Nation*. In addition to prize-winning op-ed columns and editorial writing for *The Washington Post*, he has written for *The Wall Street Journal*, *The New York Times*, and Foxnews.com. A widely celebrated speaker he is also the author of seven books. Several of them have been bestsellers, including *Thurgood Marshall: American Revolutionary* and his most recent book, *Muzzled: The Assault on Honest Debate*.

Eyes on the Prize

America's Civil Rights Years, 1954–1965

Juan Williams

With the Eyes on the Prize Production Team

Introduction by Julian Bond

A Robert Lavelle Book

PENGUIN BOOKS

PENGUIN BOOKS
Published by the Penguin Group
Penguin Group (USA), 375 Hudson Street,
New York, New York 10014, USA

USA | Canada | UK | Ireland | Australia | New Zealand | India | South Africa | China
Penguin Books Ltd, Registered Offices: 80 Strand, London WC2R 0RL, England
For more information about the Penguin Group visit penguin.com

First published in the United States of America by Viking Penguin Inc. 1987
Published in Penguin books 1988
Published with preface by Judi Hampton and Veva Hampton Zimmerman 2002
This edition with a new preface, introduction, and epilogue published in Penguin Books 2013

Pages 307–308 constitute an extension
of this copyright page.

THE LIBRARY OF CONGRESS HAS CATALOGED THE PREVIOUS EDITION AS FOLLOWS:
Williams, Juan.
Eyes on the prize.
Includes index.
1. Afro-Americans—Civil rights—History.
I. Title.
KF4757.W52   1987   323.4'0973
86-40271
ISBN 978-0-14-312474-0

Printed in the United States of America
10   9   8   7   6   5   4   3

"I know one thing we did right

Was the day we started to fight.

Keep your eyes on the prize,

Hold on, hold on."

—from a traditional civil rights song

This book is dedicated to the memory of Louis Allen, Thomas Brewer, James Chaney, Addie Mae Collins, Jonathan Daniels, Medgar Evers, Andrew Goodman, Jimmy Lee Jackson, Herbert Lee, the Reverend George W. Lee, Viola Liuzzo, Denise McNair, William Moore, the Reverend James Reeb, Carole Robertson, Michael Schwerner, Lamar Smith, Emmett Till, Cynthia Wesley, and the other men and women who gave their lives for civil rights during the years 1954 to 1965.

It is also dedicated to the people of South Africa. May they come to know that no man is free until all men are free.

Contents

1954   1955   1956   1957   1958   1959

Movement Protests

- First White Citizens Council meeting July 11, 1954 Mississippi
- Montgomery Bus Boycott December 5, 1955——December 21, 1956
- Tallahassee Bus Boycott May 27, 1956————————March 1958
- SCLC founded January 10–11, 1957
- Prayer Pilgrimage May 17, 1957
- Little Rock Central High School August 1957————————May 1959
- Prince Edward County abandons its school system June 26, 1959

Politics

Election year
- Eisenhower reelected with Nixon

Legal Work

- Brown I May 17, 1954
- Brown II May 31, 1955
- ICC bans segregation on interstate travel November 25, 1955
- Autherine Lucy admitted to University of Alabama February 3, 1956
- Southern Manifesto presented March 12, 1956
- Alabama outlaws NAACP June 1, 1956
- Supreme Court rules on bus desegregation November 13, 1956
- First Civil Rights bill since 1875 passed August 29, 1957
- Cooper vs. Aaron September 29, 1958

Violence

- Emmett Till killed August 28, 1955
- Home of Martin Luther King, Jr., bombed January 30, 1956
- Shuttlesworth home bombed December 25, 1956
- Martin Luther King, Jr., stabbed in Harlem September 20, 1958

African and Caribbean Independence

- Sudan-January 1, 1956
- Ghana-March 6, 1957

1960	1961	1962	1963	1964	1965

• Greensboro sit-in February 1, 1960 ──────── Sit-Ins and Boycotts all over the south and in some northern cities • SNCC founded April 17, 1960	• Civil Rights organizations meet with Robert Kennedy, re: voting June 16, 1961 • Freedom Rides Summer 1961 • Albany Movement November 1961 ──────── August 1962	• JFK federalizes Mississippi troops: Ole Miss September 29, 1962	• Birmingham April–May 1963 • Wallace schoolhouse stand June 11, 1963 • JFK meeting with Civil Rights leaders re: March on Washington June 20, 1963 • **March on Washington August 28, 1963** • Birmingham bombing September 15, 1963	• St. Augustine March–June 1964 • Founding of MFDP April 26, 1964 • Mississippi Freedom Summer and Atlantic City convention, August 1964 • Martin Luther King Jr. awarded Nobel Prize December 10, 1964	• Selma January–March 1965 • King meets with LBJ February 9, 1965

Election year • Kennedy elected with Johnson				Election year • Johnson elected with Humphrey	

• Civil Rights Act signed May 6, 1960	• Federal Court orders Hunter and Holmes to be admitted to University of Georgia January 6, 1961 Riot: January 11, 1961 • ICC desegregation ruling September 22, 1961		• Centennial of Emancipation Proclamation January 1, 1963	• 24th Amendment eliminates polling tax on Federal elections January 23, 1964 • Supreme Court ruling on Prince Edward County May 25, 1964 • Johnson signs Civil Rights Bill July 2, 1964	• Voting Rights Act signed August 6, 1965

		• Los Angeles Riot April 27, 1962 • Ole Mississippi Riot October 2, 1962	• Medgar Evers killed June 12, 1963 • JFK killed November 22, 1963	• Riots: New York, New Jersey, Chicago, and Philadelphia • Goodman, Schwerner, Chaney killed June 21, 1964	• Malcolm X killed February 21, 1965 • Reeb dies March 11, 1965 • Watts Riots August 11–16, 1965

• Zaire-June 30, 1960 • Somali-July 1, 1960 • Dahomey-August 3, 1960 • Upper Volta-August 5, 1960 • Ivory Coast-August 8, 1960 • Chad-August 11, 1960 • Congo Brazzaville-August 15, 1960 • Gabon-August 17, 1960 • Senegal-August 20, 1960 • Mali-September 22, 1960 • Nigeria-October 1, 1960	• Sierra Leone-April 27, 1961 • Tanzania-December 9, 1961	• Jamaica-August 6, 1962 • Trinidad/Tobago-August 31, 1962 • Uganda-October 9, 1962	• Kenya-December 12, 1963	• Malawi-July 6, 1964 • Zambia-October 24, 1964	

**Preface to the
25th Anniversary
Edition**

The inspiration for this book dates to March of 1965. Even as he joined the throng of protesters crossing the Edmund Pettus Bridge in Selma, Alabama, my brother, Henry Hampton, knew he was participating in a historic event—and in a movement—that he would one day want to chronicle. It would take almost twenty-five years, but he never lost sight of that mission and in February 1987 his now legendary public television series *Eyes on the Prize* premiered and this companion volume was published.

The television series won instant acclaim, and in the months that followed it garnered numerous awards, including multiple Emmys, a George Foster Peabody Award, and a duPont. Critics and viewers alike recognized its power, and it became one of the most watched and most talked about public television series in history.

Likewise, this companion volume has enjoyed both critical and popular success, and in the years since its initial publication it has been hailed as the definitive comprehensive history of the early civil rights years. I am gratified by its ongoing popularity among the reading public as well as its use in high schools and colleges around the country. I am honored and pleased to see this twenty-fifth anniversary edition published, and I would like to thank Cindy Kuhn and Frances Kennedy for their efforts in the process of updating it.

Eyes on the Prize—both the book and the television show—dares us to examine our values, to question our perceptions, and to overcome our prejudices and remain in active dialogue with one another about injustice, intolerance, and racism. The stories in *Eyes* are about ordinary Americans who displayed extraordinary courage in a time that must not be forgotten. *Eyes* is also about the grass roots strategies and leadership values that created and sustained a more representative democracy. We are still on that journey, though times and generations have changed. This book and the *Eyes on the Prize* series remain a guide to making our nation's dream of freedom for all a reality.

Henry Hampton passed away prematurely on November 22, 1998, too soon for those of us who knew and loved him. His death has strengthened our resolve to expand Blackside's work and to continue Henry's mission to encourage a national dialogue on crucial social issues. More than anything Henry loved telling the stories of everyday Americans and their struggles to uphold the democratic aims of our country. I dedicate this anniversary edition of *Eyes on the Prize* to his memory; to the memory of our sister, Veva; and to that of our parents, Dr. and Mrs. Henry Hampton, whose sacrifices made it possible for us to contribute in this way. I applaud once again the *Eyes* production team who, coupled with Henry's vision, was critical to the success of the films and thank Juan Williams for his inspiring work in this book. Most important, I honor all the heroes of the civil rights movement, both known and unknown, who kept their eyes always on the prize.

—*Judi Hampton*

Acknowledgments   This book and its companion six-part television series are part of a project conceived by Henry Hampton, executive producer of Blackside, Inc., a Boston film company. Henry Hampton is an extraordinary man who, over the course of seven years, managed to turn his dream of capturing the spirit of the civil rights movement into reality. Not only that, but he managed to impart that spirit to his dedicated and remarkably talented staff. The inevitable money problems lurked around each turn, ready to devour not only the project but also the businessman. But Hampton never faltered. On the contrary, he displayed supreme strength in his idea and this project. Henry Hampton fought the good fight and won.

This book would not have been possible without the skilled and intelligent editorial direction of Robert Lavelle. Indeed, in every phase of the book's evolution—from conception and organization to research, writing, and editing—Robert has been the guiding force. His wise counsel and superb editorial skills were boundless, and I am greatly in his debt.

Among the additional key contributors to the book are Bennett Singer, who flawlessly and patiently assisted with research, writing, and editing; Frances Norris, who worked tirelessly to collect the pictures displayed here; Laurie Kahn-Leavitt, the project's senior researcher, who was consistently helpful and always willing to offer precise suggestions for improvement; Hannah Benoit, who worked her magic on the prose by line-editing the manuscript; and Diane Taraskiewicz, a copy editor whose sharp editorial eye was invaluable.

David Garrow read early drafts of the manuscript and provided an invaluable historical perspective. In addition, John Dittmer and Steven Lawson both reviewed the manuscript with historians' eyes. Clay Carson, Vincent Harding, and Darlene Clark Hine (along with David Garrow) advised the project's entire staff on this period of American history. During the research phase, the book received additional guidance from Tony Freyer, Wiley Branton, Aldon Morris, and J. Mills Thornton.

Thanks also to the staff of the Moorland-Spingarn Research Center at Howard University, specifically Dr. Elinor Sinnette and Charlynn S. Pyne; the staffs of the Schomburg Collection in New York City; the John F. Kennedy Library in Boston; the Columbia University Oral History Project; the Boston Public Library; and the Widener Library at Harvard University.

I would particularly like to thank the film producers, editors, and researchers who worked busily on the *Eyes on the Prize* television series but were always willing to share their knowledge and research to the benefit of this book.

Steve Fayer, a fine writer, read the material and offered valuable insights. Judy Richardson offered both inspiration and guidance in our attempt to keep the book true to the spirit of the movement. Ruth Batson helped us write a story that would reach out to as broad an audience as possible.

Doe Coover, the project's literary representative, and Patricia Mulcahy, our editor at Viking, both believed in the project early on. They helped make sure we all worked well together as a team. Pat displayed much-needed confidence that we could get the project done well and on time, and she shared her enthusiasm for the work with the other members of Viking-Penguin's thoroughly professional staff. Karen Bates-Logan and Gail Ross were very helpful to the project as well.

I would also like to thank Jeanne Jordan, a most literate film editor, who kept the book team going with good cheer as well as insights into people and events; Gregory Witcher, who tolerated me as a distracted houseguest for nearly a year; and Herbert Denton, my friend and mentor.

And finally, my heartfelt thanks go to my wife, Delise; to my children, Antonio and Regan; and to my parents, Roger and Alma Williams.

—*Juan Williams*
Washington, D.C., September, 1986

Project Acknowledgments

To complete a project like *Eyes on the Prize* requires not only dedicated and talented professionals but also support from those outside who believe in the idea. Our friends and supporters were many, and I cannot do justice to their contributions. But without the generous help of the following people, *Eyes on the Prize* would not have happened: Ruth Batson, Joe Breiteneicher, Bob Hohler, Laya Wiesner, Tom Layton, Susan Silk, Jane Rogers, Duane Silverstein, Jack Mendelsohn, Karen Bates-Logan, Faith Griefen, Judy and Carl Sapers, Kitty Preyer, Anna Faith Jones, Melinda Marble, Donna Dunlop, Jacqui Burton, Suzanne Weil, Barry Chase, Beverly Hassell, Janet Axelrod, Carrolle Perry, Betty Stebman, Lynn Walker, Adele Vincent, Jon Else, Peter Edelman, Sally Lilienthal, Vernon Jordan, Loretta Williams, Eliot Hubbard, Robert Preyer, Michael and Lillian Ambrosino, Paul and Marion Fishman, Vincent Harding, David Garrow, Ron Hull, Josh Darsa, Gene Katt, Janet Taylor, Walter Palmer, John Ramsey, Kay Villers, Jim and Glenda Manzi, Doe Coover, Wendy Puriefoy, Paul Ylvisaker, Ann Raynolds, Gyöngy Laky, Phyllis Friedman, and the hundreds of others who gave of themselves to make this project work.

In addition, my deep thanks go to the many foundations and corporations for their generous support. The names of these key supporters can be found on the staff page at the end of this book.

—*Henry Hampton, Executive Producer*
Boston, Massachusetts, September, 1986

Introduction

The civil rights movement in America began a long time ago. As early as the seventeenth century, blacks and whites, slaves in Virginia and Quakers in Pennsylvania, protested the barbarity of slavery. Nat Turner, Sojourner Truth, Frederick Douglass, William Lloyd Garrison, John Brown, and Harriet Tubman are but a few of those who led the resistance to slavery before the Civil War. After the Civil War, another protracted battle began against slavery's legacy—racism and segregation. But for most Americans, the civil rights movement began on May 17, 1954, when the Supreme Court handed down the *Brown v. Board of Education of Topeka* decision outlawing segregation in public schools. The court unlocked the door, but the pressure applied by thousands of men and women in the movement pushed that door open wide enough to allow blacks to walk through it toward this country's essential prize: freedom.

This book, and the television project that it accompanies, brings America's civil rights years to life with stories about the people and places of that time. Here are the heroes and heroines, the brilliant strategies, the national politics and politicking, the violence, the people who defended segregation as a Southern "tradition," and the faces of the unheralded people, black and white, who were the soul of the movement. Most of us are familiar with the heroic leadership of Martin Luther King, Jr. But the passage of time has obscured the lesser-known folks who created the movement that produced King—such people as Mose Wright, Fannie Lou Hamer, and Charles Houston. This story is really their story, for the movement itself belonged to them. The civil rights drama involved thousands of acts of individual courage undertaken in the name of freedom.

To read these stories was to me both painful and inspiring. I lived through these times. I was fourteen years old when the Supreme Court handed down the *Brown* decision. Like most young black people of the day, I didn't realize the far-reaching significance of the court's pronouncement. The highest court of the land had said that racially segregated schools were unconstitutional. In my naïveté I thought, "Well, of course segregation is wrong." And that was that. In 1955 I was fifteen years old, one year older than Emmett Till when he was killed while visiting relatives in Mississippi. When he supposedly flirted with a white woman, he broke a taboo that was as real in rural Pennsylvania, where I grew up, as it was in the Deep South. What happened to Emmett Till could have happened to me. I was inspired by the great Montgomery bus boycott that took place in Alabama in 1955 and 1956. And of course I followed the news accounts in 1957 when the federal government had to call out the army to enroll nine black children at Central High School in Little Rock, Arkansas. It wasn't until my days at Morehouse College in Atlanta, however, that I realized what the movement was all about and what it was up against.

On February 1, 1960, four students in Greensboro, North Carolina, kids about my age, decided that they'd had enough of racial barriers. They sat at a whites-only lunch counter at the local Woolworth's store, requested service, and refused to move until they got it. The sit-in movement had begun. A friend of mine, Lonnie King, handed me a newspaper with the story of the student sit-in prominently displayed. He suggested that we get something going in Atlanta, Georgia. A small group of us got together and organized the Committee on Appeal for Human Rights, and we held our first sit-in on March 15, 1960. On that day, I joined hands with thousands of other Americans in different cities, in different states, who took risks during those years to create the civil rights movement.

The movement changed my life. As a boy, I thought the most I could ever achieve was a teaching or administrative post in a black school. My father had been president of Lincoln University, which represented a status seldom attained by black Southerners, and he hoped I might follow in his footsteps. Anything more ambitious was unrealistic for a black child. But I would venture far beyond the limited horizons glimpsed from the segregated fifties. I would serve in the Georgia legislature for more than twenty years. I would teach at the University of Virginia for twenty years, a school I could not have attended as a student. And I would go to the White House as a guest of a black president.

My life—and that of Barack Obama—were among the millions of black and white lives profoundly affected by the great movement that spanned the years 1954 to 1965. This book chronicles that change as never before. First, it takes readers beyond the popular belief that a few larger-than-life figures such as Martin Luther King, Jr., and John F. Kennedy were the movement's most important players. That is not to diminish these men, but, as you will learn, they were not solely responsible for this era or its successes. That insight is important, because it reaffirms the truth that in America a movement of the people—and not the actions of one or two leaders—can effect change. And it is particularly important because nowadays few people believe it.

This book demonstrates its truth. In fact, such a movement could happen again, given the right conditions. It won't happen automatically, and no one, not even the most charismatic leader, can make it happen. No one can really set out to make it happen. For example, the four young men who sat in a Greensboro restaurant to protest restaurant segregation had no notion of where their actions would lead. But their courage inspired others. No one was waiting for a leader—that would only have killed their initiative.

I remember a meeting I once attended with Martin Luther King, Jr., at a hotel in downtown Atlanta. All of the hotel employees, the maids and bellmen, were lined up in the halls to catch a glimpse of him. I heard one person say, "Gee, we're glad you've come, Dr. King, to take care of our problems." In fact, King had come there for a meeting. I'm sure he cared about those people, but the fact that they had problems was not foremost on his mind. They would never get their problems solved if they waited for Martin Luther King, Jr., to do it for them. When people stopped waiting for someone else and formed their own movement in the 1950s, the problem of legal segregation was overcome. That movement molded a Martin Luther King, Jr., and perhaps a future movement will create another leader of comparable stature.

Not only does this important book remind us that ordinary Americans made the movement, it also reminds us of the role played by the Constitution of the United States. That document provided the framework within which people could act to change the nation for the better. The story of the civil rights movement is a great testament to the Constitution's strength. Although, as you will see here, that code of law had for some time been bent and twisted to deny black Americans their rights, it also provided the basic tool used by the movement to win justice. Even when movement activists broke local laws, they remained conscious of their adherence to the Constitution's provisions. They knew that segregation was wrong on the basis of the nation's highest law. People were willing to go to jail, to fight through the legal system for change, because the Constitution was their ultimate shield.

The era from 1954 to 1965 stands in sharp contrast to the complexity of the years that followed. The movement's philosophy had been one of nonviolence and commitment to achieving change within the American system of law. After 1965, that vision became clouded. The post-1965 rage of many blacks and the fires their anger left burning across America's cities sometimes obscure the glory of the movement's earlier years. I viewed an early screening of the film version of *Eyes on the Prize* with my children, and afterward my then seventeen-year-old son asked me where the more militant blacks had been during the 1950s when blacks were told to sit in the back of the bus or were refused service at a hamburger stand. I told him that many were on the sidelines. They always insisted they would not take any insults, that they would fight back. But when it came time for sit-ins or freedom rides, they stood aside, explaining they were too violence-prone to act nonviolently.

Some of that empty anger can still be heard today. People ask what the civil rights movement has done to help black America. There is still a great gulf between blacks and whites in educational attainment and income. Poverty and un-employment beleaguer a great many, and the birthrate among unmarried black women is high. The travails of black America continue despite the best efforts of the civil rights movement and in spite of the accomplishments it can claim. The legacy of slavery, segregation, and discrimination continues to press heavily on black America. This book is critically important to this nation today, 150 years after the Emancipation Proclamation, because it reminds every reader that black Americans have shown great tenacity and courage in continuing to strive for their rights as Americans, despite this national legacy.

Eyes on the Prize is a vital and necessary book for everyone who wants to understand what it means to live in this American democracy. This book is a close, precise look at the years 1954–1965. It is also lively, compelling reading. It reminds us of the great potential we all have as Americans to change our world. It is about Americans who were willing to risk their jobs, their homes, and even their lives to create an extraordinary movement. Between 1954 and 1965, an ever-widening group of Americans marched, picketed, demonstrated, and organized to bring about an end to legal segregation. The social movements of the sixties—the antiwar movement, the women's movement, and others—all followed in the wake of the civil rights movement. We have now gained perspective on America's civil rights years and can begin to appreciate the enormity of the accomplishment.

—*Julian Bond*

Eyes on
the Prize

Black and white fourth graders in Washington, D.C., 1954.

Chapter One

God Bless the Child

The Story of School Desegregation

"A lawyer's either a social

engineer, or he's a parasite on

society."

Charles Houston, 1935

Although Charles Houston carried a 16-mm movie camera with him wherever he went, no one would mistake him for a typical northern tourist visiting the South. First, he was a black man, and blacks didn't take sightseeing trips through the South in 1935. Second, he wasn't filming the scenic countryside or historic Civil War sites. His subject was schools: the buildings, teachers, buses, and students. Charles Houston was vice dean of Howard University's School of Law in Washington, D.C. He was recording the dramatic disparity between black schools and white schools in South Carolina. In that state, as in all southern states, black children were not allowed to attend the same schools as white children.

Houston was filming for the National Association for the Advancement of Colored People (NAACP). In 1930, South Carolina spent ten times as much on educating each white child as on each black child. Other southern states did little better—Florida, Georgia, Mississippi, and Alabama devoted five times more money to the education of white children than to that of black children.

Houston knew that it would take more than statistics to convince a nation that segregation was wrong. His film showed what those statistics meant to the lives of some of the twelve million blacks in America, nine million of whom lived in the South. He contrasted the unheated cabins and tarpaper shacks that served as schools for black children with the tidy brick and stone structures where white children learned.

Houston called his documentary, "Examples of Educational Discrimination Among Rural Negroes in South Carolina." He used it as a teaching tool for his law students at Howard University, as a documentary when he spoke on college campuses or at NAACP events, and as another piece of the argument he was preparing on the racial injustice in America's schools—an argument he planned to take to court. His name may be little known, but the results of his efforts were profound.

Charles Hamilton Houston was born on September 3, 1895, eight months before the Supreme Court decided the case of *Plessy v. Ferguson*. This case essentially told the South that segregation was legal. Houston would spend most of his adult life fighting to overturn that decision.

The only child of William Houston and Mary Hamilton, Charlie (as he was known) received the best education a young black child could then expect in segregated Washington, D.C. At the turn of the century, there was a severe housing shortage in the nation's capital. Thousands of blacks lived on the streets with little or no medical attention. Jobs for minorities were scarce, and separate facilities for blacks—beaches, restaurants, schools—were the unwavering custom. But Charlie's parents made sure their son was well educated. His mother left her job as a schoolteacher to take better-paying work as a hairdresser. His father attended Howard University in the evening, earned a law degree, and established a successful law practice serving middle-class blacks in Washington.

Mary Hamilton Houston was proud of her race. Although she looked white, she always made it clear that she was a Negro. Her clients in Washington were among the wealthiest and most powerful whites in the city. Mrs. Houston refused to allow her white clients to call her by her first name as they did most blacks in their service, and she always insisted on entering their homes through the front door.

William Houston worked diligently to secure a better life for his family. He eventually became a part-time instructor at Howard University. With what he earned from his law practice, Mary's income from her hairdressing trade, and an economical lifestyle, the Houstons were able to move into one of Washington's black middle-class neighborhoods.

Charlie Houston attended one of the finest all-black high schools in the country, where he became class valedictorian. Unlike most other black high schools, which were essentially vocational trade schools, the M Street High School's curriculum was based on college entrance requirements. There was no question that William and Mary would send their son to college.

At age sixteen Charlie left Washington to attend Amherst College in Massachusetts. He was the only black student in the class of 1915. Though his social life was limited, he proved himself academically. He was elected to Phi Beta Kappa and graduated with honors.

Houston returned to Washington to decide what to do with his life. His father helped him secure a position as the temporary replacement for a Howard English instructor on leave. Charlie taught the usual English courses, but also developed a new one: Negro Literature.

Shortly before the United States entered World War I, Charlie knew that he would probably be drafted. He did not relish the thought of fighting to make the world safe for democracy when America was neither safe nor democratic for its black citizens. He knew that, as a black man, he would be assigned to a segregated unit and kept on labor details. Houston decided that if he had to go into the army, he would go as an officer. Arguing that the army's all-black units should be led by black officers and not by whites as was the custom, Houston and other Howard faculty members and students petitioned the federal government to establish a

Charlie Houston with his parents, William Houston and Mary Hamilton, 1915.

black officers' training camp. Through persistence they were successful, and in 1916, at age twenty-one, Houston left Washington for officers' training camp in Des Moines, Iowa.

William Houston had always hoped that Charlie would one day join him at his law firm. But as dearly as he loved his father, Charlie was uncertain whether he wanted to enter the legal profession. The injustices he witnessed in the army helped him make up his mind.

In the army, Houston became a judge-advocate in military cases involving blacks. Essentially, a judge-advocate acted as a prosecuting attorney, digging up evidence to support a guilty verdict. But Houston learned that it didn't take much evidence to successfully prosecute black soldiers. In one case, after a thorough investigation, he concluded there was insufficient evidence to convict. The defendants were acquitted and, much to his surprise, Houston was told by his white commanding officer that he was "no good." The judge-advocate was expected to secure a conviction even without adequate evidence. In an even more disturbing case, Houston was appalled to watch the army summarily destroy the military career of an exemplary black officer and sentence him to a year of hard labor for disorderly conduct and insubordination. The inequity of the army's judicial system and the disproportionate harshness of the sentence raised Houston's ire. He later wrote, "I made up my mind that I would never get caught again without knowing something about my rights; that if luck was with me, and I got through this war, I would study law and use my time fighting for men who could not strike back."

1st Lt. Charles Hamilton Houston, 368th Infantry, American Expeditionary Forces, 1918.

Houston survived a tour of duty in France. On his return to Washington, he witnessed a series of race riots in his overcrowded hometown. He had returned to a country where black veterans were not always thanked for their efforts abroad. Blacks were attacked and even lynched in the South by whites who believed they had to be "put back in their place." Determined to "fight for those who could not strike back," Houston applied to Harvard University Law School. Once again he left Washington for Massachusetts, arriving in Cambridge in the fall of 1919.

An outstanding student, Charlie was the first black elected to the editorial board of the *Harvard Law Review*. He studied under Dean Roscoe Pound, then one of the leading proponents of "sociological jurisprudence," a new approach to law that relied on sociological evidence as well as legal precedent when arguing a case. Another of Houston's mentors was Felix Frankfurter, a founder of the American Civil Liberties Union and later a justice of the United States Supreme Court. Houston received his law degree in 1922 and continued at Harvard on scholarship, earning a doctoral degree a year later.

In 1924, Houston joined his father's law firm, fulfilling the elder Houston's long-held wish. The two had very different working styles. William, though a generous man, did not believe in giving free legal advice. "The services rendered are worthy of the fee," he would often say. He ran the office in a businesslike fashion—checking the accounts, balancing the books, and cutting back on expenses whenever and wherever possible. Charlie, on the other hand, took on cases for which the firm could expect little or no payment. For him the law was a tool for aiding the oppressed. But the divergent temperaments of father and son never hampered their close relationship.

Charlie began teaching again at Howard University, this time in the School of Law. He wanted not only to practice the law but to train others in it as well. Houston believed that black people needed black lawyers to represent them. He believed that if the legal system were to change, it would be because of the disciplined and consistent pressure exerted by a cadre of black lawyers.

Howard University, in Washington, D.C., was the largest all-black college in the United States. The college was established in 1867 to educate blacks excluded from other universities because of the color of their skin. While Harvard and a few other northern colleges offered admission to a select number of blacks, not a single southern white university opened its doors to black students.

Howard's law school would be pivotal if blacks were ever to make the justice system work for them. Houston's first years as a law professor could not be described as brilliant, but he quickly became a proficient teacher, and he developed a conviction that the legal education of blacks must be improved.

"The real problem in those days," says James Nabrit, whom Houston eventually convinced to join Howard's faculty, "was that we didn't have the facilities to argue these [civil rights] cases . . . We didn't have the lawbooks, we didn't have the precedent cases, we didn't have the sample briefs and records of procedure, and we couldn't use the facilities or contacts of the bar associations since they wouldn't let us belong." At that time, blacks were not admitted to the local Washington affiliate of the all-white American Bar Association. Houston realized the importance of continuing education for lawyers and of a local bar association with a well-stocked library. With a handful of other D.C. lawyers, he established the Washington Bar Association for blacks.

In 1927, Houston was named director of a national survey conducted by Howard University on the training and activities of black lawyers in America. Perhaps the study's most telling finding was that America had few black lawyers well versed in constitutional law. Without a thorough understanding of the Constitution, a

Black schools in the
South.

lawyer could not successfully argue civil rights cases in federal court. Houston convinced Howard's president, Mordecai Johnson, that the university should offer a fully accredited, full-time law program, and that a thorough understanding of constitutional law should be mandatory for all students.

"In all our classes," says Edward P. Lovett, one of Houston's students who later worked with him, "whether it was equity or contracts or pleadings, stress was placed on learning what our rights were under the Constitution and statutes—our rights as worded and regardless of how they had been interpreted to that time. Charlie's view was that we had to get the courts to change."

In 1929, at age 34, Houston was appointed vice dean of Howard's law school. He was asked, in effect, to turn the school around.

Because so few of Howard's law students could afford full-time tuition, most worked days and attended classes at night, just as Houston's father had. But the flexibility of Howard's curriculum came at a price. Howard law school graduates were mocked by judges for the poor quality of their work. The school's reputation was dubious and it was not accredited by the American Bar Association.

Reforming Howard's law program would not be easy. First, Houston closed down the night school, causing newspapers to editorialize bitterly against him. How were poor blacks to afford law school now? Wasn't this the program his own father had attended? Houston's response was firm: If students couldn't afford to attend full-time, they could work full-time and save money to attend in the future.

Houston also tightened the entrance requirements. He traveled throughout the country looking for the most promising black undergraduates to recruit for Howard, and he accepted only the best. He hired eminent legal scholars as guest lecturers and, after scrutinizing the curriculum, decided to extend the academic year. As he phased out the evening law program, Houston also phased out the part-time faculty. He demoted one full-time professor to instructor and invited respected black legal scholars to join the faculty.

Within two years of Houston's reign, the American Bar Association gave Howard Law School full accreditation, and the Association of American Law Schools elected the school to membership without qualification.

As vice dean, Charles Houston demanded much from his students. Thurgood Marshall, a Houston student who went on to become a Supreme Court justice, once said, "First off, you thought he was a mean so-and-so. He used to tell us that doctors could bury their mistakes, but lawyers couldn't. And he'd drive home to us that we would be competing not only with white lawyers but really well-trained white lawyers, so there just wasn't any point in crying in our beer about being Negroes. And I'll tell you—the going was rough. There must have been thirty of us in that class when we started, and no more than eight or ten of us finished up. He was so tough we used to call him 'Iron Shoes' and 'Cement Pants' and a few other names that don't bear repeating. But he was a sweet man once you saw what he was up to. He was absolutely fair, and the door to his office was always open. He made it clear to all of us that when we were done, we were expected to go out and do something with our lives."

Houston thought that the only worthy role for a lawyer was that of social engineer—someone who understood the Constitution and knew how to use it to

A Disturbing Pattern

When the Civil War ended in 1865, President Andrew Johnson appointed provisional governors throughout the defeated South. In 1865 and 1866 the state legislatures there enacted "black codes" that severely limited the new-found freedom of blacks. "Freedmen" were restricted in the kind of work they could do, where they could meet, and even the gestures and remarks they could make to white people. Whites could still whip blacks with impunity.

In the late 1860s, General Carl Schurz conducted an investigation of post-Civil War conditions in the South for the White House.

WHITE SUPREMACY!

Attention, White Men!

Grand Torch-Light Procession

At JACKSON,
On the Night of the
Fourth of January, 1890.

The Final Settlement of Democratic Rule and White Supremacy in Mississippi.

GRAND PYROTECHNIC DISPLAY!
Transparencies and Torches Free for all.

All in Sympathy with the Grand Cause are Cordially and Earnestly Invited to be on hand, to aid in the Final Overthrow of Radical Rule in our State.

Come on foot or on horse-back; come any way, but be sure to get there.
Brass Bands, Cannon, Flambeau Torches, Transparencies, Sky-rockets, Etc.

A GRAND DISPLAY FOR A GRAND CAUSE.

The emancipation of the slave is submitted to only in so far as chattel slavery in the old form could not be kept up. But although the freedman is no longer considered the property of the individual master, he is considered the slave of society . . . Wherever I go—the street, the shop, the house, the hotel, or the steamboat—I hear people talk in such a way as to indicate that they are yet unable to conceive of the Negro as possessing any rights at all. Men who are honorable in their dealings with their white neighbors will cheat a Negro without feeling a single twinge of their honor. To kill a Negro, they do not deem murder; to debauch a Negro woman, they do not think fornication; to take property away from a Negro, they do not consider robbery. The people boast that when they get freedmen's affairs in their own hands, to use their own expression, "the niggers will catch hell."

better the living conditions of underprivileged citizens. That was the kind of lawyer he wanted Howard to produce.

Oliver Hill, a former student of Houston who became an NAACP lawyer, said, "He was a man you either liked intensely or you hated."

While at Howard, Houston assisted the NAACP with many of its most important civil rights cases. With his students helping to prepare many of these cases, Houston had turned Howard's law school into a civil rights laboratory.

During this time, Houston traveled through the South with his movie camera. The NAACP was amassing data that showed just how appallingly inadequate black schools were in the South. The film became part of the data gathered during a well-funded NAACP legal campaign. In 1922, a white Harvard undergraduate named Charles Garland decided it was morally wrong to accept a fortune he was about to inherit because he had done nothing to create it. With his $800,000 inheritance he created a foundation to support liberal and radical causes. In 1929, the Garland Fund granted $100,000 to the NAACP to launch a campaign dedicated to giving the southern Negro his "constitutional rights, his political and civil equality, and therewith a self-consciousness and self-respect which would inevitably tend to effect a revolution in the economic life of the country." The first payment of $8,000 went toward legal research. Unfortunately, the NAACP received only one additional payment of $10,000 before the Garland Fund's money was lost in the great stock market crash of 1929.

In 1933, Nathan Ross Margold, a white, Harvard-trained lawyer for the NAACP, published a document that outlined a legal strategy he had developed. This strategy sought an end to segregated schools in the United States. The document became known as the Margold Report; it reacted against a legal theory called the "separate-but-equal" doctrine, which lay at the very heart of institutionalized racism in America.

The separate-but-equal doctrine was established by an 1896 case, *Plessy v. Ferguson*, in which the Supreme Court ruled that separation of the races is within the bounds of the Constitution so long as equal accommodations are made for blacks. The plaintiff, Homer Plessy, was white in appearance but was known to have had a black great-grandmother. He bought a train ticket from New Orleans to Covington, Louisiana, a small town near the state line, and sat in the whites-only car. When he refused to move to the car where blacks sat, the police dragged him from the train, according to news accounts, and arrested him. He sued the railroad, arguing that segregation was illegal under the Fourteenth Amendment, which was ratified in 1868 to ensure equal protection for the newly freed slaves.

The Supreme Court ruled against him, arguing that "separate-but-equal" was all that was required of the railroad under the Civil Rights Act of 1875. That law guaranteed all Americans the right to public accommodations, but did not outlaw segregation.

The *Plessy* decision gave legal validity to the system of segregation called "Jim Crow," after a black minstrel caricature popularized in song during the 1830s. Over the years the name worked its way into the American vocabulary, coming to represent the day-to-day segregation of blacks from whites. Cities, towns, and states passed statutes and ordinances that "legitimized" the Jim Crow way of life. There were Jim Crow schools, Jim Crow restaurants, Jim Crow water fountains, and Jim Crow customs—blacks were expected to tip their hats when they walked past whites, but whites did not have to remove their hats even when they entered a black family's home. Whites were to be called "sir" and "ma'am" by blacks, who in turn were called by their first names by whites. People with white skin were to be given a wide berth on the sidewalk; blacks were expected to step aside meekly.

But, as the Margold Report pointed out, the *Plessy* decision was sloppily thought out and poorly written. The justice writing the majority opinion had relied on cases and legal precedent that predated the Civil War and the Fourteenth Amendment. Margold outlined a strategy to challenge gradually the constitutionality of the decision. But the Great Depression so severely strained the nation's social fabric that the NAACP decided to shelve the plan until times improved.

Not until 1935 did the NAACP feel ready to resume its legal campaign against segregation. At that time Walter White, the organization's director, convinced Charles Houston to take a leave of absence from Howard University and direct the NAACP's crusade. Houston accepted the challenge.

At the Howard School of Law, Houston had made no secret of his main goal. He wanted to make the American legal system work for blacks, and to do so he was training a cadre of top-notch black lawyers. As the chief legal counsel to the NAACP, Houston now had his pick of those well-trained legal minds. For the next five years he worked seven days a week. It was not uncommon for him to put in a sixteen- or even eighteen-hour day. He once commented that "the test of character is the amount of strain it can bear."

Using the Margold Report as a starting point, Houston worked out his own detailed, long-range strategy. They would begin by attacking segregation in professional and graduate schools. If they could amass victory after victory, selecting the right cases to litigate and establishing precedent in a clear, ever-broadening line, they could then work their way through colleges, high schools, and finally elementary schools.

Houston chose to start at the higher educational level because there the injustice was most obvious and, to the public at large, change would be least threatening. In 1935, all Jim Crow states had white elementary schools and black elementary schools, white high schools and black high schools, even white and black colleges. But because so few blacks continued beyond college, most states did not provide them with separate law schools, medical schools, or other graduate-school programs.

"The test of character is the amount of strain it can bear."

Houston decided to begin with the law schools. Judges were, of course, lawyers, and as such could be expected to recognize the folly of having separate law schools. If the cases were presented properly, the courts would have only two options: admit black students to white law schools, or demand that states provide black students with adequate out-of-state scholarship monies. Houston was convinced that, under the Fourteenth Amendment, states could not legally export their obligation to provide equal facilities for blacks by offering out-of-state scholarships. He wanted to test his theory by finding the right case and working it through the system, all the way to the United States Supreme Court if necessary.

His former student, Thurgood Marshall, was by then a lawyer in Baltimore. He told Houston about Donald Gaines Murray, a young man denied admission to the University of Maryland's all-white law school because he was black. In June 1935, Marshall and Houston argued Murray's case in Baltimore city court. Houston contended that, clearly, there were no black law schools in the state of Maryland and, if a black citizen of the state wanted to study law there, he should have the opportunity to do so. Houston also argued that Maryland could not shirk its responsibility by offering a suddenly announced scholarship for Murray to study in another state. Murray aspired to practice law in Maryland, and an out-of-state legal education would thus not constitute equal treatment under the separate-but-equal doctrine. Marshall then showed the municipal court that it would be ruling within constitutional precedent by allowing Murray to enter the school.

The presiding judge ordered the University of Maryland to admit Donald Gaines Murray to its school of law. Although the state of Maryland appealed the case, the lower court's ruling was upheld.

The *Murray* case was an important victory for the nascent NAACP legal campaign—one of the first cracks in the wall of segregation. Houston and Marshall had forced a graduate school to integrate. In 1936, many of the southern states along the Mason-Dixon line began allocating more money to graduate and profes-

The Origins of Jim Crow

The name Jim Crow was first heard by the American public in 1832 when Thomas "Daddy" Rice, one of the first whites to perform comic representations of blacks, danced across the stage of New York's Bowery Theater and sang the lyrics of the song that would become America's first international hit:

Weel a-bout and turn a-bout
And do just so.
Every time I weel a-bout
I jump Jim Crow.

Rice's portrayal of the lame black man soon became a standard comic character of minstrel shows. By the middle of the nineteenth century, the name Jim Crow had evolved into a synonym for blacks and their "comic" way of life.

Much lore surrounds the actual identity and inspiration for Jim Crow. Some historians believe he was a soldier spotted by Rice in Kentucky or Ohio. Others say that he was a slave from Cincinnati, Ohio, or Charleston, South Carolina. Some scholars believe the name came from "old man Crow," a legendary slaveholder, while others suggest that it sprang from the simile "black as a crow."

By the early 1900s, Jim Crow described a far-reaching, institutional segregation that affected every aspect of

American life. Schools, restaurants, trains and all forms of transportation, theaters, drinking fountains—virtually all public and many private facilities practiced total separation of the races. The state of Florida went so far as to require "Negro" and "white" textbooks, and in South Carolina black and white cotton-mill workers were prohibited from looking out the same window.

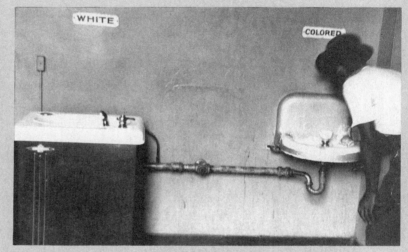

sional programs in black schools. Noting Marshall's solid performance in his first major case, Houston convinced his former student to work for the NAACP full-time as its Maryland/Washington, D.C. representative.

Marshall and Houston were a powerful combination. Marshall could disarm a room full of suspicious lawyers with a joke and temper Houston's seriousness with a lively sense of humor. A diligent worker, Marshall extracted more information from a casual conversation than most lawyers did from a legal brief. Houston read law books with precision and an eye to the future; his skill was more than matched by Marshall's ability to read people and their motives.

Off and on during 1936, Houston and Marshall traveled through the South. They gathered evidence, met with NAACP regional officers, and looked for cases with which they might challenge school segregation. Marshall's car became an office on wheels. As he describes it, "Charlie would sit in my car—I had a little old beat-up '29 Ford—and type out the briefs. And he could type up a storm—faster than any secretary—and not just with two fingers going. I mean he used 'em all. We'd stay at friends' homes in those days, for free." Teacher and student spent countless hours together in the Jim Crow South, discussing legal strategy, philosophy, and life.

Charles Houston
arguing in court.

In 1936 Houston journeyed to Missouri to argue another law school case similar to *Murray*. Lloyd Lionel Gaines, a black man of 25, was seeking admission to the all-white law school at the University of Missouri. The state claimed it would build a law school on the campus of all-black Lincoln University if Gaines would agree to apply there. No funds were yet allocated for such a law school and establishing it might take years, but the state said it would commence with the procedure as soon as Gaines filed his application. If he did not want to wait, they were prepared to pay his tuition at an out-of-state law school. Gaines lost his case in the Circuit Court of Boone County, as he had anticipated, and Houston appealed on his behalf to the United States Supreme Court. It took nearly two-and-a-half years, however, for the Court to hear the *Gaines* case.

The hearing was finally scheduled for November 9, 1938. On November 8 of that year, Houston rehearsed his argument for the *Gaines* case at Howard University before scholars and students. It was the first of many such Supreme Court rehearsals at Howard. Over the next fourteen years, NAACP attorneys would often present their major cases to the students and faculty before setting foot in the courtroom. It was a useful exercise for the attorneys and invaluable experience for the students who sat in. During the *Gaines* rehearsal Robert Carter and Spottswood Robinson, both students at the time, were in the audience. In years to come, both men would remember the valuable lessons Charles Houston taught them.

The next day, Houston stood before the Supreme Court and delivered a demand for true equality. He argued that it wouldn't be enough simply to set up a school and call it a law school; for the separate-but-equal doctrine to stand, the black and white schools had to be truly equal.

The Supreme Court ruled in Gaines' favor. He was entitled to attend the University of Missouri School of Law. The Supreme Court opinion made it clear that states had an obligation to provide an equal education for their citizens, black and white; that they could not send black students out of the state instead of providing in-state facilities to educate them; and that they could not ask students to wait while they built those schools within the state.

"Lawsuits mean little unless supported by public opinion."

The ruling had far-reaching implications. If the state had to furnish an equal legal education to its black citizens, then did the state also have to supply equal undergraduate colleges, high schools, and elementary schools? What of other public facilities—parks, hospitals, libraries?

In 1940, after working full time for five years as the NAACP's chief legal counsel, Charles Houston decided to return to his father's law firm. In a letter to his father, he wrote, "I have had the feeling all along that I am much more of an outside man than an inside man. . .I usually break down under too much routine. Certainly, for the present, I will grow much faster and be of much more service if I keep free to hit and fight wherever the circumstances call for action." In Washington, Houston resumed his part-time position as a member of the NAACP's National Legal Committee. At only thirty years of age, Thurgood Marshall was named as Houston's replacement at the association's national headquarters.

Free from the organizational constraints of the NAACP, Houston took on more controversial causes. In 1944, President Franklin Roosevelt appointed him to the President's Committee on Fair Employment Practices. Houston quit twenty months later, charging that the administration, now led by Harry Truman, was not truly committed to job equality. He also pursued scores of court cases dealing with such issues as segregation within the military, discrimination by taxicab operators, and racial prejudice in labor unions.

Perhaps more than any other desegregation lawyer in the 1940s, Houston realized the importance of speaking to people. "Lawsuits mean little unless supported by public opinion," he once said. "The really baffling problem is how to create the proper kind of public opinion. The truth is there are millions of white people who have no real knowledge of the Negro's problems and who never give the Negro a serious thought." In February, 1948, while giving one of his many lectures for the NAACP in Washington, he met Gardner Bishop, a black barber with a fourteen-year-old daughter named Judine.

Bishop represented a Washington, D.C., organization that came to be known as the Consolidated Parents Group. Two months before Bishop introduced himself to Houston, the group had launched a strike, keeping all their children home from the Browne Junior High School. Built to accommodate 800 students, the school was packed with 1,800, while the nearby white junior high school had hundreds of empty seats. Browne had so many students that they attended in two shifts.

The Consolidated Parents Group was made up mostly of poor blacks. They were skeptical of the "upper-class Negroes" of the NAACP, but held Charles Houston in high esteem. The group sent Gardner Bishop to ask if Houston would represent them in a lawsuit. Houston accepted without hesitation and without a fee.

Meanwhile, Thurgood Marshall, the NAACP's new special counsel, set up an organization to serve as the association's legal arm. In 1946, the newly formed Legal Defense Fund picked up where the Houston-Marshall team had left off— challenging segregated graduate schools. The association still planned to demand equal schools under the separate-but-equal *Plessy* doctrine. But two crucial post-war cases emboldened them to attack the doctrine itself.

The first involved a black mailman named Herman Sweatt, who in 1946 applied to the law school at the University of Texas in Austin. The school offered to set up a legal education program in three small basement rooms downtown, where Sweatt would be taught by part-time faculty members. The NAACP contended that Sweatt was not being offered a legal education equal to that which Texas provided for its white students. Before the trial began, 2,000 whites from the university rallied in support of Sweatt and cheered when the president of the student body said the institution should practice the democracy it preached. But the lower court ruled against Sweatt, and the long appeal process began.

The second case involved a sixty-eight-year-old black professor who had been refused admission to the doctoral program in education at the University of Oklahoma. Several years later, Marshall told a group of black newspaper executives about the graduate school desegregation campaign. "The Dixiecrats and the others said it was horrible. The only thing Negroes were trying to do, they said, was to get social equality. As a matter of fact, there would be intermarriage, they said. The latter theory was the reason we deliberately chose Professor McLaurin. We had eight people who had applied and who were eligible to be plaintiffs, but we deliberately picked Professor McLaurin because he was sixty-eight years old and we didn't think he was going to marry or intermarry—they could not bring that one on us, anyhow."

The special district court that decided the case ordered the state "to provide the plaintiff with the education he seeks as soon as it does for applicants of any other group." But when McLaurin finally matriculated at the university, he was required to sit at a desk surrounded by a railing marked "reserved for colored." He also had to eat at a separate table in the cafeteria and was restricted to his own table at the library. Marshall appealed the case to the Supreme Court, arguing that McLaurin was not being offered an equal education. Although he attended the same classes, ate the same food, and studied from the same books as the other students, he was not getting an equal education because of the daily harassments and restrictions.

The *McLaurin* and *Sweatt* cases were heard by the Supreme Court on the same day in April, 1950. The eleven southern states joined forces and filed an *amicus curiae* (a "friend of the court" brief that supports one party in an argument). The states maintained that *Plessy* was the governing principle and that all of the precedents supported a decision against the mailman who wanted to be a lawyer. But Thurgood Marshall and the NAACP got support from an unexpected source: the Justice Department filed an *amicus* brief in both cases, arguing that *Plessy* was wrong and that the Supreme Court should overrule it. It was a radical step.

Just six weeks before the Supreme Court decided these two important cases, Charles Houston lay in a hospital in Washington, D.C. He had suffered a severe heart attack. For two-and-a-half years he had worked diligently on the Consolidated Parents Group case. With his health failing rapidly, Houston asked his client, Bishop, to see his friend and colleague James M. Nabrit, the lawyer who was then secretary of Howard University and later became its president.

Nabrit proposed a different approach to the case. Instead of asking for black schools equal to those available to whites, Nabrit suggested that they challenge the very concept of racial segregation in the school system.

"When [Charlie] was on the death bed, he sent for me and asked me to take these cases," Nabrit remembers. "I [said], 'I am going to decide on the legal theory myself.' So he said, 'What do you mean?' I said, 'You know, for the last three years, Charlie, I have been trying to get you all to agree that you would take these cases and fight them on the grounds that segregation itself is unconstitutional . . . If I take these cases I am telling you now I am going to abandon this separate-but-equal theory you have, and I am going to draft a new theory. I am going to try these cases on the theory that segregation *per se* is unconstitutional.' He said, 'I'm glad to hear you [say] that, 'cause I'll rest better, 'cause I've about come to that position myself,'" Nabrit recalls.

Nabrit met with Gardner Bishop and told him that he would not pursue the equalization case the way Houston had mapped it out, but if Bishop would gather a group of plaintiffs willing to attack segregation directly, Nabrit would be glad to represent them. Bishop agreed. The case came to be known as *Bolling v. Sharpe. Bolling* was twelve-year-old Spottswood Bolling, Jr. C. Melvin Sharpe was the president of the Board of Education of the District of Columbia.

On April 20, 1950, Charles Houston died at the age of fifty-four. The pallbearers at his funeral were friends, colleagues and brothers in the legal struggle for racial equality—Benjamin F. Amos, Joseph Waddy, George Marion Johnson, Edward P. Lovett, Phineas Indritz, Oliver W. Hill, and Thurgood Marshall.

On June 5, 1950, the Supreme Court handed down its decisions on the *Sweatt* and *McLaurin* cases, concurring with the lawyers Charles Houston had trained twenty years earlier. However, the justices carefully wrote their decisions as narrowly as possible. The Court did not overturn *Plessy*; it applied its findings only to graduate schools. But it did say, in effect, that separate-but-equal education was not just a slogan. The equality had to be genuine or the separation was unconstitutional.

The Legal Defense Fund had come very close to getting the Supreme Court to overturn *Plessy*. Like Nabrit and Houston, many of the NAACP lawyers wondered if the time had come to launch an all-out campaign that would force the Court to decide the very constitutionality of the separate-but-equal doctrine. The rulings by the federal courts indicated to some that the existence of segregated schools, no matter how good they were, implied inferiority—that separate could never be equal.

However, if the lawyers challenged the doctrine and lost, it could be many years before the Legal Defense Fund could prepare a new case and broach the doctrine's constitutionality once again. The Supreme Court is generally loath to reconsider one of its own decisions.

Thurgood Marshall called a series of meetings with legal scholars and members of the Legal Defense Fund. In June of 1950, the NAACP held a conference in New York City. It was attended by forty-three lawyers and fourteen branch and state conference presidents. After much discussion, they agreed that, in all their future education cases, they would seek to obtain schooling on a nonsegregated basis.

Hedging their bets, the lawyers decided to attack segregation on two fronts. First, they would confront *Plessy v. Ferguson* head on and argue that the separate-but-equal doctrine was unconstitutional under the Fourteenth Amendment. But in case that strategy failed, they would also argue that schools should be truly equal under the *Plessy* doctrine and that the only way to equalize the schools was to integrate them. The lawyers referred to this approach as their "bow with two strings."

To show that separate schools could never be equal, the NAACP had to prove that the consequences of segregation—the psychological, intellectual, and financial damage—precluded equality. The Legal Defense Fund lawyers called on all the NAACP offices to gather cases from across the nation to use as ammunition for the constitutional cannon they were about to fire. They wanted cases from different states and different situations. A broad attack would make it harder for the Court to hand down a decision limited to a particular case. With 2.2 million black students in the nation's all-black elementary schools, the search didn't take long.

South Carolina's Clarendon County provided the first chance to attack segregation in the elementary schools. There were nearly three times as many black students as white students in Clarendon, but the white students received more than sixty percent of the educational funds. The per capita spending for white students was $179 per year; for black students, $43. Not much had changed since Charles Houston toured that part of the state on his filming trip in the 1930s. In late 1950, the NAACP brought a suit against the school board for not putting enough money and teachers into the black schools. Twenty black parents, led by the Reverend J. A. DeLaine, signed the suit. The first name was that of thirty-four-year-old Harry Briggs, a father of five, so the case bears his name.

Whites throughout Clarendon County exerted pressure on those who had brought the suit. Bank loans were called in, people were fired, and stores refused to supply farmers with seed for planting and machines for harvesting.

Liza Briggs, the wife of Harry Briggs, recalls, "I was working at the Summerton Motel. The White Council of Summerton came down and told [my boss] if he didn't fire the women who signed the petition that they would close the business down. They wouldn't let the trucks come and deliver. So they called us in and asked . . . that we take our names off the petition in order to work . . . I told him 'no,' I didn't want to do that because we would be hurting the children, and I'd rather give up my job and keep my name on there. So in about two weeks' time I was fired. Not only me, the rest of them who had anything to do with the

"Segregation is the way in which a society tells a group of human beings that they are inferior to other groups..."

petition, they all was fired."

Knowing that their new approach to these education cases required proof of damage caused by segregation, Robert Carter of the Legal Defense Fund contacted black psychologist Kenneth Clark, a fellow Howard University graduate who had done his doctoral work at Columbia University. For several years Clark had been studying the effects of segregation on children by using dolls in interviews with students. It was highly unorthodox evidence to present in a courtroom, but the situation called for unusual legal ammunition.

William Coleman, one of the NAACP attorneys, was extremely skeptical of using Clark's findings. He thought that talking about dolls in a courtroom would be a joke. But Thurgood Marshall was willing to use Clark's approach. "I told the staff that we had to try this case just like any other one in which you would try to prove damages to your client. If your car ran over my client, you'd have to pay up, and my function as an attorney would be to put experts on the stand to testify to how much damage was done. We needed exactly that kind of evidence in the school cases."

Thurgood Marshall, Robert Carter, and Kenneth Clark rode the train from New York City to Clarendon County. Black and white dolls in hand, Clark went to Scott's Branch, a joint elementary and high school for black children. The childrens' parents sent two men along to protect the psychologist from harassment by whites.

Clark tested sixteen black children, aged six to nine. Ten of the children looked at the black and white dolls Clark showed them and said they liked the white doll better. Eleven of them added that the black doll looked "bad." Nine of the youngsters said the white doll looked "nice." While all the children stated correctly which doll was black and which was white, seven of the sixteen students said they saw themselves as the white doll.

Clark recalls, "The most disturbing question—and the one that really made me, even as a scientist, upset—was the final question: 'Now show me the doll that's most like you.' Many of the children became emotionally upset when they had to identify with the doll they had rejected. These children saw themselves as inferior, and they accepted the inferiority as part of reality." The results matched those from similar tests Clark had conducted throughout the South.

"Segregation was, is, the way in which a society tells a group of human beings that they are inferior to other groups of human beings in the society," Clark said in a recent interview. "It really is internalized in children, learning they cannot go to the same schools as other children, that they are required to attend clearly inferior schools than others are permitted to attend. It influences the child's view of himself."

Clark's data and the findings of other social scientists formed one "string" of the NAACP's "bow." The studies showed that the damage wrought by the mere existence of segregation causes inequality. Separate could never be equal, no matter how comparable the separate schools were. The other string of the bow was the statistical evidence showing that, within the separate-but-equal system, the black schools were grossly unequal: In Clarendon County, the net worth of the three black schools for 808 children was one-fourth the value of two schools that housed 276 white children. There was one white teacher for every twenty-eight white students; one black teacher for every forty-seven black students.

Even so, the federal district court ruled that the separate-but-equal doctrine was not violated. In a two-to-one decision, the court found Clark's psychological data irrelevant to the case. As for the inequities in the facilities for black children, the court asked that the county correct the differences and send a report to the court.

The lone dissent came from Judge J. Waties Waring, a white man who had long opposed segregation. "There is absolutely no reasonable explanation for racial prejudice," Waring wrote. "It is all caused by unreasoning emotional reactions and these are gained early in childhood . . . Segregation in education can never produce equality and . . . is an evil that must be eradicated."

The Legal Defense Fund lawyers had not expected to win the case at this level. But they had presented evidence that showed the consequences of segregation and that would later help them through the appeals process. Waring's dissent offered them hope. Marshall appealed the *Briggs* decision to the Supreme Court, but he had to wait nearly two years for the appeal to be heard.

A week after the trial ended, some of the lawyers from the *Briggs* case packed their suitcases and headed for Topeka, Kansas, to take on the next case.

Seven-year-old Linda Brown, who lived in Topeka, had to cross railroad tracks in a nearby switching yard and wait for a rickety bus to take her to a black school. It wasn't the worst that black children had to endure, but soft-spoken Oliver Brown was fed up with his child having to go to the other side of town when there was a good school much closer to home—a white school.

"The issue came up and it was decided that Rev. Brown's daughter would be the goat, so to speak," remembers Arthur Fletcher, then a member of the Topeka NAACP and later an assistant secretary of labor in the Nixon administration. "He put forth his daughter to test the validity of the [law], and we had to raise the money."

The children of the *Brown* case: (top row) Harry Briggs, Jr., Ethel Belton, (bottom row) Dorothy Davis, Linda Brown, and Spottswood Bolling.

The Dolls Test:

An Interview with Kenneth Clark

In 1939 and 1940, psychologist Kenneth Clark and his wife, Mamie Phipps, tested black children in Washington, D.C., and New York City to determine how the children perceived themselves. The test revealed that the Washington students, who attended segregated schools, had lower self-esteem than the black children in New York. The researchers published their study in the Spring, 1940 issue of the *Journal of Experimental Education*, unaware that fourteen years later the Dolls Test would become important evidence against segregation in *Brown vs. Board of Education*.

We did the Dolls study before we had any idea that it would be relevant to public policy. In fact, we conducted the study fourteen years before *Brown*. The NAACP lawyers learned about it and asked us if we thought it was relevant to what they were planning to do in terms of the *Brown* cases. We said it was up to them to make that decision— that we hadn't done the testing for litigation, but to communicate to our colleagues in psychology the influence of race, color, and status on the self-esteem of children.

The Clarendon County testing was requested by the lawyers who had read the material we had published. The lawyers wanted to know if their plaintiffs, the black children in Clarendon County, would show the same results as those we had tested earlier. I wasn't all that happy about going to Clarendon County, because of the violence and threats of violence. My wife didn't want me to go. She was from the South and she was more aware of the potential for violence than I. But we had to test those children. The head of the NAACP in South Carolina went with me. I used the same methods as in the earlier studies, and the results were the same.

I remember one child in Arkansas, a little boy, from the earlier study. When I asked him the key question ["Which doll is most like you?"], he looked up and smiled, laughed, and pointed to the brown doll, and said, "That's a nigger. I'm a nigger." I found that as disturb-

ing, if not more disturbing, than the children in Massachusetts who would refuse to answer that question, or would cry and run out of the room. The children in the South did not reject the feelings of inferiority that the question implied [by having to identify with the doll they had deemed inferior]. In fact, they sort of accepted it as part of the reality of their lives. The children in the North more overtly and emotionally rejected their feelings of inferiority.

Some of the lawyers felt the case should not be "contaminated" by psychological evidence. Other lawyers, particularly Robert Carter, argued that you couldn't overthrow [*Plessy*]* by just sticking to the law. To show damage and a violation of equal protection under the Fourteenth Amendment, you had to show that being segregated actually damaged the children. Carter felt that the test results were evidence of the damaging effect of segregation on children. I couldn't play any part in their discussion, but [Thurgood] Marshall made the decision and accepted the test results as part of the evidence. I was very, very happy when Thurgood called me at the college on May 17, 1954, and told me not only that the decision [to eliminate segregation] had come down but that Justice Warren had specifically mentioned the psychological testimony as key.

*Plessy v. Ferguson (see p. 9).

Arguing *Brown v. Board of Education of Topeka* would be Robert Carter, Thurgood Marshall's top assistant, and Jack Greenberg, a young white lawyer from the Bensonhurst section of Brooklyn. Greenberg sought out experts to testify to the detrimental effects of segregation on black children. The first was a white professor at the University of Kansas City, Hugh W. Speer. Despite criticism from his colleagues for cooperating with "outside agitators" like the NAACP, Speer agreed to testify. He told the court that, in Topeka, the school budgets and facilities provided for black students and for white students were inequitable. But these differences were not great in themselves, he added. The scarring injury of school segregation was inflicted by the racial isolation itself: "If colored children are denied the experience in school of association with white children, who represent ninety percent of our national society in which colored children must live, then the colored children's curriculum is being greatly curtailed. The Topeka school curriculum . . . cannot be equal under segregation."

Speer's testimony was supported by that of Horace B. English, a professor of psychology at Ohio State University. English testified that blacks were not necessarily slower learners than whites. The problem facing black students, he said, was that "if we din it into a person that it is unnatural for him to learn certain things, if we din it into a person that he is incapable of learning, then he is less likely to learn."

Wilbur B. Brookover, a social psychologist Greenberg enlisted in Michigan, told the court that segregation made black children feel "subordinate, inferior."

The defense attorney dismissed these arguments as frivolous. When white children don't make the football team, aren't they pained? he queried. When white children don't get asked to the big dance, don't they feel isolated? He added that some blacks who went to segregated schools seemed no worse for it— accomplished people like Langston Hughes and W. E. B. DuBois.

In his ruling, Judge Walker Huxman noted that he was impressed by the plaintiff's expert witnesses. But he added that, under the doctrine of separate-but-equal, the Topeka School Board had maintained a school system for blacks and the spending discrepancies between the two school systems were not large. He ruled that no laws were being violated and dismissed the plaintiff's suit.

However, in his opinion Judge Huxman wrote that "segregation of colored children in public schools has a detrimental effect upon the colored children—the impact is greater when it has the sanction of the law—for the policy of separating the races is usually interpreted as denoting the inferiority of the Negro group." That admission, coupled with the Legal Defense Fund's steady pressure on graduate schools, kept alive the hope of one day dismantling the separate-but-equal doctrine.

Throughout the nation, the NAACP continued to gather cases. Spottswood Robinson, one of the Howard University law students who watched Charles Houston rehearse the *Gaines* case there in 1938, was now a special agent for the NAACP in Virginia. Robinson had been litigating case after case against unequal school facilities for blacks. By 1948 Robinson and other NAACP lawyers had forced improvements in some black schools and won equalization of black and white teacher pay in one Virginia county. But they hadn't yet attacked the inequities in Prince Edward County. Moton High School, in that county's town of Farmville, held twice as many students as it was designed for and had no cafeteria or gym. The county's only concession to the blacks' complaints was to erect tar-paper and wooden shacks to hold the overflow of students. The highest paid teacher at Moton earned less than the lowest paid white teacher in the county.

Whites in Prince Edward County generally disdained the growing pressure from some black ministers and parents for a new school. A *Saturday Evening Post* writer reported from Farmville that a white city leader had said, "If the Negroes wanted a library or a swimming pool we'd . . . help them get it. But they're not interested. They want pool rooms and dance halls . . . That's what they've got— and they're happy with it. We have a saying around here: Be a Negro on a Saturday night and you'll never want to be a white man again."

In April 1951, a Moton High School junior named Barbara Rose Johns plotted a rebellion at the school. For months she had watched the local school board rebuff black parents' repeated demands for educational improvements. She decided it was time for the students to take matters into their own hands. First she had an accomplice telephone the school's principal and ask him to go to the Greyhound bus terminal under the pretext of picking up two truants. While he was gone she forged the principal's signature on notes ordering the teachers to bring all students to the auditorium for a special assembly. Saying that the students were planning a surprise event, Johns convinced the teachers to leave the auditorium. She then told the students the truth: She wanted them to go on strike to demand a better school. The town jail could hold a few of them, she challenged, but not all 450 of them. The students burst into cheers that quickly hushed when the principal reappeared.

Although he entreated them not to strike, he didn't order them back to class. Instead, he left the auditorium and allowed the young rebels to finish their deliberations. The schoolchildren decided to strike the following day.

Robert L. Carter
NAACP Legal Defense
Fund, Inc.

Thurgood Marshall
NAACP Legal Defense
Fund, Inc.

Thurgood Marshall
(center) and other
lawyers for the *Brown*
case entering the
Supreme Court, February
4, 1953.

On the third day of the Moton strike, at Barbara Johns' request, Spottswood Robinson went to Farmville to meet with the students. He planned to tell them that, in this part of the state, there were few moderate whites who might be receptive to their strike, and that without the support of moderate whites they had little chance of success. Instead, Robinson was won over by the fiery girl of sixteen he found leading the strike. The students were united behind her and had drawn up a list of their demands. Robinson told them that if they could get the support of their parents to attack segregation head-on and not settle for equalization, then the NAACP would represent them.

NAACP organizer Lester Banks met with the youngsters' parents. They agreed to the Legal Defense Fund's terms. A month after the two-week school strike began, Robinson filed *Davis v. County School Board of Prince Edward County*. The first name on the list of plaintiffs was that of Dorothy E. Davis, the fourteen-year-old daughter of a Prince Edward County farmer. Spottswood Robinson and his clients—117 Moton High School students—asked that the state of Virginia abolish its mandate of segregated schools.

After the strike Barbara Johns moved to Montgomery, Alabama, to live with her uncle, the Reverend Vernon Johns, lest she attract angry reprisals from whites. Pastor of the Dexter Avenue Baptist Church, Johns was fighting the ill treatment of blacks on Montgomery's city buses. He retired soon after Barbara came to live with him, and was replaced by a young minister named Martin Luther King, Jr.

Despite the efforts of students and parents, the NAACP lost the Moton High School case. In 1953, the three-man Federal District Court unanimously ruled that separate schools resulted not from racism but from Southern "mores." The Legal Defense Fund appealed the case to the United States Supreme Court.

The Supreme Court was well aware of the Legal Defense Fund's efforts to challenge school segregation. As the cases worked their way through the appeals process, more and more information was laid at the doorstep of the country's highest court.

Two important school segregation cases were already waiting to be heard by the Court. *Brown v. Board of Education of Topeka* had been there for a while, and it seemed the Court was stalling. The more diverse the cases were, the more difficult it would be to garner a broadly written opinion that might abolish segregated schooling in all of America. The Legal Defense Fund staff assumed that the Court was not yet ready to decide the constitutionality of the separate-but-equal doctrine. But in June 1952, the Court announced that it would hear *Briggs v. Clarendon County* together with *Brown* in its coming autumn term.

On Behalf Of The South

In 1962, James Jackson Kilpatrick, then the editor of *The News Leader* in Richmond, Virginia, wrote *The Southern Case for School Segregation*. In the following excerpt, he responds to the Supreme Court's *Brown* decision and addresses what he sees as the inability of northerners to understand the mind of the South. Kilpatrick, author of *The American South* and *The Writer's Art*, is now a contributing editor of William Buckley's *National Review* and a frequent commentator on national television and radio programs.

My father came from New Orleans. His father, a captain in the Confederate Army, returned from the War and established a prosperous business in ship chandlery there. And though I myself was born in Oklahoma, Father having moved there just prior to World War I, we children visited along the Delta in our nonage . . . Our life in Oklahoma was New Orleans once removed; it was a life our playmates accepted as matter-of-factly as children of a coast accept the tides: The Negroes *were;* we *were*. They had their lives; we had ours. There were certain things one did: A proper white child obeyed the family Negroes, ate with them, bothered them, teased them, loved them, lived with them, learned from them. And there were certain things one did not do: One did not intrude upon their lives, or ask about Negro institutions, or bring a Negro child in the front door.

. . . For three hundred years, the South has lived with this subconsciousness of race. Who hears a clock tick, or the surf murmur, or the trains pass? Not those who live by the clock or the sea or the track. In the South, the acceptance of racial separation begins in the cradle. What rational man imagines this concept can be shattered overnight?

. . . White infants learn to feel invisible fences as they crawl, to sense unwritten boundaries as they walk. And I know this much, that Negro children are brought up to sense these boundaries, too. What is so often misunderstood, outside the South, is this delicate intimacy of human beings whose lives are so intricately bound together. I have met Northerners who believe, in all apparent seriousness, that segregation in the South means literally that: *segregation*, the races stiffly apart, never touching. A wayfaring stranger from the New York *Herald Tribune* implied as much in a piece he wrote from Virginia after the school decision. His notion was that whites and Negroes did not even say "good morning" to each other. God in heaven!

In plain fact, the relationship between white and Negro in the segregated South, in the country and in the city, has been far closer, more honest, less constrained, than such relations generally have been in the integrated North. In Charleston and New Orleans, among many other cities, residential segregation does not exist, for example, as it exists in Detroit or Chicago. In the country, whites and Negroes are farm neighbors. They share the same calamities—the mud, the hail, the weevils—and they minister, in their own unfelt, unspoken way, to one another. Is the relationship that of master and servant, superior and inferior? Down deep, doubtless it is, but I often wonder if this is more of a wrong to the Negro than the affected, hearty "equality" encoun-

tered in the North.

. . . Many of these [Jim Crow] practices, so deeply resented in recent years by the Negro, may have had some rational basis when they were instituted in the post-Reconstruction period. When the first trolleys came along, the few Negroes who rode them were mostly servants; others carried with them the fragrance of farm or livery stable. A Jim Crow section perhaps made sense in those days. But in my own nonage, during the 1920s, and in the years since then, few Southerners ever paused to examine the reasons for segregation on streetcars. We simply moved the little portable sign that separated white from Negro as a car filled up, and whites sat in front of the sign and Negroes sat behind it. This was the way we rode streetcars. After *Brown v. Board of Education*, when the abiding subconsciousness of the Negro turned overnight into an acute and immediate awareness of the Negro, some of these laws and customs ceased to be subject to reason anyhow; they became, confusingly, matters of strategy; they became occupied ground in an undeclared war, not to be yielded lest their yielding be regarded as needless surrender. Many aspects of our lives have gone that way since. The unwritten rules of generations are now being, in truth, unwritten; in their place, it is proposed by the apostles of instant integration that there be no rules at all. It seems so easy: "What difference does the color of a man's skin make?" "Why not just treat them as equals?" "There is no such thing as race."

Ah, but it is not so easy. The ingrained attitudes of a lifetime cannot be jerked out like a pair of infected molars, and new porcelain dentures put in their place. For this is what our Northern friends will not comprehend: The South, agreeable as it may be to confessing some of its sins and to bewailing its more manifest wickednesses, simply does not concede that at bottom its basic attitude is "infected" or wrong. On the contrary, the Southerner rebelliously clings to what seems to him the hard core of truth in this whole controversy: *Here and now,* in his own communities, in the mid-1960s, the Negro race, as a race, plainly is not equal to the white race, as a race; nor, for that matter, in the wider world beyond, by the accepted judgment of ten thousand years, has the Negro race, as a race, *ever* been the cultural or intellectual equal of the white race, as a race.

This we take to be a plain statement of fact, and if we are not amazed that our Northern antagonists do not accept it as such, we are resentful that they will not even look at the proposition, or hear of it, or inquire into it.

Then, on October 8, just days before the *Brown* and *Briggs* cases were to be heard, the Court issued a postponement. They had decided to include *Davis v. Prince Edward County*.

At Marshall's office in New York, the NAACP's legal staff hurriedly reworked their briefs. They now had three cases to be heard together and only until December 8 to prepare for the hearing. Then, with only a few weeks left until the trial began, the Court added two more cases. Fittingly, one was the District of Columbia case begun by Charles Houston. After Houston's death, Nabrit had redesigned the Consolidated Parents' Group legal fight and filed a case that challenged separate-but-equal directly: *Bolling v. Sharpe*. The other case was added just two-and-a-half weeks before the trial was to begin: *Gebhart v. Belton*, from the state of Delaware.

The cases were consolidated under the name of the first case the Court had decided to hear—*Brown v. Board of Education of Topeka*. But it was no accident that *Brown* was chosen to head the list. "We felt it was much better to have representative cases from different parts of the country," Justice Tom Clark explained, "so we consolidated them and made *Brown* the first so that the whole question would not smack of being a purely Southern one."

Ten days before the oral arguments began, Thurgood Marshall arrived in Washington. His suite at the Statler Hotel became the NAACP command post. People came in and out, argued into the night, refined their ideas, and tried to anticipate what the opposition would do. Marshall had participated in fifteen Supreme Court cases, more than any other member of the Legal Defense Fund. He'd won thirteen. This was by far the most important case he'd ever argued.

The preparations included a dry-run at Howard Law School. It was only fitting that they should meet at Howard on the eve of their greatest battle. Howard was where many of them had learned the law and where Charlie Houston had trained so many in this cadre. The dry-run was set up just like a court. Half a dozen or so mock judges were selected, and the attorneys took turns presenting their oral arguments and answering the toughest questions the mock judges could throw at them. Afterwards, the assembled group of students, lawyers, and faculty evaluated the answers of the attorneys and tried to strengthen their cases.

On December 9, 1952, spectators filled every seat in the Supreme Court and four hundred more people lined the corridors seeking admission.

The Court now had an array of arguments, locales, and attorneys with which to decide the critical question of the constitutionality of segregated public schools. The five cases would allow the gradations of attitudes among blacks to be aired, as each of the lawyers chose his own approach to the essential target—better schools for black children.

In the first case, Robert Carter argued the unconstitutionality of unequal educational opportunities for blacks. The *Sweatt* and *McLaurin* cases had established that educational opportunities are defined not by physical factors alone but by intangible ones as well, including racial segregation that might place a student at a disadvantage in the classroom.

Marshall took the same approach when arguing *Briggs*. His brief, however, contained an important appendix. Because many of the NAACP lawyers found Kenneth Clark's psychological experiments on the effects of segregation too controversial and his method suspect, Marshall, who valued the importance of the data, decided to present only a written summary of Dr. Clark's findings, along with an *amicus* brief filed by some of the most eminent social scientists in the country.

The opposing attorney, John W. Davis, saw little to fear in the *Briggs* brief. During the trial, he wrote to a fellow attorney in South Carolina, "I have read the brief and appendix submitted by our opponents and there seems to be nothing in them which requires special comment. I think it perfectly clear from interior evidences that the witness [Kenneth] Clark drafted the appendix which is signed by the worthy social scientists. I can only say that if that sort of 'guff' can move any court, 'God save the state!'"

John W. Davis had argued more than 250 cases before the Supreme Court—more than any attorney in the twentieth century. At age seventy-nine, the sharp-witted Davis typically put in twelve-hour days preparing for trial and was considered one of the most accomplished attorneys in America. He contended that the state of South Carolina had no reason to "reverse the findings of ninety years." He also cited W. E. B. DuBois' writings as evidence that not all blacks believed school desegregation would help their race.

Marshall responded that Davis failed to explain why blacks were "taken out of the mainstream of American life." Later, he added, "It seems to me that in a case like this the only way that South Carolina, under the test set forth in this case, can sustain that statute is to show that Negroes as Negroes—all Negroes—are different from everybody else."

The arguments continued for three days. No clear victor emerged. Records of private discussions between the justices indicate that Chief Justice Fred M. Vinson was at first inclined to rule against ending segregation. A decision siding with the civil rights lawyers would mean the Court must repudiate its fifty-year adherence to the separate-but-equal doctrine originated in the *Plessy* case. The Fourteenth Amendment to the Constitution guaranteed equal protection of the rights of all citizens. The plaintiffs argued that separate schools violated the rights of black children, but the defense countered that Congress intended the separation of the races to continue under the equal protection clause.

On December 11, six days after the hearings began, the Court convened to consider the evidence. Their deliberations dragged on. The justices delivered a list of questions about the cases and questions about the Fourteenth Amendment to both sides. Nine months passed without a decision.

In September 1953, Chief Justice Vinson died unexpectedly of a heart attack at the age of sixty-three. For a month the Court was without a chief justice. President Eisenhower then nominated Earl Warren to the bench. Eisenhower owed Warren a debt from the 1952 Republican convention, when Warren's political maneuvering assured Eisenhower's nomination.

To the NAACP, Warren was an enigma. In newspaper interviews, he extolled equality for all under the law and fair employment. But in 1942, when California's attorney general, he had supported locking away Japanese-Americans in internment camps during World War II.

In December 1953, one year after hearing the first oral arguments, the Court heard the attorneys respond to the questions the justices had posed after hearing the first set of arguments. The new chief justice said little; he observed and gathered information.

It is not clear when Warren made up his mind, but it is clear that he wanted a unanimous decision. If the Supreme Court were to appear divided on this controversial issue, the ruling would be much more difficult to implement. According to Richard Kluger's book, *Simple Justice*, Warren had a difficult time securing that unanimity. Justice Stanley Reed wanted to write a dissenting opinion. Reed's clerk, George Mickum, recalls that his boss struck a deal with Warren: Reed would vote with the majority if the Warren court would allow segregation to be dismantled gradually rather than all at once.

The Supreme Court customarily announced all its opinions on Mondays. But because the Court gave no advance notice about what cases it would be deciding, the plaintiffs were seldom present to hear the final decisions. Even the press avoided these dry proceedings, waiting in the newsroom downstairs rather than in the courtroom. As the justices read their opinions, copies were distributed to the newspeople.

On Monday, May 17, 1954, the fourth opinion delivered was *Brown v. Board of Education of Topeka*. Earl Warren read the first major ruling since he joined the high court. The Court could not determine, Warren said, whether Congress intended segregation to end under the Fourteenth Amendment. As for the separate-but-equal doctrine, the chief justice noted that it was written in 1896 and "we must consider public education in the light of its full development and its present place in American life.

"Does segregation of children in public schools solely on the basis of race, even though the physical facilities and other tangible factors may be equal, deprive children of the minority group of equal educational opportunities?" he continued. "We believe it does . . . To separate them from others of similar age and qualifications solely because of their race generates a feeling of inferiority as to their status in the community that may affect their hearts and minds in a way very unlikely ever to be undone.

"We conclude, unanimously, that in the field of public education the doctrine of 'separate but equal' has no place. Separate educational facilities are inherently unequal."

In Atlanta, Georgia, students at the Russell High School gather around a radio to hear the news that segregation in public schools has been ruled unconstitutional.

Reporters scurried to file news bulletins that interrupted radio shows and stopped the presses of the nation's afternoon papers. The Court had called for a fundamental change in American life: Blacks were to be treated as equals in the public schools. Georgia governor Herman Talmadge, a fervent spokesman for white supremacists, declared the ruling "a mere scrap of paper." He predicted that abolishing segregation would "create chaos not seen since Reconstruction days." *Newsweek*, describing Governor Talmadge's position, wrote, "Talmadge stands immovable on the school issue. 'I think about 98 percent of the white and colored people of the state prefer segregation,' he says. The school decision, he believes, will lead to a breakdown in segregation, and that inevitably will result in intermarriage and the 'mongrelization of the races.'" Governor James F. Byrnes of South Carolina agreed. "Ending segregation," he said, "would mark the beginning of the end of civilization in the South as we have known it."

New York Times columnist James Reston wrote that, in its ruling, the Court had relied "more on social science than legal precedents, [and] insisted on equality in hearts and minds rather than the equal school facilities." He contended that the decision read more like "an expert paper on sociology than a Supreme Court decision."

That week's *Time* magazine noted, "In its 164 years the Court had erected many a landmark of U.S. history . . . none of them except the Dred Scott case (reversed by the Civil War) was more important than the school segregation issue.

None of them directly and intimately affected so many American families."

In an editorial, the May 19 *Washington Post* said, "It is not too much to speak of the Court's decision as a new birth of freedom. It comes at a juncture in the affairs of mankind when this reaffirmation of basic human values is likely to have a wonderfully tonic effect. America is rid of an incubus which impeded and embarrassed it in all its relations with the world. Abroad as well as at home, this decision will engender a renewal of faith in democratic institutions and ideals."

To black Americans, the Court's action on school segregation was a sign of hope. But they had listened to promises from white America before. There were no grand celebrations. As Charles Houston had said years earlier, "Nobody needs to explain to a Negro the difference between the law in books and the law in action."

"We conclude, unanimously, that in the field of public education the doctrine of 'separate but equal' has no place."

The lawyers who had argued the case, however, were jubilant. After years of work, they understood the magnitude of their achievement. Thurgood Marshall was meeting with Roy Wilkins of the NAACP when they heard the story of the Court's decision on the Associated Press. The two men silently embraced. That evening, retired Judge J. Waties Waring, who had been forced into early retirement because of his controversial dissent in the *Briggs* case, held a small celebratory dinner party at his home in New York. In attendance were Walter White, head of the NAACP, Robert Carter, one of the lawyers on the *Brown* case, and South African writer Alan Paton. The team of lawyers from the Legal Defense Fund knew they had won the most important civil rights case of the twentieth century.

Nearly twenty-five years later, Thurgood Marshall, a supreme court justice himself, remembered the role of Charles Houston in this victory. "A large number of people never heard of Charles Houston . . . [but] when *Brown against the Board of Education* was being argued in the Supreme Court . . . there were some two dozen lawyers on the side of the Negroes fighting for their schools . . . Of those lawyers, only two hadn't been touched by Charlie Houston . . . That man was the engineer of all of it."

Cotton sharecroppers at work in Mississippi.

Chapter Two

Standing For Justice

Mississippi and the Till Case

"Before Emmett Till's murder, I had known the fear of hunger, hell and the Devil. But now there was a new fear known to me—the fear of being killed just because I was black."

From *Coming of Age in Mississippi*, Anne Moody's autobiography

B lack Monday. That was what southern segregationists came to call the day the Supreme Court ruled on *Brown v. Board of Education*. "On May 17, 1954, the Constitution of the United States was destroyed because of the Supreme Court's decision," said Mississippi senator James Eastland. "You are not obliged to obey the decisions of any court which are plainly fraudulent [and based on] sociological considerations."

In Linden, Alabama, state senator Walter C. Givhan railed against the NAACP's campaign to end school segregation. What, he asked his white audience, is the real purpose of the campaign? "To open the bedroom doors of our white women to Negro men."

When the Supreme Court handed down its decision, it did not include instructions on how the order was to be implemented. Desegregation began almost immediately in Washington, D.C., and Baltimore, but most of the nation waited for the Court to provide specific instructions on how to end school segregation.

Ku Klux Klan cross-burning rally.

A year later, the Court still had not acted. Instead, the justices asked the lower federal courts, closer to the local school districts, to ensure that those districts "admit to public schools on a racially nondiscriminatory basis with all deliberate speed the [black children]."

To many blacks, the Court's delay and the vague wording of its eventual decree were a bitter disappointment. "I remember the great elation that I had—how wonderful I felt the country was and the Constitution [after the 1954 ruling] . . . ," said one civil rights attorney. "I felt an equally strong sense of depression and bitterness a year later when the Court came out with the 'all deliberate speed' formulation. I had the feeling that we'd won a hollow victory."

President Eisenhower distanced himself from the Court's actions. "It makes no difference whether or not I endorse it," he said. "The Constitution is as the Supreme Court interprets it and I must conform to that and do my very best to see that it is carried out in this country." But later he commented that his appointment of Earl Warren was "the biggest damn-fool mistake I ever made." He told one of his aides in the White House, "I am convinced that the Supreme Court decision set back progress in the South at least fifteen years."

In Mississippi, unarguably the most supremacist and segregated state in the country, whites' anger over the ruling fueled violent segregationist backlash. Gangs of whites committed beatings, burnings, and lynchings—murder by mob. The Supreme Court decision also spurred the formation of a new kind of white hate group, composed of urban, middle-class whites determined to fight desegregation. They called themselves the Citizens' Council, and civil rights activists dubbed them the "white-collar Klan," after the Ku Klux Klan.

The Klan's members were generally poor, rural white men. Wearing white robes and hoods that covered their faces, they set crosses ablaze on the lawns of integrationist "troublemakers." If that tactic failed to intimidate, they resorted to beatings and murder. The Citizens' Councils, which began to proliferate throughout the South, sought to control blacks more through economic reprisals than by violence. One Council leader said that their purpose was "to make it difficult, if not impossible, for any Negro who advocates desegregation to find and hold a job, get credit, or renew a mortgage."

Several blacks were killed by white men in Mississippi in 1955. Racially motivated murder was not new to the state, but at least three of the killings that year were different.

Two of the victims, the Reverend George W. Lee and Lamar Smith, were NAACP organizers trying to register black voters. Until 1940 there were more blacks than whites in Mississippi, and in 1955 blacks still outnumbered whites in many counties. To segregationists, the vote was too powerful a weapon to be in the hands of so many "nigras." The usual reasons for murder ranged from stealing food to talking back to a white person. These latest victims were blacks who were standing up for their rights.

The victim of the third killing was a teenage boy. His death was different for so many reasons that his murder made the front page of virtually every black newspaper in the nation.

Emmett Till was a fourteen-year-old from the South Side of Chicago. In August, 1955, Emmett and his cousin Curtis Jones were visiting relatives near Money, Mississippi. They were staying with Curtis' grandfather, Mose Wright. In the town of Money, a black girl had recently been "flogged" for the dubious offense of "crowding white people" in a store.

Friends and family knew Emmett as a brash, prank-loving eighth grader at McCosh Elementary School. He was doing well enough in school, even with the speech defect he had developed from a bout with nonparalytic polio at age three. The neighborhood kids on St. Lawrence Avenue said his stutter didn't make Emmett Till shy; he liked to dress smart and talk smart. He was a mama's boy, an only child.

Chicago in 1955 was a post-World War II boom town, a magnet for blacks from the South. The *Chicago Defender*, a weekly black newspaper, ran gossip columns called "News From Home," covering counties in every southern state.

A Citizens' Council meeting—its purpose was "to make it difficult, if not impossible, for any Negro who advocates desegregation to find and hold a job, get credit, or renew a mortgage."

Emmett Till and his
mother, Mamie Bradley.

Bryant's Grocery and
Meat Market in Money,
Mississippi.

Carolyn Bryant, the
woman Emmett Till met in
the grocery store, sits next
to her husband Roy and
their children.

For its fiftieth anniversary that year, the paper printed a full-page drawing that showed an exodus of black people—men loaded down with baggage and tools, women with children on their hips, all marching north to Chicago. The city was "the shining El Dorado of freedom and good jobs to millions of southern Negroes," the paper editorialized.

Emmett Till's neighborhood was a working-class black area with its share of storefront preachers and apartment buildings crowded with relatives from Alabama, Louisiana, and Mississippi. The music that drifted through the alleyways ranged from old gospel hymns to the modern strains of Fats Domino. Religion, like the numbers and gin, was an important part of black Chicago's life. That summer blacks and whites sat together at the Jehovah's Witnesses convention at Comiskey Park. Mayor Richard Daley spoke at the opening of the black National Baptist Convention of America. His appearance there was significant to the transplanted southern blacks who were not yet accustomed to the idea that in Chicago they could cast a ballot—even if there was talk of vote-fraud. There was a strong enough black political presence in the city to ensure that blacks received at least low-level jobs in city government. That same summer the city even sponsored a "Salute to Negroes in Government." Roy Wilkins, the new executive secretary of the NAACP, spoke on that occasion of the opportunity the war had given blacks because they were now veterans; they had proven they were Americans, and now they were proving it in local government. As veterans they were entitled to veterans' benefits, help with schooling and housing, and an end to segregation.

Emmett Till knew segregation. McCosh Elementary was a public school with black students only. When Mamie Bradley, Emmett's mother, made plans to send him south for the summer on the Illinois Central, she knew he would have to ride in the train's colored section. But the segregation Emmett knew in the North was nothing like the segregation he rode into in Mississippi. His only warning came from his mother, a Mississippi native who had left for Chicago with her family when she was two years old. She told her boy not to fool with white people down south: "If you have to get on your knees and bow when a white person goes past, do it willingly."

His cousin, Curtis Jones, recalled that Emmett liked to pull pranks. One Wednesday evening in August, 1955, Emmett and Curtis drove Mose Wright's '41 Ford to Bryant's Grocery and Meat Market, a country store with a big metal Coca-Cola sign outside.

There the boys met up with some other black children, and Curtis Jones began a game of checkers with a seventy-year-old black man sitting by the side of the building. Outside the store, Emmett was showing off a picture of a white girl who was a friend of his in Chicago. Till bragged to the titillated boys that this white girl was *his* girl, and Jones recalls that one of the southern boys said, "'Hey, there's a [white] girl in that store there. I bet you won't go in there and talk to her.' So he went in there to get some candy. When he was leaving the store, he told her, 'Bye, Baby.' And that's when the old man [the checker-player] started telling us that she would go to her car, get a pistol, and blow his [Emmett's] brains out."

The boys jumped in their car as Carolyn Bryant came out the swinging screen doors. They sped out of the little town.

By the next day the incident had become just a good story to the two northern boys. But the tale went beyond those in the car. One girl who had heard it through the grapevine warned, "When that lady's husband come back there is going to be trouble." Roy Bryant was out of town at the time, trucking shrimp from Louisiana to Texas.

The boys kept the encounter a secret from Mose Wright, hoping it would blow over. Three days passed, and the boys forgot about Emmett's "Bye, Baby" to the pretty white woman. But after midnight on Saturday, a car pulled off the gravel road and headed through the cotton field to Mose Wright's unpainted cabin. Roy Bryant was back from his trucking job. He and his brother-in-law J. W. Milam had come to Wright's cabin to get that "boy who done the talkin'." Mose told the men that the boy was from "up nawth" and didn't know a thing about how to act with white folks down south. He told them that the boy was only fourteen, that this was only his second visit to Mississippi. Why not give the boy a good whipping and leave it at that? As the men dragged Emmett outside, one of them asked Mose Wright, "How old are you, preacher?"

"Sixty-four."

"If you cause any trouble, you'll never live to be sixty-five," said the man. They pushed Emmett into the back seat of the car and drove away.

Precisely what happened next is unknown. Two months after the trial, however, William Bradford Huie, a white Alabama journalist, paid Milam and Bryant $4,000 to tell their story. The two Mississippians attempted to justify the murder by claiming that they didn't intend to kill Till when they picked him up at Mose Wright's house, that they had only wanted to scare him. But when the young boy refused to repent or beg for mercy, they said, they *had* to kill him.

"What else could we do?" Milam told Huie. "He was hopeless. I'm no bully; I never hurt a nigger in my life. I like niggers in their place. I know how to work 'em. But I just decided it was time a few people got put on notice."

Milam drove Emmett to the Tallahatchie River, Huie wrote, and made the boy carry a seventy-five-pound cotton-gin fan from the back of the truck to the river bank before ordering him to strip. Milam then shot the boy in the head.

The Milam and Bryant account of the incident left several questions unanswered. One witness, for example, reported seeing Till and the two accused with a group of other men, both black and white, before the murder. Who were they? How and why would Milam and Bryant coerce blacks into helping them? Why would they need other whites along if they had only wanted to intimidate the boy? And, would a tongue-tied fourteen-year-old boy really make baiting comments, as Milam and Bryant allege, to the men who were viciously beating him?

What we do know is that Mose Wright heeded the kidnappers' order. He did not call the police. But the next morning, Curtis Jones went to the plantation owner's house and asked to use the phone. He told the sheriff Emmett Till was gone.

Till's body was found three days later. The barbed wire holding the cotton-gin fan around his neck had become snagged on a tangled river root. There was a bullet in the boy's skull, one eye was gouged out, and his forehead was crushed on one side.

Milam and Bryant had been charged with kidnapping before the gruesome corpse was discovered. They were now charged with murder. The speed of the indictment surprised many. But white Mississippi officials and newspapers said that all "decent" people were outraged at what had happened and that justice would be done. Milam and Bryant could not find a local white lawyer to take their case. The Mississippi establishment seemed to be turning its back on them.

Meanwhile, the tortured, distended body pulled from the river became the focus of attention. It was so badly mangled that Mose Wright could identify the boy only by an initialed ring. The sheriff wanted to bury the decomposing body quickly. But Curtis Jones called Chicago, passing word to Till's mother first of Emmett's death and then of the imminent burial. She demanded that the corpse be sent back to Chicago. The sheriff's office reluctantly agreed, but had the mortician sign an order that the casket was not to be opened.

As soon as the casket arrived in Chicago, however, Mrs. Bradley did open it. She had to be sure, she said, that it was really her son, that he was not still alive and hiding in Mississippi. She studied the hairline, the teeth, and in vengeance

Chicago Defender coverage of the Till killing.

declared that the world must see what had been done to her only child. There would be an open-casket funeral.

The thirty-three-year-old mother collapsed to the concrete train platform, crying, "Lord, take my soul." She had to be taken from the station in a wheelchair.

"Have you ever sent a loved son on vacation and had him returned to you in a pine box, so horribly battered and water-logged that someone needs to tell you this sickening sight is your son—lynched?" Mamie Bradley asked reporters afterwards.

That body would shock and disgust the city of Chicago, and after a picture of it was published in the black weekly magazine, *Jet*, all of black America saw the mutilated corpse.

Till's mother sobs hysterically as her son's casket arrives in Chicago.

On the first day that the casket was open for viewing, thousands lined the streets outside the Rainer Funeral Home. The funeral was held on Saturday, September 3; 2,000 people gathered outside the church on State Street. Mrs. Bradley delayed burial for four days to let "the world see what they did to my boy."

It is difficult to measure just how profound an effect the public viewing of Till's body created. But without question it moved black America in a way the Supreme Court ruling on school desegregation could not match. Contributions to the NAACP's "fight fund," the war chest to help victims of racial attacks, reached record levels. Only weeks before, the NAACP had been begging for support to pay its debts in the aftermath of its Supreme Court triumph.

The Cleveland Call and Post, a black newspaper, polled the nation's major black radio preachers and found five of every six preaching on the Till case. Half of them were demanding that "something be done in Mississippi now," according to the paper.

White Mississippians responded differently as the case became a national cause. As northerners denounced the barbarity of segregation in Mississippi, the state's white press angrily objected to the NAACP's labeling of the killing as a lynching. *Jackson Clarion Ledger* writer Tom Ethridge called the condemnation of Mississippi a "Communist plot" to destroy southern society. Civil rights activists were frequently accused of being Communists or Communist sympathizers.

Public opinion in Mississippi galvanized in reaction to the North's scorn. Five prominent Delta attorneys now agreed to represent Milam and Bryant. A defense fund raised $10,000. Signs of support suddenly appeared from the same local officials who had at first put distance between themselves and the men charged with the boy's brutal murder. The sheriff, declaring that the body was too badly

Roy Bryant, charged with the murder of Emmett Till.

decomposed to be positively identified as Till's, did no investigative work to help the prosecution prepare its case. A special prosecutor had to be appointed by the state, but he was given no budget or personnel with which to conduct a probe.

On September 19, less than two weeks after Emmett Till was buried in Chicago, Milam and Bryant went on trial in a segregated courthouse in Sumner, Mississippi. The press, particularly the black press, was in the courtroom. Reporters from across the country knew that, in light of the Supreme Court's ruling on school desegregation, this could make a good story—a telling example of how the South was reacting to the changing status of blacks.

No one knew if any black witnesses would dare testify against the white men. Curtis Jones, who in later years became a Chicago policeman, recalls that his mother forbade him to return to Mississippi to testify at the trial of his cousin's accused murderers. "My mother was afraid something would happen to me like something happened to Emmett Till," he said.

Without a witness, there would be no case. But in 1955, for a black man to accuse a white man of murder in Mississippi was to sign his own death warrant. Violence had long been used in the South as a means of intimidating blacks into passivity, but this murder was particularly brutal and all the more threatening. White Mississippi, angry at the northern press' interest in the case, was closing ranks. The word spread throughout the black community: Keep your mouth shut.

Mose Wright had not slept at his home since the kidnapping. He feared the men might return. His wife, Elizabeth, never went back to the cabin after that night. "Tell Simmie [her son] to get any corset and one or two slips or a dress or two and bring them to me," she wrote in a note to her husband from her hiding place. After the indictment, Wright received anonymous warnings to leave the state before the trial began. He was told to take his family and "get out of town before they all get killed."

But Wright didn't leave the state. Although he had been intimidated by the kidnappers the night they took Emmett, he was now going to be a witness for the prosecution. A black man was going to testify.

Just before the trial began, black reporters had gotten word that Wright would be a witness. Twenty years earlier, in another Mississippi courthouse, when a black boy accused of raping a white woman got up to testify, a white man in the courtroom pulled out a revolver and started shooting. Anticipating the fury that Wright's testimony would prompt, the black reporters made plans for the moment, just in case the whites in the courtroom turned on the few blacks. James Hicks, a reporter covering the trial for the *Amsterdam News*, described their plan this

J. W. Milam, also accused of Till's murder.

The NAACP in Mississippi:

An Interview with Myrlie Evers

In the mid-1950s, Myrlie Evers was secretary to her husband, Medgar Evers, Mississippi's field secretary for the National Association for the Advancement of Colored People (NAACP). Mississippi was probably the most challenging state for an NAACP organizer.

Although more blacks lived in Mississippi than in any other state—or perhaps because of that fact—segregationists controlled black people not only through legal restrictions but also through intimidation.

A biracial organization, the NAACP was founded in 1909 "to

achieve, through peaceful and lawful means, equal citizenship rights for all American citizens by eliminating segregation and discrimination in housing, employment, voting, schools, the courts, transportation, recreation." A white Boston lawyer, Moorfield

The Emmett Till case shook the foundations of Mississippi, both black and white—with the white community because it had become nationally publicized, with us blacks, because it said even a child was not safe from racism and bigotry and death.

Medgar was field secretary for the NAACP, and he and others who worked with him had the responsibility of going into these areas where there might have been problems and investigating these cases. I can recall so well that Medgar cried when he found that this happened to Emmett Till. He cried out of the frustration and the anger of wanting to physically strike out and hurt. I myself felt anger, frustration, almost a hopelessness at that time that things were going to continue to happen. But it said something else to me too—that Medgar's life was in danger twenty-four hours a day, because at that particular

time, he was the only person who was in the forefront of investigations, getting the word of these hypocrisies out to the public.

Medgar played a very important role in the Emmett Till case. As field secretary for the NAACP, part of his responsibility was to investigate murders. He and Amzie Moore and a few others dressed as sharecroppers and went to the plantations to ask people about the murderers or the accused murderers. [His responsibilities included asking] what had happened, making contact with local officials, and getting the press out.

It was a very dangerous job. Medgar was also responsible not only for finding witnesses but helping to get them out of town. I remember one case where he put a witness in a casket, in conjunction with a mortuary, and got the person out of town, out of the state,

Storey, was the organization's first president. With its northern roots, the NAACP grew slowly among southern blacks. But by 1919, southern membership in the NAACP surpassed that in the North. Even so, southern segregationists never stopped thinking of the NAACP as a group of "outside agitators."

When Emmett Till was murdered, Medgar Evers had been an officer for the NAACP less than one year. He went to Money, Mississippi, to investigate the murder and found witnesses and evidence for the prosecution. He was in the courtroom in Sumner during the trial.

across the border to Tennessee and then north.

I bled for Emmett Till's mother. I know when she came to Mississippi and appeared at the mass meetings how everyone poured out their hearts to her, went into their pockets when people had only two or three pennies, and gave . . . some way to say that we bleed for you, we hurt for you, we are so sorry about what happened to Emmett. And that this is just one thing that will be a frame of reference for us to move on to do more things, positively, to eliminate this from happening ever again. It was a sad and terrible time. It's too bad to have to say that sometimes it takes those kinds of things to help a people become stronger and to eliminate the fear that they have to speak out and do something.

Medgar Evers, Field Secretary for the NAACP, Jackson, Mississippi, 1955.

way. "We had worked it out where I was going to get the gun [from a bailiff seated in front of the black reporters], somebody else was going to take this girl [Cloyte Murdock Larsson, a reporter for *Jet*] to the window, she was going to go out the window two floors down . . . then we were just going to grab the chairs . . . and fight our way out—if we could."

A packed courtroom watched intently as sixty-four-year-old Wright took the witness stand. The prosecuting attorney asked him to identify the men who had come to his home and taken young Till away with them. Before a white judge, an all-white jury, and armed white guards, Wright pointed to J. W. Milam. "Thar he," said Wright, identifying Milam as one of the men. He then pointed to the other defendant, Roy Bryant, as the second man.

"It was the first time in the history of Mississippi that a Negro had stood in court and pointed his finger at a white man as a killer of a Negro," said Michigan congressman Charles Diggs, who attended the trial. Actually, Wright's testimony was not literally the first such instance, but it was indeed a rare and courageous act for that time and place.

Afterwards, recalling that moment, Wright said he could "feel the blood boil in hundreds of white people as they sat glaring in the courtroom. It was the first time in my life I had the courage to accuse a white man of a crime, let alone something terrible as killing a boy. I wasn't exactly brave and I wasn't scared. I just wanted to see justice done."

After Mose Wright testified, other blacks came forward. Willie Reed, the son of a sharecropper, told the court that around six o'clock that morning he was on his way to buy meat for breakfast when he saw Emmett sitting in the back of a passing pickup truck. Two other blacks and four white men were also in the truck, but Reed recognized only Till and J. W. Milam. The truck drove to a shed on the plantation, and Reed said he then heard cries coming from inside. He ran to the home of his aunt, Amanda Bradley. The cries became wails and pained grunts, and then a chant of "Mama, Lord have mercy, Lord have mercy."

"Who are they beating to death down at the barn, Aunt Mandy?" Reed asked Mrs. Bradley. Then he saw Milam, with a gun in his holster, come out of the shed to get water from the well. Three other white men came out and joined him. Eventually, the truck was backed up to the shed, Reed said, and three black men helped the others roll something wrapped in a tarpaulin into the back of the pickup. Later he saw the blacks washing out the back of the truck, the blood-red water soaking into the Mississippi soil.

Amanda Bradley testified to hearing the sound of a beating coming from the shed.

An Interview With Congressman Charles Diggs

When the voters of Michigan sent Charles Diggs, Jr., to the United States House of Representatives in 1954, he became the first black congressman in the state's history. He was not, however, the first black congressman in the United States. During the period of Reconstruction, from 1865 to 1877, the United States government tried to rebuild the South after the political and economic devastation of the Civil War. Black citizens held prominent government positions throughout the nation, including the posts of mayor, governor, lieutenant governor, state supreme court justice, U.S. senator, and U.S. congressman.

Congressman Diggs, elected as a Democrat, was one of only three blacks in the 84th Congress. He traveled to Sumner, Mississippi, to attend the trial of the men accused of killing Emmett Till.

I think the picture in *Jet* magazine showing Emmett Till's mutilation was probably the greatest media product in the last forty or fifty years, because that picture stimulated a lot of interest and anger on the part of blacks all over the country.

When I read about the Till case, I became immediately interested, first because it was in Mississippi, which was the bottom line for the arch segregationists in the United States. Second, it was the home state of my father and my grandfather, and all the people on the Diggs side of the family. Third, being a pioneer member of Congress, I thought that I could serve the purpose well and be a witness to the prosecution of a case of this type.

There was a great deal of tension at the trial. The court was located in a very, very rural community. They were not used to the kind of attention that was generated by the Till case. The racial dimensions brought in a whole lot of people from the outside, black and white, from the North.

I think it was almost a foregone conclusion that these people would not be found guilty . . . I certainly was angered by the decision, [but] I was not surprised by it. And I was strengthened in my belief that something had to be done about the dispensation of justice in that state.

In talking about the Till trial, you have to repeat the atmosphere. This is Mississippi in 1955, with a long history of intimidation of witnesses and fear on the part of blacks to testify, in racial situations in particular. For someone like Mose Wright and others to testify against white defendants in a situation like this was historic.

The Black Press At The Trial:

An Interview with James Hicks

In the early days of the civil rights movement, the black press was a powerful and unifying force. During the 1930s and 1940s, many local black newspapers began to publish national editions, and by the late 1940s, sixty percent of their circulation crossed state lines. By 1955 there were more than 200 black magazines and newspapers being published in the United States. Newspapers such as the *Chicago Defender*, the *Pittsburgh Courier*, and the *Baltimore Afro-American* and magazines such as *Jet* and *Ebony* reached black readers in every corner of the country.

In 1955, the *Amsterdam News* was one of the most successful black newspapers in the country. During the trial of J. W. Milam and Roy Bryant, James Hicks reported for the *Amsterdam News* as well as for the National Negro Press Association. James Hicks died in 1986.

I had covered the courts in many areas of this country, but the Till case was unbelievable. I mean, I just didn't get the sense of being in a courtroom. The courtroom was segregated . . . The local people who tried to get in had to stand back until the whites came in and filled the place up. They sat in the back of the courtroom.

The black press sat at a bridge table far off from the bench. The white press sat right under the judge and jury, but we had a bridge table. They sat the boy's mother at the bridge table.

I was the one that got Congressman Diggs in, because the sheriff wouldn't let him in. The congressman had sent a telegram to the judge to say he'd like to come down and observe this trial. The judge was the one white person that appeared to be fair-minded. He wired Diggs back and told him to come down.

When the people started coming into the courtroom, they filled up the white section, then the blacks filled up what was left. When Congressman Diggs came down, the room was filled. He couldn't get in.

Congressman Diggs gave me his card to give to the judge. I went straight up and started for the judge's bench. He hadn't come in yet but on the way up to the bench I was stopped by one of the veterans who had been deputized. He said, "Where you going, nigger?"

And I said, "I'm going to see the judge." I pulled open my coat pocket which had Diggs' card in it. "I was going to hand it to the judge . . . you give it to him then." He called another deputy over and said, "This nigger said there's a nigger outside who says he's a congressman . . . " So this guy said, "A nigger congressman?" "That's what this nigger said, ha! ha! ha!"

I said to myself, "My God!" I had never seen anything like this in my life. The deputy went to the sheriff, who said, "I'll bring him in here, but I'm going to sit him at you niggers' table." And when he brought Congressman Diggs in, that's where he sat.

When Mose Wright was called to testify, he was asked if he could identify anybody in the courtroom that had come to his house that night and got Emmett Till . . . We had been told by some people in our motel that "the stuff is going to hit the fan when Mose Wright stands up and identifies J. W. Milam and the other fellow." So when the question was put to him, he looked around and said in his broken language, "Thar he." There was terrific tension in the courtroom, but nothing happened. I mean, no outbreak came. I think that was because of the judge. The judge was pounding his gavel and saying "order, order."

James Hicks (at near end of table) sits with others at the black press table in the courtroom. Also at the table, third to Hicks' right, is Congressman Charles Diggs. Across from Diggs sits Mamie Bradley, Till's mother.

Emmett's mother identified the body pulled from the Tallahatchie River as her son.

After they testified, the witnesses were hurried out of town by sympathetic observers. Congressman Diggs took Willie Reed; other blacks escorted the Bradleys. Mississippi's NAACP field secretary, Medgar Evers, and reporter James Hicks worked together to get Mose Wright out of the state shortly after he testified.

The two defendants never took the stand. The defense consisted of half a dozen character witnesses. At the end of the five-day trial, John C. Whitten, one of the five defense attorneys, made his simple pitch to the all-white, all-male jurors: "Your fathers will turn over in their graves if [Milam and Bryant are found guilty] and I'm sure that every last Anglo-Saxon one of you has the courage to free these men in the face of that [outside] pressure."

The prosecutor, District Attorney Gerald Chatham, countered that the killing was a "cowardly act—it was a brutal, unnecessary killing of a human being."

The jury deliberated a little more than an hour. It was September 23, 1955, the 166th anniversary of the signing of the Bill of Rights. When the jurors returned to the court at 5:43 P.M., Judge Curtis Swango asked for the verdict.

"Not guilty," said J. W. Shaw, the jury foreman. Later, Shaw would assert, "I feel the state failed to prove the identity of the body."

Reaction was swift. Blacks staged major rallies in Baltimore, Chicago, Cleveland, Detroit, New York, Youngstown, and Los Angeles. Roy Wilkins of the NAACP told a crowd in Harlem, "Mississippi has decided to maintain white supremacy by murdering children. The killer of the boy felt free to lynch because there is in the entire state no restraining influence of decency, not in the state capital, among the daily newspapers, the clergy, not among any segment of the so-called lettered citizens."

Dr. Archibald J. Carey, a former delegate to the United Nations, said the "shattering damage done to our nation's prestige in world affairs by the Mississippi jury rates each of them as America's public enemy number one."

Around the country, major white dailies editorialized bitterly against the verdict. Some compared events in Mississippi to the Holocaust of Nazi Germany; one writer called Till America's Anne Frank. The uproar was fueled further when a grand jury refused to indict Milam and Bryant on separate charges of kidnapping.

Through the extensive press coverage, all America saw the injustice that had taken place. But black Americans, particularly in the South, saw something else as well—something that in retrospect is easily overlooked. They saw black people stand in a court of law and testify against white people.

The all-white jury deliberated less than seventy-five minutes before issuing its "not guilty" verdict.

When asked to identify the men who had abducted his nephew, Mose Wright turned to the accused. "Thar he," he said as he pointed to each man.

Other witnesses at the trial included Willie Reed (second from left, standing next to his father, Walter), Mamie Bradley (next to the Reeds), and Amanda Bradley (far right). Also shown are Congressman Charles Diggs (second from right) and Dr. T. R. M. Howard (third from right).

A Dixie White's View

On September 24, 1955, the *Chicago Defender*, a black newspaper, ran this story by Lew Sadler.

Sadler was a white radio announcer in Mississippi when the Till trial took place. He broadcast on-the-spot coverage when Roy Bryant and J. W. Milam were indicted and arraigned.

Say Dixie Whites Are Not Bad Folks
By Lew Sadler

Greenwood, Mississippi — During the middle of the week, a reporter who said he was with your paper stopped by the station here to talk to me. He said he had heard my "on the spot" report over the air from Sumner, Miss., the day Milam and Bryant were taken to Sumner for arraignment.

I was busy on the mike at the time and didn't have much opportunity to talk to him. He did take two photos of me at the mike, and before I had a few off-minutes he was gone.

Now, did [he] really want to hear what I had to say, or [was he] just curious about something? Would you like to have something to run with those photos if you use them? . . .

All right, why are the people of the South . . . Mississippi in particular, being prosecuted because of all this trouble? Didn't our sheriff have the two suspects in custody long before the Till boy's body, if it was his body, was found?

Does that look as if our law was slanted?

It has been said by someone far more intelligent than I that "The Southern Negro is sitting in the white man's wagon, and the white man is having to do the driving."

That is no secret to any white or colored person here in the South. So it's easy to see that they're on our backs, and we're not complaining. But why do the people of the North insist that we hold them on our laps?

My wife was raised by a Negro woman, as have so many other ladies of the South. That still is the case. You can drive by our parks and yards and see how many white children are cared for by, not white nurses, but colored women.

I've seen many times the mother come home from work, and the kids would hold on to the Negro woman's legs letting themselves be dragged to the sidewalk and on into the car before letting go, because they didn't want her to leave. Does that look like we are allergic to Negroes?

The owner of this station has a brother who owns a station in Natchez, Miss., and when something needs to be done here he will send for James, a Negro who works for the Natchez station, to come here, nearly 200 miles to do it, rather than pull in someone else. Doesn't that sound like we are loyal to a good Negro?

When we need a baby sitter at home, we have a Negro woman come in, rather than a white girl. We do not lock up the baby's bank either. Does that sound like we do not trust the Negroes?

A person does not have to drive very far through town to see Negro and white children playing together. Does that sound like we do not want our children playing and mixing with Negroes?

There are Negroes living in the town, as well as white people living in the colored section. So does that sound like we are trying to segregate the colored or whites?

I could give you many individual cases of many varieties of the help we have given the Negroes, including last winter when I gave James, the boy I was telling you about before from Natchez, my only pair of leather gloves. (By the way I've never had an extra $3 to get another pair.)

So please, as a favor to the South, while you are getting the news try to dig just a little deeper and you may come up with something that will enlighten the North to the fact that we of the South have a "good-neighbor" policy of our own.

The only line we draw is at the door of our schools. Poll the Negroes of the South and you'll find the Southern Negro feels the same. As I said before . . . they're on our backs, and we aren't complaining, but why do you insist they be in our lap too?

Emmett Till and the Younger Generation

In her autobiography, *Coming of Age in Mississippi*, writer and civil rights activist Anne Moody recalled learning of Emmett Till's death when she was a young girl. She did housekeeping for a white woman after school, and her mother warned her not to let on to Mrs. Burke that she had heard about the Till killing. "Just do your work like you don't know nothing," her mother said. In this excerpt, Moody describes a scene at her former employer's home.

When they had finished and gone into the living room as usual to watch TV, Mrs. Burke called me to eat. I took a clean plate out of the cabinet and sat down. Just as I was putting the first forkful of food in my mouth, Mrs. Burke entered the kitchen.

"Essie, did you hear about that fourteen-year-old boy who was killed in Greenwood?" she asked me, sitting down in one of the chairs opposite me.

"No, I didn't hear that," I answered, almost choking on the food.

"Do you know why he was killed?" she asked and I didn't answer.

"He was killed because he got out of his place with a white woman. A boy from Mississippi would have known better than that. This boy was from Chicago. Negroes up North have no respect for people. They think they can get away with anything. He just came to Mississippi and put a whole lot of notions in the boys' heads here and stirred up a lot of trouble," she said passionately.

"How old are you, Essie?" she asked me after a pause.

"Fourteen. I will soon be fifteen though," I said.

"See, that boy was just fourteen too. It's a shame he had to die so soon."

She was so red in the face, she looked as if she was on fire.

When she left the kitchen I sat there with my mouth open and my food untouched. I couldn't have eaten now if I were starving. "Just do your work like you don't know nothing" ran through my mind again and I began washing dishes.

I went home shaking like a leaf on a tree. For the first time out of all her trying, Mrs. Burke had made me feel like rotten garbage. Many times she had tried to instill fear within me and subdue me and had given up. But when she talked about Emmett Till there was something in her voice that sent chills and fear all over me.

Before Emmett Till's murder, I had known the fear of hunger, hell and the Devil. But now there was a new fear known to me—the fear of being killed just because I was black. This was the worst of my fears. I knew once I got food, the fear of starving to death would leave. I also was told that if I were a good girl, I wouldn't have to fear the Devil or hell. But I didn't know what one had to do or not do as a Negro not to be killed. Probably just being a Negro period was enough, I thought.

Mose Wright returned to Mississippi to testify against Milam and Bryant on kidnapping charges before a second grand jury. That done, Wright never went back. He gave away his prize hunting dog, abandoned his old car at the train station, and took the Illinois Central's colored car to Chicago.

Black leaders called for a "refugee fund" to help blacks leave the South, a black "March on Dixie," and a boycott of goods produced in Mississippi.

The southern papers reacted defensively to the onslaught of denunciations. The *Delta Democrat Times* of Greenville, Mississippi, editorialized that "to blame two million Mississippians for the irresponsible act of two is about as illogical as one can become." They wrote that the prosecution's case was weak and that a guilty verdict would not have stood up in any appeals court in the nation.

The murder of Emmett Till had a powerful impact on a new generation of blacks. It was this generation, those who were adolescents when Till was killed, that would soon demand justice and freedom in a way unknown in America before.

The *Montgomery Advertiser* in Montgomery, Alabama, picked up the Till story and gave it prominent display. Three months later, the black population of Montgomery began an historic boycott of their municipal bus system.

Mose Wright did not go down in the history books as a leader of the civil rights movement. But his individual act of courage, like the acts of so many unknown citizens, was just as important to the movement as the charismatic leadership of people like Martin Luther King, Jr.

For some time after her son's murder, Mamie Bradley traveled and lectured throughout the country, calling herself a "nobody" and her dead son a "little nobody who shook up the world." She spoke for millions of blacks who had moved north trying to forget the indignities of the South. Speaking in Cleveland, Mrs. Bradley said, "Two months ago I had a nice apartment in Chicago. I had a good job. I had a son. When something happened to the Negroes in the South I said, 'That's their business, not mine.' Now I know how wrong I was. The murder of my son has shown me that what happens to any of us, anywhere in the world, had better be the business of us all."

During the height of the thirteen-month Montgomery bus boycott, the Montgomery Improvement Association held mass meetings twice each week.

Chapter Three

We're Not Moving To The Back, Mr. Blake

The Montgomery Bus Boycott

Ain't gonna ride them buses no more,

Ain't gonna ride no more.

Why don't all the white folk know

That I ain't gonna ride no more.

Sung by Montgomery
boycotters, 1955

In the 1950s, racial segregation in the South was a pervasive way of life. Bigotry extended beyond the economic and educational spheres into the smallest details of everyday living. Separate restaurant and entertainment facilities for blacks and whites were the norm, and state laws openly outlawed racial integration. A black person could not so much as drink from a public water fountain unless it was specifically marked for "coloreds" only.

The city buses were a microcosm of this segregated society. Black passengers, after paying their fares at the front of the bus, had to leave it and re-enter through the back door. They were allowed to sit only in the rear, and had to give up their seats whenever a white rider was left standing.

Many forms of discrimination were felt privately, by individuals. But thousands of blacks and whites rode the buses together daily—and their close proximity there only made their separateness that much more distinct. Day by day blacks stood together in the rear of crowded buses while the agents of their indignity sat comfortably right in front of them.

Indignity suffered alone is debilitating; indignity shared can transform itself into power. Perhaps it was not just by chance that the public buses became one of the first arenas in the organized fight against segregation.

In 1953, the black community in Baton Rouge, Louisiana, successfully petitioned the city council to pass an ordinance allowing blacks to be seated on a first-come, first-served basis on city buses. Blacks would still have to begin their seating at the back of the bus while whites would sit up front, but no seats were to be actually reserved for whites. The white bus drivers, however, ignored the ordinance, continuing to save seats for whites. In an effort to demand compliance with the new ordinance, the black community staged a one-day boycott of the buses. But by day's end, the Louisiana attorney general declared the new ordinance illegal and ruled that the drivers did not have to change the seating practices on the buses. The strike ended unsuccessfully.

Three months later, led by the Reverend T. J. Jemison and other community leaders, blacks in Baton Rouge launched a second bus boycott. The action lasted only about one week, yet it induced city officials to offer a compromise: first-come, first-served seating as stipulated in the nullified ordinance, but with two side seats up front reserved for whites and one long seat in back set aside for blacks. The compromise was accepted by Rev. Jemison and the other boycott leaders.

This boycott marked one of the first times a community of blacks had organized a sustained, direct action against segregation and won. In light of the subsequent

Thousands of blacks and whites rode these segregated buses daily.

triumphs of the civil rights movement, the Baton Rouge victory was a small one. But the work of Rev. Jemison and the other boycott organizers in Baton Rouge had far-reaching implications for the movement that was just beginning to take root. Although the success in Baton Rouge was overshadowed by the landmark 1954 Supreme Court decision on school desegregation, the lessons learned in Louisiana were not lost. They were soon put to use some 400 miles away in Montgomery, Alabama, where perhaps the most significant boycott of the civil rights movement was about to begin.

The white residents of Montgomery considered themselves progressive in matters of race relations. News of the brutal murder of Emmett Till and the resulting trial received substantial coverage in Montgomery, but many white residents felt that Sumner, Mississippi was a rural backwater compared to their urban environment.

Montgomery's public bus system, like that in Baton Rouge, was racially segregated. Although Montgomery's black riders accounted for more than seventy-five percent of all passengers, they were regularly forced to surrender their seats to whites. The policy of the Montgomery City Lines bus company was written in keeping with city and state ordinances on segregation. Drivers were to designate the front part of the bus for whites and the rear section for blacks in proportion to the number of blacks and whites on the bus at any given moment. As more whites came onto the bus, the driver moved an imaginary color line further back. Blacks sitting directly behind the whites-only section would be told to get up and move further into the bus. The official policy was that if there were no seats available for blacks to move back to as additional white passengers got on, blacks were not required to give up their seats.

But in practice, whenever a white person needed a seat, the driver would look in the rearview mirror and yell at the "nigras" to move to the back of the bus. Crowded blacks would often have to stand behind empty seats.

Jo Ann Robinson was an English professor at all-black Alabama State College. At Christmas time, 1949, her arms loaded with gifts, Robinson was rushing to Dannelly Field airport for a trip home to Cleveland. Absentmindedly, she sat in the front section of a nearly empty bus. The driver walked over to Robinson, drew back his hand as if to strike her, and barked, *"Get up from there! Get up from there!"* Sobbing, she bolted past the driver and off the bus, packages falling from her arms.

"I felt like a dog," she said later. "And I got mad, after this was over. I realized that I was a human being and just as intelligent and far more [educationally] trained than that bus driver . . . I cried all the way to Cleveland."

Robinson returned to Montgomery intent on stirring a major protest aimed at the bus company and city officials. But when she related the humiliating incident to members of the Women's Political Council, an organization of black professional women, she was disappointed at their response. Such rudeness, they told her, was simply a fact of life in Montgomery. They had fought against it before, but to no avail. Every day, 40,000 blacks put their dimes in the collection boxes of the Montgomery City Lines along with 12,000 whites. But as the whites took their seats, black riders had to get off the bus and re-enter through the back door.

In 1953 Montgomery was run by three commissioners: the mayor, a commissioner of public affairs, and a commissioner of public works. Jo Ann Robinson and other blacks in the city demanded to meet with the commissioners. The black leaders, including Edgar Daniel (E. D.) Nixon, former head of the local NAACP, once again decried the segregated seating and complained that bus stops were farther apart in black neighborhoods than in white areas. They also wanted to know why the city refused to hire black bus drivers. The commissioners listened but took no action. Then Robinson and others in the Women's Political Council met with bus company officials. The white men told the black women that city and state laws required segregation on the buses. They did, however, make a single concession to the thirty-seven percent of the city's residents who were black: the buses would stop at every corner in black neighborhoods, just as they did in the white sections of town.

On May 17 of that year, the *Montgomery Advertiser* carried a headline announcing the Supreme Court ruling outlawing segregation in public schools. Inspired anew, Jo Ann Robinson wrote to Montgomery's mayor, W. A. Gayle. "Mayor Gayle, three quarters of the riders of these public conveyances are Negroes," Robinson argued, now as president of the Women's Political Council. "If Negroes did not patronize them they could not possible operate . . . there has been talk from 25 or more local organizations of planning a city-wide boycott of buses."

It was a bold letter, but no one in Montgomery knew if black riders could actually be united to stage a boycott. A few years earlier, the minister of the Dexter Avenue Baptist Church had tried to prompt a group of blacks to walk off a bus in protest. The driver had ordered Rev. Vernon Johns to get up and let a white man sit down. Johns stood up and challenged the other blacks to march off the bus with him. They told him they weren't moving. "You ought to knowed better," said one.

Asking blacks to protest for their rights in Montgomery was asking a lot. They could expect to be fired from their jobs and harassed on the streets, and could possibly become the victims of an economic boycott on the part of white segregationists. A successful bus boycott would need to be mapped out carefully and executed with discipline. Rev. Johns' niece, Barbara Johns, had successfully launched a school boycott back in Virginia in 1951. In 1955, the Women's Political Council had worked out plans for a bus boycott in Montgomery.

All they needed was the right moment. Their hope was that soon the right person—someone who could not only withstand the scrutiny and anger of whites but who could inspire black Montgomery to take action—would be arrested. The organizers would then spread the news throughout the black community in hopes that enough people would respond to muster a boycott.

Early in 1955, fifteen-year-old Claudette Colvin was dragged from a bus by police and arrested after she and an elderly woman refused to give up their seats in the middle section of the bus. The old woman left when the driver went to fetch the police, but Colvin stayed in her seat. "I done paid my dime, I ain't got no reason to move," she said repeatedly.

E. D. Nixon and the NAACP came to the girl's defense, and the association's Youth Council adviser, Rosa Parks, took a particular interest. She herself had been thrown off a Montgomery bus eleven years earlier for refusing to enter through the back door. The driver of that bus, James F. Blake, had kept her money, told her to step outside, and driven away. Now Parks and Nixon, along with Jo Ann Robinson, wanted to take Colvin's case to federal court to demonstrate that segregated buses were illegal under the United States Constitution. They began to raise money for Colvin's defense and to arrange speaking engagements throughout the town to garner support.

But just before the court date, Nixon discovered that Colvin had "taken a tumble," as they said in Montgomery—she was pregnant. Fearing the white press would portray her as a "bad girl" just trying to cause trouble, he decided it would be foolhardy to appeal Colvin's case to a higher court. She was not the "right person" in whom to invest money, time, and the great hope of ending segregation. That person would have to be above reproach.

Nixon would reach the same decision twice that year about other women who had refused to be humiliated on the bus and gotten themselves arrested. "I had to be sure that I had somebody I could win with . . . to ask people to give us half a million dollars to fight discrimination on a bus line, I [had to be] able to say, 'We got a good leg in,'" he later explained.

Rosa Parks in Montgomery, Alabama.

The Highlander Folk School

Rosa Parks at the Highlander Folk School.

During the Great Depression, Myles Horton, a teacher and community activist, developed a simple philosophy: people are not powerless. With guidance, they can solve their own problems.

Horton put his philosophy into practice in 1932 when he founded the Highlander Folk School in Monteagle, Tennessee. The problems of oppressed workers in the Appalachian Mountains were the initial items on Highlander's agenda. The school offered workshops on labor unions, workers' rights, and race relations.

During the 1950s and '60s, the center evolved into a training ground for civil rights activists. Because the school's resources were limited, Horton concentrated on identifying new leaders, training them, and sending them back home to work for change. Rosa Parks attended a workshop at Highlander the summer before the Montgomery bus boycott. "At Highlander," Parks recalled, "I found out for the first time in my adult life that this could be a unified society, that there was such a thing as people of differing races and backgrounds meeting together in workshops and living together in peace and harmony. It was a place I was very reluctant to leave. I gained there strength to persevere in my work for freedom, not just for blacks but all oppressed people." Other civil rights leaders who attended Highlander workshops include James Bevel, John Lewis, Diane Nash, and Marion Barry.

With its emphasis on practical training for daily life, Horton's novel approach to education paid off. In 1955, Highlander began a remarkably successful program in which black adults learned to read and write—and thereby qualified to vote. A black hairdresser, Bernice Robinson, taught the first class, which was held two nights a week in the back of a small store. Horton chose a nonprofessional teacher so that the sessions would not be dominated by old-fashioned pedagogical methods. Robinson taught the fourteen students what they wanted to learn: how to write their names, how to write letters to their sons in the army, how to write a check. "We decided we'd pitch it on a basis of

them becoming full citizens and taking their place in society and demanding their rights, and being real men and women in their own right," Horton said. When the first class ended, eight students passed the voting test. Soon, other "citizenship schools" opened across the South.

Not surprisingly, Highlander faced stiff opposition from segregationist whites. In 1957, the IRS revoked the school's tax-exempt status. In 1959, Arkansas attorney general Bruce Bennett led a hearing to determine whether Highlander was part of a communist conspiracy. And in 1960, the school's charter was revoked. Horton was found guilty of selling beer without a license and of violating a Tennessee law that forbade blacks and whites from attending school together.

But Highlander withstood the attack. Horton re-opened his center in Knoxville; later he moved it to New Market, Tennessee. Though the school has turned its attention to new issues—among them nuclear waste and strip mining—the Highlander approach remains the same: education of the people, for the people, by the people.

Since Claudette Colvin's arrest and conviction, Rosa Parks had attended a workshop on race relations at the Highlander Folk School in Monteagle, Tennessee. The school was established during the depression to train poor people in the South to help themselves and their community. Virginia Durr, wife of a progressive white attorney, Clifford Durr, knew Rosa Parks well. She followed Parks' activities in the NAACP and put up the money to send her to Highlander. Parks said later of her Highlander experience, "That was the first time in my life I had lived in an atmosphere of complete equality with the members of the other race . . . I did enjoy going up there. I felt it could be done without the signs that said 'White' and 'Colored'—without any artificial barriers of racial segregation."

In 1955, Rosa Parks was a quiet but strong-willed woman of forty-three. She had worked for several years as the secretary of the Montgomery chapter of the NAACP, and continued to work with the association's Youth Council. When Parks was a student, Montgomery had no high school for black children. Her family sent her to the laboratory school at Alabama State College. Unable to find work commensurate with her education, Parks became a seamstress. She did some part-time tailoring for Clifford and Virginia Durr, and, in the winter of 1955, was working as a tailor's assistant at a department store.

On Thursday, December 1, amid blinking Christmas lights in the downtown shopping district, Rosa Parks boarded a Cleveland Avenue bus at Court Square. She sat down in the first row of the middle section of seats, an area open to blacks as long as no whites were left standing. At the next stop—the Empire Theatre—some whites got on, filling all the whites-only seats. One white man was left standing.

The bus driver was James Blake, the same man who had evicted Parks from a bus in 1943 for refusing to use the back door. He told Parks and the other three blacks in the fifth row to get up so that the white man could sit down. Nobody moved.

"Y'all better make it light on yourself and let me have those seats," said Blake. Three of the people rose, but Parks, though she shifted to allow the man next to her to get up, didn't move from her seat.

"When he saw me still sitting," Parks recalls, "he asked if I was going to stand up, and I said, 'No, I'm not.' And he said, 'Well, if you don't stand up, I'm going to have to call the police and have you arrested.' I said, 'You may do that.'"

Parks was taken in a police car to the city jail, where she was booked for violating the law banning integration. She longed for a drink of water to soothe her dry throat. "But they wouldn't permit me to drink out of the water fountain," she recalls. "It was for whites only."

She used her one phone call to telephone her mother, who was living with Rosa and her husband. Could she tell Rosa's husband and ask him to come get her out of jail? News of Parks' arrest soon reached E. D. Nixon, the man who had headed the NAACP when Rosa Parks was its secretary. Nixon in turn tried to reach Fred Gray, one of the city's two black lawyers. Gray wasn't home, so Nixon called Clifford Durr, a former member of the Federal Communications Commission who had recently returned to Montgomery from Washington.

"He said, 'If you don't stand up, I'm going to have to call the police and have you arrested.' I said, 'You may do that.'"

"About six o'clock that night the telephone rang," Virginia Durr remembers, "and Mr. Nixon said he understood that Mrs. Parks had been arrested, and he [had] called the jail, but they wouldn't tell him why she was arrested. So they thought if Cliff called, a white lawyer, they might tell him. Cliff called, and they said she'd been arrested under the segregation laws . . . so Mr. Nixon raised the bond and signed the paper and got Mrs. Parks out."

Nixon had a proposition for her. "Mrs. Parks," he said, "with your permission we can break down segregation on the bus with your case." Parks consulted with her husband and mother, who had long told her that she was going to get herself lynched by working with Nixon and the NAACP. Parks decided to let Nixon make her case into a cause. "I'll go along with you, Mr. Nixon," she said.

At home, Nixon made a list of black ministers in Montgomery. Lacking influence with the current leaders of the NAACP, some of whom snubbed him because he had only a sixth-grade education and worked on a train as a sleeping-car porter, Nixon decided that clergymen, important leaders in the black community, could do as much if not more to mobilize people. Of these ministers, he was best acquainted with the Reverend Ralph Abernathy, whom he knew through past work with the NAACP.

At 5 A.M. Friday, the morning after the arrest, Nixon called Abernathy, the twenty-nine-year-old minister of the First Baptist Church. Abernathy knew most of the other ministers and black civic leaders in Montgomery. After discussing the situation, Nixon called eighteen other ministers and arranged a meeting for Friday evening to discuss Parks' arrest and figure out what they might do about it.

Meanwhile, Fred Gray had called Jo Ann Robinson Thursday night and told her of Parks' arrest. Robinson knew Parks from the Colvin case and believed she would be the ideal person to sustain a test case against segregation. Robinson called the leaders of the Women's Political Council. They urged her to initiate a

This is for Monday, December 5, 1955

Another Negro woman has been arrested and thrown into jail because she refused to get up out of her seat on the bus for a white person to sit down.

It is the second time since the Claudette Colbert case that a Negro woman has been arrested for the same thing This has to be stopped.

Negroes have rights, too, for if Negroes did not ride the buses, they could not operate. Three-fourths of the riders are Negroes, yet we are arrested, or have to stand over empty seats. If we do not do something to stop these arrests, they will continue. The next time it may be you, or your daughter, or mother.

This woman's case will come up on Monday. We are, therefore, asking every Negro to stay off the buses Monday in protest of the arrest and trial. Don't ride the buses to work, to town, to school, or anywhere on Monday.

You can afford to stay out of school for one day if you have no other way to go except by bus.

You can also afford to stay out of town for one day. If you work, take a cab, or walk. But please, children and grown-ups, don't ride the bus at all on Monday. Please stay off of all buses Monday.

One of the 35,000 handbills Jo Ann Robinson stayed up all night mimeographing. The next morning, she called on her students at Alabama State College to help distribute the anonymous handbills throughout Montgomery.

Jo Ann Robinson in the 1950's.

boycott in support of Parks, starting the following Monday, Parks' trial date.

Robinson went to Alabama State College, cut stencils, and mimeographed 35,000 handbills. It took all night. In the morning she asked a few of her students to help load the handbills into her car. She drove to elementary and high schools where students she had telephoned earlier were waiting. The students distributed the handbills in school to be taken home to parents.

Robinson did not put her name or that of the Women's Political Council on the handbills. She feared city and state officials would realize she had used the mimeograph machine at Alabama State and, in revenge, cut off funds for the all-black school. The flier read, "This is for Monday, Dec. 5, 1955 — Another Negro woman has been arrested and thrown into jail because she refused to get up out of her seat on the bus and give it to a white person. It is the second time since the Claudette Colvin case that a Negro woman has been arrested for the same thing. This has to be stopped . . .

"The woman's case will come up on Monday. We are therefore asking every Negro to stay off the buses Monday in protest of the arrest and trial. Don't ride the buses to work, to town, to school, or anywhere on Monday . . . "

Thousands of the anonymous leaflets passed secretly through Montgomery's black neighborhoods—in stores, schools, bars, and churches.

By the time the ministers and civil rights leaders met on Friday evening, word of the boycott had spread throughout the city. The Reverend L. Roy Bennett, president of the Interdenominational Ministers Alliance, headed the meeting. He concluded that there was no time for debate—the boycott was on for the following Monday. He wanted the ministers to begin organizing committees to orchestrate the action. Some in attendance objected, calling for debate on the pros and cons of a boycott. Almost half of them left the meeting in frustration before any decisions could be reached. But those remaining eventually agreed to spread word of the one-day boycott in their Sunday sermons and to hold a mass meeting Monday night to decide if the boycott should continue.

E. D. Nixon was not at this meeting he had arranged—he was at work as a Pullman-car porter on the Montgomery-Chicago route. But before leaving for work, Nixon had taken one of the handbills mimeographed by Jo Ann Robinson and called a white reporter, Joe Azbell, at the *Montgomery Advertiser*.

"He said, 'I've got a big story for you and I want you to meet me,'" recalls Azbell. "Now, E. D. doesn't talk in long sentences, he's very short and brusque . . . He said, 'Can you meet me?' I said, 'Yeah, I can meet you.' So we met down at Union Station and he showed me one of these leaflets . . . And he said,

Organizing Before the Boycott:

An Interview with Jo Ann Robinson

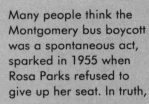

Many people think the Montgomery bus boycott was a spontaneous act, sparked in 1955 when Rosa Parks refused to give up her seat. In truth, the boycott was anything but spontaneous. Here, Jo Ann Robinson, a prime mover of the boycott, reflects on her role and gives an indication of just how well black people had prepared themselves to fight segregation.

The Woman's Political Council was an organization begun in 1946 after dozens of black people had been arrested on the buses. We witnessed the arrests and humiliations and the court trials and the fines paid by people who just sat down on empty seats. We knew something had to be done.

We organized the Women's Council and within a month's time we had over a hundred members. We organized a second chapter and a third, and soon we had more than 300 members. We had members in every elementary, junior high, and senior high school. We had them organized from federal and state and local jobs; wherever there were more than ten blacks employed, we had a member there. We were organized to the point that we knew that in a matter of hours we could corral the whole city.

The evening that Rosa Parks was arrested, Fred Gray called me and told me that her case would be [heard] on Monday. As president of the main body of the Women's Political Council, I got on the phone and called all the officers of the three chapters. I told them that Rosa Parks had been arrested and she would be tried. They said, "You have the plans, put them into operation."

I didn't go to bed that night. I cut those stencils and took them to [the] college. The fellow who let me in during the night is dead now . . . he was in the business department. I ran off 35,000 copies.

I talked with every member [of the Women's Council] in the elementary, junior high and senior high schools and told them to have somebody on the campus. I told them that I would be there to deliver them [the handbills]. I taught my classes from 8:00 to 10:00. When my 10:00 class was over, I took two senior students with me. I would drive to the place of dissemination and a kid would be there to grab [the handbills].

After we had circulated those 35,000 circulars, we went by the church. That was about 3:30 in the afternoon. We took them to the minister . . . The

An empty bus during the Montgomery bus boycott.

[ministers] agreed to meet that night to decide what should be done about the boycott after the first day. You see, the Women's Council planned it only for Monday, and it was left up to the men to take over after we had forced them really to decide whether or not it had been successful enough to continue, and how long it was to be continued.

They had agreed at the Friday night meeting that they would call this meeting at Holt Street Church and they would let the audience determine whether or not they would continue the bus boycott or end it in one day.

Monday night, the ministers held their meeting. The church itself holds four or five thousand people. But there were thousands of people outside of the church that night. They had to put up loudspeakers so they would know what was happening. When they got through reporting that very few people had ridden the bus, that the boycott was really a success—I don't know if there was one vote that said 'No, don't continue that boycott'—they voted unanimously

to continue the boycott. And instead of it lasting one day as the Women's Council had planned it, it lasted for thirteen months.

The spirit, the desire, the injustices that had been endured by thousands of people through the years . . . I think people were fed up, they had reached the point that they knew there was no return. That they had to do it or die. And that's what kept it going. It was the sheer spirit for freedom, for the feeling of being a man or a woman.

Now when you ask why the courts had to come in, they had to come in. You get 52,000 people in the streets and nobody's showing any fear, something had to give. So the Supreme Court had to rule that segregation was not the way of life . . . We [met] after the news came through. All of these people who had fought got together to communicate and to rejoice and to share that built-up emotion and all the other feelings they had lived with during the past thirteen months. And we just rejoiced together.

'I want to tell you what we're going to do. We're gonna boycott these buses. We're tired of them fooling with our women—they done it for the last time.' So I said, 'Okay.' [Nixon] said, 'You gonna put this on the front page?' And I said, 'Yeah, I'm gonna try to.'"

The story of the impending boycott ran on the *Advertiser's* front page Sunday morning, spreading the news to blacks who might have missed the leaflets. The ministers reinforced the call from the pulpit that morning. But uncertainty lingered among boycott organizers. Would Montgomery's blacks unite for the boycott or continue to ride the buses from fear of white retaliation? The clergymen had barely been able to agree on supporting the one-day strike. To add to their worries, it looked as though it were going to rain.

On Monday morning the sky was very dark. City police were claiming that blacks had organized "goon squads" to keep other blacks from riding the buses. The police chief said he would have two motorcycle policemen trailing every bus to hold off the "goons."

By 5:30 A.M., however, a torn piece of cardboard appeared on a bus shelter at Court Square, a main downtown bus stop. It said, "PEOPLE DON'T RIDE THE BUSES TODAY. DON'T RIDE IT FOR FREEDOM."

That morning, Martin Luther King, Jr., was called to his front window by his wife, Coretta. Fresh from Boston University's doctoral program in theology, King was the new minister at the Dexter Avenue Baptist Church. He had replaced Rev. Vernon Johns in 1954. "I was in the kitchen, drinking my coffee, when I heard Coretta cry, 'Martin, Martin, come quickly . . . '," King wrote later, remembering the day. "As I approached the front window, Coretta pointed joyfully to a slowly moving bus: 'Darling, it's empty!' I could hardly believe what I saw. I knew the South Jackson line, which ran past our house, carried more Negro passengers than any other line in Montgomery . . . " And then another bus passed their house—empty. They knew the boycott was going to be a success.

Montgomery's eighteen black-owned taxi companies had agreed to transport blacks for the same fare they would pay on the bus—ten cents—and on this Monday morning the cabs were crammed with black people. An *Alabama Journal* reporter described the day. "Negroes were on almost every street corner in the downtown area, silent, waiting for rides or moving about to keep warm, but few got on buses . . . scores of Negroes were walking, their lunches in brown paper sacks under their arms. None spoke to white people. They exchanged little talk among themselves. It was an almost solemn event."

A local black historian who watched the day's events later reported, "The 'old unlearned Negroes' were confused. It seemed they could not figure out if the police [riding along with the buses] would arrest them or protect them if they attempted to ride the buses . . . the few Negroes who boarded the buses were more confused. They found it difficult to get off without being embarrassed by other Negroes who waited at the bus stops throughout the city. Some were seen ducking in the aisles as the buses passed various stops."

In court on Monday morning, a large crowd of blacks looked on as Rosa Parks was found guilty of violating the segregation laws and given a suspended sentence. She was fined ten dollars and had to pay four dollars in court fees.

"PEOPLE DON'T RIDE THE BUSES TODAY. DON'T RIDE IT FOR FREEDOM."

That afternoon, the preachers met with black leaders to prepare for that night's community meeting. Several feared a repeat of the raucous Friday night meeting, when half of the group had walked out. Rev. Bennett was not popular with everyone in attendance; his abrupt style of leadership often caused internal bickering. One community leader, Rufus Lewis, worried that the boycott's momentum might wither. Lewis, who had started a unique private nightclub for blacks—only registered voters could become members—understood what motivated people and had a solid grasp of Montgomery politics.

To plan efficiently and really let the city know that something new was being done, the group decided to set themselves up as a new organization. Rev. Abernathy suggested the group be called the "Montgomery Improvement Association." Rev. Bennett declared that the group should elect a president. Rufus Lewis saw this as his chance to move the well-entrenched Bennett aside in a diplomatic way.

Quickly, Lewis nominated Martin Luther King. King was the minister at the church Lewis attended, so Lewis had heard him speak often. More importantly, King was new in town. Others at the meeting also saw the advantages of having Rev. King lead the group. For several months Ralph Abernathy had been trying to get the new minister involved in civil rights work, but King was too busy getting his church in order.

"Rev. King was a young man," E. D. Nixon recalls, "a very intelligent young man. He had not been here long enough for the city fathers to put their hand on him. Usually they'd find some young man just come to town . . . pat him on the shoulder and tell him what a nice church he got. [They'd say,] 'Reverend, your suit don't look so nice to represent the so-and-so Baptist Church' . . . and they'd get him a suit . . . you'd have to watch out for that kind of thing."

With King as their new leader, the organizers faced the difficult question of whether or not the boycott should continue beyond Monday. The one-day boycott had shown a strength of unity not seen before in Montgomery. But an extended boycott would be a direct assault by blacks on the system of Jim Crow—a serious and potentially dangerous assault.

Several of the ministers rose to suggest that the boycott might best be left as a one-day success. The strike might disintegrate if rain fell or the police started to harass the boycotters. Abernathy recalls that no one in the meeting believed the boycott would last beyond the end of the work week—four more days.

E. D. Nixon, in a thunderous voice, said the black ministers should confront the whites no matter what. The time had come to take a stand. Nixon was angry that his successor as head of the NAACP refused to become involved in the boycott unless he got approval from the national office.

"What's the matter with you people?" Nixon said, his big hands gesturing at the assembled ministers. "Here you have been living off the sweat of these washerwomen all these years and you have never done anything for them. Now you have a chance to pay them back, and you're too damn scared to stand on your feet and be counted! The time has come when you men is going to have to learn to be grown men or scared boys."

The group agreed to wait until that night's meeting and let the people decide if the boycott should continue. No one was sure how many people would show up. The meeting was to be held at the Holt Street Baptist Church, because it was large and because it was in the black section of town. People might feel safer if they didn't have to travel through white communities to attend such a controversial meeting.

Rosa Parks with E. D. Nixon (far left).

Twenty-six-year-old Martin Luther King, Jr., the newly elected president of the Montgomery Improvement Association, had about twenty minutes to prepare what he later described as one of the most important speeches of his life.

That evening, Joe Azbell drove to Holt Street to cover the meeting. "The Holt Street Baptist Church was probably the most fired up, enthusiastic gathering of human beings that I've ever seen," recalls Azbell. "I came down the street and I couldn't believe there were that many cars. I parked many blocks from the church just to get a place for my car. I went on up to the church, and they made way for me because I was the first white person there . . . I was two minutes late and they were [already] preaching, and that audience was so on fire that the preacher would get up and say, 'Do you want your freedom?' And they'd say, 'Yeah, I want my freedom!' [The preacher would say,] 'Are you for what we're doing?'; 'Yeah, go ahead, go ahead!' . . . and they were so excited . . . I've never heard singing like that . . . they were on fire for freedom. There was a spirit there that no one could capture again . . . it was so powerful.

The Reverend Martin
Luther King, Jr.,
addressing a mass
meeting of boycotters.

Twenty-six-year-old
Martin Luther King, Jr.
(right), with the twenty-
nine-year-old Ralph
Abernathy, on the steps
of Rev. King's Dexter
Avenue Baptist Church.

"And then King stood up, and most of them didn't even know who he was. And yet he was a master speaker . . . I went back and I wrote a special column, I wrote that this was the beginning of a flame that would go across America."

Azbell was particularly moved by King's speech, at once a rousing call to action and a warning to disavow violence. "There comes a time," King said, "that people get tired. We are here this evening to say to those who have mistreated us so long that we are tired—tired of being segregated and humiliated; tired of being kicked about by the brutal feet of oppression . . . For many years we have shown amazing patience. We have sometimes given our white brothers the feeling that we like the way we were being treated. But we come here tonight to be saved from that patience that makes us patient with anything less than freedom and justice. One of the great glories of democracy is the right to protest for right . . . if you will protest courageously and yet with dignity and Christian love, when the history books are written in future generations the historians will pause and say, 'There lived a great people—a black people—who injected new meaning and dignity into the veins of civilization.' That is our challenge and our overwhelming responsibility."

The Reverend Ralph Abernathy spoke with humor and a down-home fundamentalism that balanced King's more philosophical tone.

In his reporter's notebook, Azbell scribbled that the strongest applause and show of emotion came when the young preacher intoned, "We will not retreat one inch in our fight to secure and hold onto our American citizenship."

After King's speech, Rosa Parks was introduced to the crowd, who gave her a standing ovation. Then Rev. Abernathy rose to recite the demands the Montgomery Improvement Association had decided upon in the name of the boycotters. His words silenced the throngs packed into the pews, the balcony above, and the streets outside.

The first demand was for courteous treatment on the buses. The second called for first-come, first-served seating, with whites in the front and blacks in the back. The third requested the hiring of black drivers on black bus routes.

Rev. Abernathy asked for the vote. Throughout the church, people began to stand, at first in ones and twos. Soon, every person in the Holt Street Baptist Church was standing in affirmation. The thousands outside cheered. The answer was a resounding "yes."

"The fear left that had shackled us across the years—all left suddenly when we were in that church together," Abernathy said, recollecting the moment.

Though unafraid, people who left Holt Street Baptist Church that December night were uncertain about how the city's white leaders would respond to their demands. The Montgomery police were their prime concern. The police had already begun harassing blacks waiting for cab rides. A few months earlier, a white policeman had shot a black man who had refused the bus driver's order to leave the bus and reboard through the back door. When the man demanded his dime back, the police officer intervened and suddenly fired his gun, killing the man.

What would the police do to the boycotters, whose defiance was now organized and citywide? How would the mayor and the Citizens' Council and the Ku Klux Klan accept this mass demonstration of black pride, so new and foreign?

The answers came quickly. On Thursday, December 8, only four days into the boycott, the Montgomery Improvement Association (MIA), including King and attorney Fred Gray, met with the city commissioners and representatives of the bus company. The MIA presented its three demands: courtesy on the part of the bus drivers; the hiring of black bus drivers; and segregated seating on a first-come, first-served basis. King made it clear that they were not seeking an end to segregation through their boycott. "That's a matter for the legislature and the courts," he said before the meeting. "We feel we have a plan within the [existing] law."

The bus company's manager, James H. Bagley, and its attorney, Jack Crenshaw, denied that drivers were regularly discourteous, rejected the idea of black drivers, and stated that the proposed seating plan was in violation of state statute and city code. Attorney Gray responded to this last point by showing that the seating plan was in no way a violation of existing segregation laws. In fact, the seating arrangements the MIA proposed were already in practice in other Alabama cities, including Mobile, whose bus system was run by the same company as Montgomery's.

But attorney Crenshaw was adamant. According to King, Commissioner Frank Parks was ready to accept the seating proposal, but Crenshaw argued, "I don't see how we can do it within the law. If it were legal I would be the first to go along with it, but it just isn't legal. The only way that it can be done is to change your segregation laws."

Commissioner Clyde Sellers, staunchly opposed to integration, was not about to compromise. And Crenshaw offered perhaps the most damaging argument when he said, "If we granted the Negroes these demands, they would go about boasting of a victory that they had won over the white people, and this we will not stand for." It was this "give them an inch and they'll take a mile" attitude that would unite many white people in Montgomery against the boycott.

Crenshaw's words inflamed Rev. King. "Feeling that our demands were moderate," he later wrote, "I assumed that they would be granted with little question . . . the experience taught me a lesson . . . even when we asked for justice within the segregation laws, the 'powers that be' were not willing to grant it. Justice and equality, I saw, would never come while segregation remained, because the basic purpose of segregation was to perpetuate injustice and inequity."

At this same meeting, Commissioner Sellers hinted to the boycott leaders that the city's 210 black cab drivers would be heavily fined if they didn't charge every passenger the minimum forty-five-cent fare.

The boycott leaders now had to face the possibility that the taxicabs—their main source of alternate transportation—would no longer be available at low fares. King called Baton Rouge, Louisiana, to speak with those who had successfully staged a bus boycott months before. Rev. T. J. Jemison had worked out a detailed strategy for transporting boycotters, a complex system of carpooling with drop-off and pick-up points and a communications network to connect those needing rides with those offering them. He suggested that the MIA form a private taxi system. This could be done only if blacks in Montgomery could be convinced to use their cars to ferry maids and laborers to work.

At a mass meeting of bus boycotters Thursday night, Rev. King asked for volunteers. They would need drivers and automobiles. The preachers would be willing to drive their own cars, he assured audience members, who at first were quiet to the suggestion of sharing their automobiles with others. To many blacks, car ownership was a status symbol that distinguished them from the less privileged.

Jo Ann Robinson volunteered to drive her car—the one she had used to carry the handbills heralding the boycott. Other members of the Women's Council raised their hands; so did many homemakers. Mrs. A. W. West offered to transport workers in her green Cadillac. More than 150 people volunteered. Later, three whites from a nearby Air Force base would volunteer, and numerous white women would help their maids and babysitters get to work.

The MIA appointed a Transportation Committee to work with some black postal workers who knew the layout of the streets. They developed an efficient plan for transporting the boycotters. Within one week of the meeting at which people volunteered their cars, the MIA had organized forty-eight dispatch and forty-two pick-up stations.

The boycott had withstood its first assault. But setting up this elaborate system required funding. Mass meetings were held twice a week to keep the boycotters informed, to keep spirits high, and to collect contributions. Every Monday and Thursday night, a church would rock with a packed crowd. "This movement was made up of just ordinary black people, some of whom made as little as five dollars a week," reporter Azbell remembers, "but they would give one dollar of that to help support the boycott."

In time the MIA bought several station wagons to use as taxis. The churches put their names on the side of many of the cars, which became known as "rolling churches." Financial support came from other sources as well. Members of Montgomery's Jewish community offered money, as did some white southerners who often gave anonymously. As news of the boycott spread, sympathizers in the North offered assistance, and the NAACP organized fundraising events. E. D. Nixon, who was also the president of the local chapter of the Brotherhood of Sleeping Car Porters, garnered union support from the United Automobile Workers in Detroit.

"One feels history is being made in Montgomery these days."

Days turned into weeks, and the boycott continued unabated. "One feels history is being made in Montgomery these days," wrote white librarian Juliette Morgan in a letter to the *Advertiser*. "It is hard to imagine a soul so dead, a heart so hard, a vision so blinded and provincial as not to be awed with admiration at the quiet dignity, discipline and dedication with which the Negroes have conducted the boycott." Morgan compared the movement to Mahatma Gandhi's struggle against the British in India.

The comparison to Gandhi's successful struggle was apt. As a doctoral student at Boston University, King had read some of the writings of Mohandas Gandhi. Gandhi united the people of India against their colonial ruler, England, by advocating nonviolence and passive resistance—that is, by refusing to cooperate within the confines of an unjust system. King learned more about Gandhi when he met with the Reverend Glenn Smiley, and later with divinity student James Lawson, who had studied pacifism in India. But King's first uses of the nonviolent method were based more on the Bible and Christian pacifism than on the teachings of the Mahatma. As both sides of the boycott dug in for what looked like a protracted battle, King preached the importance of meeting hate with love. For the struggle to be successful, the movement needed to win the support of morally decent and compassionate people. In the face of threats, being fired from work, or even being beaten, to react with violence would undermine the righteousness of the cause.

Commissioner Sellers and his police department were undaunted. When their first attempt at breaking the boycott by pressuring cab drivers failed, they turned to other means. They would try to divide the leadership, set well-to-do blacks against poor blacks, and support segregationist organizations like the Ku Klux

As president of the Montgomery Improvement Association, King worked with the Transportation Committee to develop a plan for moving the boycotters to and from work during the bus strike.

The E. L. Posey parking lot became a transfer point for the intricate system of cabs, station wagons, and carpools that replaced the buses during the boycott.

Klan, which would strike violently at the boycotters.

In early January, Commissioner Sellers, clearly the most segregationist of the three commissioners, attended a meeting of the white Citizens' Council. He announced dramatically that he was joining the organization.

On January 21, the City Commission met with three black ministers, none of whom represented the MIA. The commission's hope was that the MIA did not truly reflect the will of blacks in Montgomery. If more "reasonable" ministers were to agree to a compromise, perhaps the boycotters would stop their protest. The compromise consisted of reserving ten seats in the front of each bus for whites, ten seats in the back for blacks, and having the remaining seats in the middle available on a first-come, first-served basis. The commission would not promise to hire black drivers for the black routes, and segregation, in this modified form, would continue. The three ministers accepted the proposal.

The commission then leaked news of the agreement to the *Advertiser*, which ran bold headlines on the Sunday paper's front page falsely announcing the end of the boycott.

But King, Abernathy, and Nixon heard about the hoax and went bar-hopping on Saturday night, passing the word that the story to appear in the morning paper was a lie—the boycott was still on. The commission had underestimated the support of the MIA by Montgomery blacks. Very few rode the buses on Monday.

When they realized that the ploy was not going to work, the ministers publicly repudiated the compromise. They told King they had not understood the proposal that had been set before them. The commissioners were enraged at what they viewed as a lack of reasonableness. And when the public learned of the failed compromise, there was increasing concern among the city's segregationists that their commissioners were not holding the line against integration. The segregationists renewed their pressure on the local politicians. Mayor Gayle, in response to this embarrassing and maddening situation, announced that he would no longer negotiate with the boycotters. He said, "There seems to be a belief on the part of the Negroes that they have the white people hemmed up in a corner and they are not going to give an inch until they can force the white people of our community to submit to their demands—in fact, swallow all of them." He called the leaders of the boycott "a group of Negro radicals." He ended his vitriolic barrage by saying, "When and if the Negro people desire to end the boycott, my door is open to them. But until they are ready to end it, there will be no more discussions."

The bus company was feeling the economic costs of the boycott and downtown businesses were also suffering. These financial burdens, combined with the tense-

White Support of the Montgomery Boycott:

An Interview with Virginia Durr

Born in 1903, Virginia Foster Durr was raised in Birmingham, where her father was a preacher. She spent summers at her grandparents' plantation in Union Springs, Alabama. Later she moved with her husband, attorney Clifford Durr, to Washington, D.C. Her brother-in-law was Hugo Black, a justice on the Supreme Court. Here, Durr tells of the difficulties whites faced when they were openly sympathetic to the Montgomery bus boycott.

I was born into a segregated system, and I took it for granted. Nobody told me any different. It really wasn't until I got to Washington that I began to realize how much at variance the South was from the rest of the country and how very wrong the system was. So when I came back to Montgomery, in 1951, after almost twenty years, I no longer took the system for granted.

The first thing that happened to whites like us who were sympathetic to the boycott was that we lost our businesses. People didn't come to us. We got a reputation. My husband got mighty little law business after he took a very decided stand. People like my husband and Aubrey Williams [publisher of the *Southern Farmer*] realized that they were cutting their own throats. Aubrey lost all of his advertising, every bit of it.

The fact that our family stood by us even though they did not agree with us was our salvation. If they had disowned us, had not stood by us, we could not have stayed. We were lucky because Clifford was kin to so many people in Montgomery County. It was difficult for them to ostracize us on account of that strong feeling of kinship.

It all gets down to economics. White men were terrified that if they took any position at all they would lose their

Virginia Durr, preparing to testify at a hearing in New Orleans.

business, as my husband had. They couldn't sell real estate to blacks or they would get in bad with the bank. You had to have a great deal of security to be willing to take that kind of ostracism and disapproval.

There was another kind of terror. Some whites were scared that they wouldn't be invited to the ball, to the parties. It's a terror of being a social failure, of not making your way in the world. Now that's not nearly as bad as being lynched or killed or beaten up. But it is a terrible fear; that's the fear that possesses most men today.

I think the women played a tremendous part in the movement, the white and the black women. For years, we had an integrated prayer group here. We'd pray together every morning. That was broken up by one of those white Nazi groups. The husbands and uncles and brothers of these women took out advertisements in the papers, and many of them repudiated their own wives.

When I heard that the boycott had been successful, I felt pure, unadulterated joy. It was like a fountain of joy. Of course the blacks felt that way, but the white friends I had felt the way I did. We felt joy and release. It was as if a great burden had fallen off us.

Members of the MIA met often to avert violence and circumvent the city commissioners' efforts to end the boycott.

Lone white bus riders were seen frequently during the boycott.

ness of the confrontation, fueled the anger of even some politically moderate whites in Montgomery. Telegrams, phone calls, and letters of support poured into city hall. Claiming overwhelming support, Mayor Gayle announced, "There is no need for us to straddle the fence any longer. I am taking a stand and so are the other commissioners."

Battle-cry responses from segregationists prompted the mayor to further angry statements. For example, he asked housewives not to drive their maids to work.

"They'd arrest you if you went six miles [an hour] in a five-mile zone," remembers Virginia Durr. "But that didn't last, because the white women got so furious at the mayor that they kept . . . writing letters to the paper saying, 'If the mayor wants to do my wash and wants to cook for me and clean up after my children let him come and do it. But as long as he won't do it I'm certainly not going to get rid of this wonderful woman I've had for fifteen years.'"

The humor of the situation escaped the mayor, now a segregationist hero for his "no-talk" and "get-tough" policy. On January 24, Mayor Gayle and Commissioner Parks (who weeks earlier had been ready to accept the MIA's proposed seating plan) both joined the white Citizens' Council. With police commissioner Clyde Sellers already a member, all three city commissioners now belonged to the council. Within weeks, the entire County Board of Revenue had also joined.

The tension in Montgomery continued to escalate. On January 30, King's house was bombed. His wife Coretta fled to a back room with her seven-week-old baby to escape injury.

On February 1, E. D. Nixon's home was bombed.

Also on February 1, Fred Gray filed suit in United States District Court challenging the constitutionality of bus segregation. As Ralph Abernathy later described the sequence of events, "Our first demand was to have more courtesy on the part of the bus drivers, to eliminate them calling our women names . . . [calling them] cows and niggers and things like that . . . we could not solve the problem because they were not willing to cooperate . . . all they had to do was change the law and make it permissible for black people to ride on the buses under those conditions . . . but that was the most important lesson of the boycott . . . the city leaders were not going to compromise, so consequently we needed a ruling from the U.S. Supreme Court."

On February 1, about 6,000 people in Montgomery belonged to the white Citizens' Council. By the end of the month, that number had doubled.

A group of prominent white lawyers in Montgomery suggested that the protest could be destroyed by prosecuting the leaders of the MIA under an old, seldom-

Martin Luther King, Jr., was arrested for the first time in his life under an old Alabama statute that denied people the right to boycott. His wife, Coretta, celebrated her husband's arrest because it would bring national attention to the cause.

The bus boycott continued for nearly thirteen months, through rain, heat, and freezing temperatures.

used law prohibiting boycotts. The Montgomery business community, however, was opposed to the idea. Frustrated by the inability of the politicians to resolve the problem, a group of businessmen tried to settle the matter by negotiating with the boycotters themselves. The group, known as the Men of Montgomery, felt that the city's image was already tarnished by the actions and reactions surrounding the boycott; it could only get worse if the ministers who led this nonviolent movement were thrown in jail. But meetings with the MIA produced no solution. On February 13, at the urging of Circuit Solicitor William Thetford, a grand jury met to consider indictments against the boycott leaders.

"If the mayor wants to do my wash and wants to cook for me and clean up after my children, let him come and do it."

On February 21, the grand jury indicted eighty-nine blacks—including King and twenty-four other ministers—for conspiring to boycott. It was, as the Men of Montgomery had feared, a story of national interest.

Also of national interest, on March 12, some 100 United States congressmen signed the Southern Manifesto, taking issue with the Supreme Court's ruling on school desegregation announced some ten months earlier.

When the trial of the boycott leaders began in Alabama, the national press got its first good look at Martin Luther King, Jr., the first defendant. Four days later, King was found guilty. The sentence was a $500 fine and court costs, or 386 days of hard labor. The judge explained that he had imposed this "minimal penalty" because King had promoted nonviolence. King was released on bond; his indictment and conviction became front-page news across the nation.

In an effort to raise money for the boycott and publicize what was happening in Montgomery, King accepted many invitations to speak throughout the country. He maintained a grueling schedule of engagements, and his message and eloquence were met with rapt attention and enthusiastic support.

Meanwhile, the boycott's leaders were pursuing their own court case. Filed by Fred Gray on February 1, the case was on behalf of five women who were challenging the constitutionality of bus segregation. The boycott leaders now considered whether they might call an end to the strike. Their best chance of victory lay with the courts, not in negotiations with city officials or the bus company. But King and others were unhappy with the way those in power had treated them. They insisted on continuing the boycott. If the court did not rule in their favor, the boycott would still offer some chance of success. The boycotters stayed off the buses. They carpooled and walked through winter, spring, and on into the summer of 1956.

In June, the five women won their suit by a two-to-one vote in the special three-judge federal District Court. But the city commissioners appealed the decision to the Supreme Court. The buses remained segregated, and the blacks did not ride them. Meanwhile, whites tried another way to choke off the boycott: preventing the "rolling churches" from getting insurance. Without insurance, these church-owned cars used to transport blacks could not operate legally.

The liability insurance was cancelled four times in as many months, and insurance agents throughout the South were pressured by the city commissioners, the white Citizens' Council, and their supporters to refuse the boycotters coverage. But King arranged for insurance through T. M. Alexander, a black agent in Atlanta. Alexander found a Lloyd's of London underwriter who agreed to sell the boycotters a policy. Blacks stayed off the buses through that autumn.

But the segregationists did not quit. In October, the mayor sought a restraining order in state court, hoping to prevent blacks from gathering on street corners while waiting for the "rolling churches." The mayor claimed that the blacks were singing loudly and bothering residents, thus constituting a public nuisance.

He won a small victory on November 13, when a court granted the order. But on that same day, the boycotters won a far greater triumph. The United States Supreme Court affirmed the lower court's decision outlawing segregation on buses. Nearly a year after Rosa Parks had defied James Blake's order to move to the back of the bus—after months of walking, carpooling, litigation, and intimidation—the boycotters had won. As Jo Ann Robinson said years later, "We felt that we were somebody. That somebody had listened to us, that we had forced the white man to give what we knew [was] our own citizenship . . . And if you have never had the feeling that . . . you are [no longer] an alien, but that this is your country too, then you don't know what I'm talking about. It is a hilarious feeling that just goes all over you, that makes you feel that America is a great country and we're going to do more to make it greater."

The segregationists challenged the ruling, arguing that it violated states' rights. The Supreme Court, however, refused to reconsider the case. The white Citizens' Council forecast racial violence.

The written mandate from the Supreme Court did not arrive in Montgomery until December 20. The next day, nearly thirteen months after the boycott began, blacks boarded Montgomery City Lines buses.

Though thousands of blacks once again rode the buses daily, the streets of Montgomery had become a battleground of another sort. Snipers fired at buses, and a pregnant black woman was shot in the leg while riding a bus. Several weeks later, Rev. Abernathy's home and church were bombed, as were four other black churches and the homes of two pastors. Citing the danger of snipers, the city

Under pressure from segregationists, insurance companies cancelled the insurance policies on the "rolling churches." A black Atlanta insurance agent, T. M. Alexander, got Lloyds of London to underwrite the boycotters' transportation system, enabling the protest to continue legally.

commissioners suspended bus operations after 5 P.M. for a week. A few days after the regular bus schedules resumed, officials imposed a second week-long bus curfew. The white opposition had reason to smile—now *they* were making the blacks walk.

Segregationists distributed fliers that they claimed were written by blacks. "Look Out," said one leaflet. "Liver-lipped Luther [King] is getting us in more trouble every day . . . We get shot at while he hides. Wake up. Mess is his business. Run him out of town."

A group calling itself the Rebel Club sought a franchise to form a whites-only bus line. That was denied, but the bombings continued.

As difficult as it proved for Montgomery to adjust to integrated buses, the city's success fired the imagination of blacks throughout the country. Boycotts began in neighboring Birmingham and Mobile, and also in Tallahassee, Florida.

An informal organization arose out of the network of southern churches that had supported the Montgomery bus boycott. On January 10 and 11, 1957, less than two months after the Supreme Court had ruled in favor of the boycotters, a meeting was called in Atlanta, Georgia. Ministers from eleven southern states met at Martin Luther King, Sr.'s Ebenezer Baptist Church. For two days they discussed the success of the boycott, the new network of churches, the importance of nonviolence both as a tactic and as a morally right position, and plans for the future.

The ministers decided that they needed to establish a formal organization to continue the struggle for civil rights. The Reverend T. J. Jemison, the leader of the 1953 Baton Rouge bus boycott and a founding member of the new organization, described how they eventually chose their name: "Since the NAACP was like waving a red flag in front of some southern whites, we decided that we needed an organization that would do the same thing and yet be called a Christian organization . . . .We chose 'Southern Christian Leadership Conference,' so they would say, 'Well, that's Baptist preachers,' so they didn't fear us."

The new organization then elected the Reverend Dr. Martin Luther King, Jr., as its president. The articulate leadership of King and the founding of the SCLC were two important results of the Montgomery bus boycott. So too was the realization that black people, united for a just cause, could successfully stand up to segregation.

As Martin Luther King wrote in his book *Stride Toward Freedom*, "The story of Montgomery is the story of 50,000 Negroes who were willing to substitute tired feet for tired souls and walk the streets of Montgomery until the walls of segregation were finally battered by the forces of justice!"

Chapter Four

Hall Monitors from the 101st

The Little Rock Story

"For a vast majority of southerners

playing at politics, it has been not

necessarily the democratic process

in action, so much as a thoroughly

delightful sport."

Thomas D. Clark in
"Economic Basis of
Southern Politics"

The Supreme Court outlawed school segregation in its 1954 *Brown* decision, but only two southern states began desegregation that year—Texas integrated one school district; Arkansas, two. In the rest of the South, not a single classroom was racially mixed. Most school officials claimed they were waiting for the Supreme Court's expected implementation decision before executing an integration plan. Five of the seven states closest to the North began desegregation in 1954. But even there, acceptance of the court's ruling was slow.

The law school at the University of Arkansas in Fayetteville voluntarily admitted blacks as early as 1948, and the university's medical school in Little Rock did the same. In fact, nearly half the student body of that city's University of Arkansas Graduate Center was black. This relatively progressive attitude toward race relations made Little Rock an unlikely stage for the crisis that developed there in 1957. But that crisis had as much to do with political grandstanding as with blacks and whites.

From the mid-forties to the mid-fifties, blacks in Little Rock made dramatic gains. Some blacks had been allowed to join the police force, and in a few neighborhoods blacks and whites lived next door to one another. In contrast to their counterparts in most southern states, thirty-three percent of all eligible Arkansas blacks were registered to vote. The library, parks, and public buses had all been integrated, and in 1955 white schools seemed ready to open their doors to blacks.

The Little Rock school board was the first in the South to issue a statement of compliance after the Supreme Court's ruling. "It is our responsibility," the board announced just five days after the decision, "to comply with federal constitutional requirements, and we intend to do so when the Supreme Court of the United States outlines the methods to be followed."

Black leaders had high hopes for a smooth transition to integrated classrooms. In the *Arkansas Gazette* and the *Arkansas Democrat*, both white-run daily newspapers, Little Rock residents read words of support for desegregation. In 1954, Daisy Bates, head of the state NAACP, called Little Rock a "liberal southern city."

But despite the recent changes, Little Rock was still a highly segregated town. If there was little racial strife in the community of over 100,000, it was mainly because most everyone knew the rules of segregation and followed them.

In the summer of 1954, Virgil T. Blossom, Little Rock's superintendent of schools, drafted a scheme for implementing desegregation. He proposed to begin with two high schools then under construction; the schools were scheduled to

Daisy Bates, the president of the NAACP in Arkansas.

open in the fall of 1956. Integration of the junior high schools would follow the next year, and finally the grade schools would be desegregated, at an unspecified date. In the fall of 1954, Blossom began explaining the plan to black and white members of the school district staff. On May 24, 1955 the school board adopted a much-diluted version of the Blossom Plan.

The board's scheme, known as the Little Rock Phase Program, limited integration to just one school, Central High, and delayed implementation until September 1957. Only a limited number of black children would be allowed to join the student body, which consisted of about 2,000 white youngsters from a working-class neighborhood. The soon-to-be-completed Hall High School would, for an unspecified time, be attended only by the largely upper-middle-class white youngsters who lived on the city's west side. The school district's lower grades would be integrated over the next six years, but students would be allowed to transfer from a school where their race was in the minority. This final provision left little chance that any of the currently all-black schools would be integrated.

The school board tried to justify its gradual approach by citing the danger of sudden change. "Since our school system has been segregated from its beginning until the present time," the officials stated, "the time required in the process as outlined should not be construed as unnecessary delay but that which is justly needed with respect to the size and complexity of the job at hand . . . By starting integration at the senior high level, the process will begin where fewer teachers and students are involved. In the adoption of [this] plan of integration, [which starts with one school and with the oldest children in the school system] . . . we provide the opportunity to benefit from our own experience as we move through each phase of this plan, thus avoiding as many mistakes as possible."

On May 31, the Supreme Court ruled that desegregation need only be implemented "with all deliberate speed." In response, Arkansas segregationists called for a state constitutional amendment that would circumvent the Court's orders. A young politician named James Johnson led the amendment campaign. His sudden gain in statewide popularity, based largely on his hard-line segregationist ideology, disturbed not only Arkansas blacks but the governor as well.

Governor Orval Faubus, elected in 1954, was neither a moderate nor a reactionary on race issues; he was an old-fashioned southern politician who tried to tell the people what they wanted to hear. Because the governor's term in Arkansas was only two years long, Faubus was always running for office. In the 1954 election, he won the support of central and northern Arkansas, and he knew that by directing funds toward local projects he could keep that support in the next

Little Rock's school superintendent Virgil T. Blossom, whose plan for gradual school desegregation was rejected by other members of the school committee. The school committee received criticism from the black community for moving too slowly on desegregation, and threats of violence from segregationists for moving too quickly.

election. His support was weakest in the southeastern part of the state, where large cotton plantations were run by whites and worked by black people. Although blacks in this Arkansas Delta could vote, their votes were controlled through economic intimidation by their white employers, who delivered the black vote to those whom they favored. Governor Faubus thought he would need their favor in the next election, and was unsettled by James Johnson's growing popularity in that region.

In Little Rock, white opposition to the Phase Program surfaced quickly. Robert Erving Brown, president of the segregationist Capital Citizens' Council, a small but vociferous organization in the city, told reporters, "The Negroes have ample and fine schools here, and there is no need for this problem except to satisfy the aims of a few white and Negro revolutionaries in the Urban League and the National Association for the Advancement of Colored People." Another Council member, attorney Amis Guthridge, voiced his objections to the plan at a school board meeting on June 27. Along with the Reverend Wesley Pruden of the Broadmoor Baptist Church, Guthridge argued that school integration would have unintended consequences—for example, would blacks be allowed to dance with whites at school dances? A week later, the board offered a written reply. "Social functions which involve race mixing will not be held . . . " the board wrote. "Integration of the PTA is a matter to be decided within those organizations; all pupils will use restroom facilities regularly provided; teachers can and will avoid situations such as love scenes in class plays featuring students of different races . . . "

NAACP attorneys Wiley Branton (left) and Thurgood Marshall.

Late in January of 1956, Governor Faubus announced a poll indicating that eighty-five percent of Arkansans opposed integrating schools in their state. He proclaimed that he could not "be a party to any attempt to force acceptance of change to which the people are so overwhelmingly opposed."

The growing opposition to desegregation both locally and throughout the state began to alarm Little Rock's blacks, many of whom were dissatisfied with the limited scope of the Phase Plan and its vague statement that integration "may start in 1957." Seeking a stronger assurance that their children would at last be guaranteed their constitutional rights, they enlisted the aid of the state NAACP. In February, Wiley Branton, chairman of the NAACP Legal Redress Committee, and U. Simpson Tate, regional attorney for the NAACP, filed suit in federal district court hoping to force immediate and thorough integration of the schools. The suit charged that black children in Little Rock were being rejected from four schools there because of their skin color.

Governor Orval Faubus
speaking at a press
conference.

"It became rather obvious to the NAACP that the Little Rock board really was not going to move forward unless they were forced to . . . " Branton recalls. "I filed that suit . . . on behalf of [thirty-three] Negro children and their parents, running through elementary, junior, and senior high school."

Leon Catlett, the school board's attorney, tried to embarrass the NAACP by pointing out that the local branch of that organization had refused to file the suit because they felt that Little Rock had relatively few racial problems and that the school board did have a plan to desegregate, albeit an imperfect one. Catlett provoked further animosity by referring to the NAACP's "nigger leaders" during the hearing and calling state NAACP president Daisy Bates by her first name.

Branton had advised NAACP attorney Tate to center his legal arguments on the school board's delaying tactics, but instead Tate based his case on the unconstitutionality of school segregation—the same premise that had won the *Brown* case. But federal district court judge John E. Miller dismissed the suit, saying that the school board had devised its plan for gradual integration in "utmost good faith." Thurgood Marshall, heading the NAACP Legal Defense Fund, joined Branton in appealing the case to the Eighth U.S. Circuit Court of Appeals in St. Louis. This time they argued that the board's delays amounted to a sly dodge of the Supreme Court mandate. But on April 27, 1957, the appeals court ruled that the Little Rock plan complied with the Supreme Court's "deliberate speed" prescription for enacting school desegregation. The judges insisted, however, that the school board allow no further delays, and they ordered the federal district court to retain jurisdiction over the case to prevent stalling.

Branton and Marshall were tempted to appeal the case to the Supreme Court, but they decided against that route. It was already the spring of 1957, and the high court would be in recess until that fall. By then, desegregation in Little Rock would be underway. Also, an unsuccessful Supreme Court appeal could have unwanted repercussions. As Branton later explained, "This would be the first case [of its kind] going to the Supreme Court . . . We thought [the school board's scheme] was a pretty sloppy plan, and we didn't want to run the risk of having the court adopt that one as a model plan for the nation." So even though the NAACP Legal Defense Fund felt the Little Rock plan was too limited and too gradual, it reluctantly embraced the scheme after the court's endorsement.

Many Arkansas whites were angry that the NAACP had taken the school board to court at all. They felt that the city had been working its way quietly but steadily toward desegregation. In retaliation, lawmakers introduced four prosegregation bills in the state legislature. One bill allowed the school board to hire lawyers to contest suits calling for school integration; another made attendance at integrated schools voluntary; the third required organizations and individuals "challenging the authority" of local or state officials to register with the state and make regular reports of their budgets; and a fourth bill created a state sovereignty commission to "perform any and all acts and things deemed necessary to protect the sovereignty of Arkansas and other states from encroachments of the federal government." The measures passed the Arkansas house by a vote of eighty-eight to one before going on to the state senate.

One critic of the bills asserted that they were "more in harmony with the principles of communist and fascist governments" than with American democracy. And although Governor Faubus supported the bills, his appointee as head of Arkansas Industrial Development Commission, Winthrop Rockefeller, charged that creation of a sovereignty commission would be tantamount to setting up an "Arkansas Gestapo." As a guardian of business interests in the state, Rockefeller worried that increasing racial strife would scare off the northern-based industry that agrarian Arkansas was then trying to lure to the state. But despite the opposition, all four bills passed the senate and became law early in 1957. The NAACP would now have to reveal its members' names and its budget to the government, while the white Capital Citizens Council would be eligible for state support through the new Sovereignty Commission.

As segregationist sentiment grew during the summer, the Little Rock school board launched a quiet campaign to pare down the number of black students eligible to attend Central High School. Branton recalls, "As the summer went by and Little Rock decided that, 'Oh, my God, this thing is on us,' they started putting up all kinds of barriers. They required black children who wanted to go to white schools to register . . . Approximately seventy-five black kids signed up to go to Central High School. And then as the opening of school approached, the Little Rock school board screened the seventy-five down to twenty-five."

Then the board tried to dissuade even those twenty-five from attending Central. According to Branton, they "began calling in parents of kids, saying, 'If you really want your son to play football, you ought to stay over there at Horace Mann [the all-black high school],' or, 'Your daughter has a magnificent voice . . . but if she goes over to the white school, and being new, she could get lost in the shuffle and won't get a chance to sing.'"

In the end, only nine black students enrolled at Central. None of the thirty-three students whose parents had sued over the slowness of the desegregation plan were among them. "The nine of the twenty-five [were] selected by the school board because they were trying to get 'good' Negroes, and none of the 'radicals' who sued them . . . ," said Branton. "They became the Little Rock Nine and carved out a place in history."

In August 1957, less than two weeks before integration was scheduled to begin, Georgia governor Marvin Griffin visited Little Rock at the invitation of the Citizens Council. He told the 300 white guests at a ten-dollar-a-plate dinner that he had no intention of complying with the Supreme Court's dictate. The only connection between the federal government and the Georgia public schools, he contended, was Uncle Sam's financial contribution to school lunches. "If they try to tell us then to integrate the races," he warned, "I will be compelled to tell them to get their black-eyed peas and soup pots out of Georgia." The crowd stood and cheered. Governor Griffin then urged them to join him in rejecting the high court's ruling. They could prevail, he said, through "the determined and cooperative efforts of a dedicated people, a steadfast general assembly and an administration committed unequivocally toward preservation of our cherished institutions . . . "

"A note was tied to it.

I broke the string and

unfolded a soiled piece

of paper. Scrawled in

bold print were the

words: 'Stone this time.

Dynamite next.'"

That night, a rock was thrown through Daisy Bates' living room window. "Instinctively, I threw myself to the floor," Bates later recounted in her book *The Long Shadow of Little Rock*. "I was covered with shattered glass . . . I reached for the rock lying in the middle of the floor. A note was tied to it. I broke the string and unfolded a soiled piece of paper. Scrawled in bold print were the words: 'Stone this time. Dynamite next.'"

Five days later, on August 27, another unexpected volley was tossed at Bates and the NAACP. Governor Faubus had privately arranged for the Mothers' League of Little Rock Central High, a newly formed segregationist group, to file for a temporary injunction in Pulaski County Chancery Court, arguing that Central High should remain white. Mrs. Clyde A. Thomason, head of the group, told the judge that black and white students were buying knives and guns in anticipation of gang warfare. The parents were afraid to send their children to the school, she said. Chancellor Murray O. Reed demanded evidence supporting Thomason's contentions; she could produce none. Then a surprise witness took the stand— Governor Orval Faubus. The governor claimed that guns and knives had recently been confiscated from Little Rock students. This time the judge did not ask for evidence, and the governor went on to say that in the past three weeks, Arkansas residents had shifted their attitudes on desegregation. "People are coming to me and saying, 'If Georgia doesn't have to integrate, why does Arkansas have to?'" Faubus said.

Governor Faubus in front of the governor's mansion with members of the Mothers' League of Little Rock Central High.

The Little Rock Nine. Front row (left to right): Jefferson Thomas, Carlotta Walls, Gloria Ray, Elizabeth Eckford, Thelma Mothershed. Back row (left to right): Melba Pattillo, Terrance Roberts, Minniejean Brown, Ernest Green.

The governor had asked that same question during a mid-August telephone conversation with the U.S. Justice Department. A department official had traveled to Little Rock to gauge the threat of violence and the need for federal intervention. But the governor could provide no evidence of likely mayhem, and Little Rock police knew of no surge in local weapons sales. The Justice Department informed the governor that it would do nothing to delay desegregation.

Chancellor Reed, however, reached a different conclusion. He granted the temporary injunction, blocking desegregation of Central High School. "In view of the testimony," he said, "and the show of the threat of violence, riots and bloodshed, and particularly the opinion of Governor Faubus, I feel I can only rule to grant the injunction." The courtroom resounded with applause. Desegregation would be delayed again—this time indefinitely.

Daisy Bates couldn't sleep that night. Rowdies kept driving by her house, honking their horns and shouting, "Daisy, Daisy, did you hear the news? The coons won't be going to Central!"

On August 30, Wiley Branton and Thurgood Marshall asked the federal district court to nullify the injunction. Judge Ronald N. Davies ruled that, in the absence of concrete evidence that violence was likely, desegregation must proceed. "When the governor couldn't block us in court," said Branton, "he announced that he'd given the matter further consideration and was going to go on statewide television. So everybody thought he was going to say that he'd done his best, and that the law is the law and everybody ought to be patient and tolerant and cooperative and this, that, and the other . . . "

Branton was wrong. On September 2, the day before the schools were to open in Little Rock, Faubus went on statewide television and announced that he intended to surround Central High with National Guardsmen because of "evidence of disorder and threats of disorder."

"[This decision] has been made after conferences with dozens of people . . . ," Faubus said. "The mission of the state militia is to maintain or restore order and to protect the lives and property of citizens. They will not act as segregationists or integrationists but as soldiers . . . it will not be possible to restore or to maintain order and protect the lives and property of the citizens if forcible integration is carried out tomorrow in the schools of this community. The inevitable conclusion, therefore, must be that schools in Pulaski County, for the time being, must be operated on the same [segregated] basis as they have been operated in the past . . . "

When Winthrop Rockefeller heard of the governor's plan, he immediately went to the capitol to see Faubus. Rockefeller argued that using the national guard would scare off businessmen his Industrial Development Commission sought to attract. But Faubus told Rockefeller he had to stop the blacks. "I'm sorry, but I'm committed," the governor said, according to a Rockefeller associate quoted in *Time* magazine. "I'm going to run for a third term, and if I don't do this, Jim Johnson and Bruce Bennett [both segregationists] will tear me to shreds [in next year's gubernatorial race]."

Daisy Bates was stunned, as was her husband, L. C. Bates, publisher of a black newspaper, the *Arkansas State Press*. "His words electrified Little Rock," Daisy Bates recounts. "By morning they shocked the United States. By noon the next day, his message horrified the world . . . From the chair of the highest office of the state of Arkansas, Governor Orval Eugene Faubus delivered the infamous words, 'Blood will run in the streets' if Negro pupils should attempt to enter Central High School."

The next day, the first day of school, 250 National Guardsmen stood on the sidewalks outside Central High. "Little Rock arose . . . to gaze upon the incredible spectacle of an empty high school surrounded by the National Guard, troops called out by Gov. Faubus to protect life and property against a mob that never materialized," wrote the *Gazette*.

As the parents of the nine black youngsters slated to enter Central conferred with NAACP officials and lawyers, the school board issued a written statement, saying that "although the federal court has ordered integration to proceed, Governor Faubus has said that the schools should continue as they have in the past and has stationed troops at Central High to maintain order . . . We ask that no Negro student attempt to attend Central or any white high school until this dilemma is legally resolved." The board then sought guidance from Judge Ronald Davies, the magistrate who just days earlier had ordered integration to go forward. Judge Davies immediately ordered them to proceed with the integration plan, saying that he was aware of the segregationist sentiment in Little Rock but that "I have a constitutional duty and obligation from which I shall not shrink."

Rebuffed by the court, the school board advised the nine black students to attend school the next day, September 4. Although Superintendent Blossom promised that the children would be protected, their parents were afraid. Because the board had asked the parents not to accompany their youngsters to school, explaining that the presence of the black parents might incite a mob, Daisy Bates made preparations to take the children to school. She telephoned eight sets of parents with instructions to have the children meet her at 12th Street and Park Avenue at 8:30 A.M., where two police cars would be waiting to drive them to school. But she failed to reach the Eckfords, parents of fifteen-year-old Elizabeth. They had no telephone, and Bates forgot to send a message.

As Elizabeth prepared for school the next morning, she heard the newscaster on the television wondering aloud whether the black children would dare to show up at the school. Birdee Eckford told her daughter to turn off the set. "She was so upset and worried," Elizabeth recalls. "I wanted to comfort her, so I said, 'Mother, don't worry.'" Her father paced the floor with a cigar in one hand and a pipe in the other—both unlit. The family prayed together, then Elizabeth set off for school in the crisply pressed black-and-white dress that she and her mother had made especially for this day. She walked to the public bus stop and rode off toward her new high school.

Elizabeth Eckford was met with shouts of hatred when she tried to attend Central High on the first day of classes.

Getting off the bus near Central High, Eckford saw a throng of white people and hundreds of armed soldiers. But the presence of the guardsmen reassured her. The superintendent had told the black students to come in through the main entrance at the front of the school, so Elizabeth headed in that direction. "I looked at all the people and thought, 'Maybe I'll be safe if I walk down the block to the front entrance behind the guards,'" she remembers. "At the corner I tried to pass through the long lines of guards around the school so as to enter the grounds behind them. One [soldier] pointed across the street . . . so I walked across the street conscious of the crowd that stood there, but they moved away from me . . . [Then] the crowd began to follow me, calling me names. I still wasn't afraid—just a little bit nervous. Then my knees started to shake all of a sudden and I wondered whether I could make it to the center entrance a block away. It was the longest block I ever walked in my whole life. Even so, I wasn't too scared, because all the time I kept thinking the [guards] would protect me.

"When I got in front of the school, I went up to a guard again," she continues. "He just looked straight ahead and didn't move to let me pass. I didn't know what to do . . . Just then the guards let some white students through . . . I walked up to the guard who had let [them] in. He too didn't move. When I tried to squeeze past him, he raised his bayonet, and then the other guards moved in and raised their bayonets . . . Somebody started yelling, '*Lynch her! Lynch her!*'"

As Daisy and L. C. Bates drove toward the appointed meeting place at 12th Street and Park Avenue, they heard a news bulletin over the car radio. "A Negro girl is being mobbed at Central High . . . ," the announcer said. L. C. jumped out of the car and ran as fast as he could to the school.

"I tried to see a friendly face somewhere in the mob . . . ," Elizabeth recalls. "I looked into the face of an old woman, and it seemed a kind face, but when I looked at her again, she spat on me."

The young woman heard someone snarl, "No nigger bitch is going to get in our school. Get out of here." The guards looked on impassively; Eckford was on her own. "I looked down the block and saw a bench at the bus stop. Then I thought, 'If I can only get there, I will be safe.'" She ran to the bench and sat down, but a cluster of ruffians had followed her. "Drag her over to the tree," said one of them, calling for a lynching.

Then Benjamin Fine, an education writer for the *New York Times*, put his arm around Elizabeth. "He raised my chin and said, 'Don't let them see you cry,'" she recalls. Finally a white woman named Grace Lorch, whose husband taught at a local black college, guided Elizabeth away from the mob. The two tried to enter a nearby drugstore to call a cab, but someone slammed the door in their faces. Then they spotted a bus coming and quickly boarded it. Lorch accompanied Elizabeth home safely, but the experience had left its mark. Afterwards, the fifteen-year-old sometimes woke in the night, terrified, screaming about the mob.

Eckford sits at a bus stop near Central High, surrounded by a hostile mob. Benjamin Fine, *New York Times* education editor, is visible directly behind Eckford, and Grace Lorch stands at right.

The other black students did not have to face the mob alone, but they, too, failed to get past the Arkansas National Guardsmen and into Central High. The next day, Judge Davies asked the Justice Department to investigate the disruptions in the integration plan. Governor Faubus, triumphant in defying the federal courts, was nonetheless nervous about how the administration might respond. He sent a telegram to President Dwight D. Eisenhower, saying that he had been "reliably informed" that United States officials were planning to arrest him. "I have reason to believe," he went on, "that the telephone lines to the Arkansas executive mansion have been tapped—I suspect federal agents." The governor also asked Eisenhower to "use your good office to modify the extreme stand" of the federal courts.

Eisenhower's return telegram assured Faubus that the federal government did not plan to jail the governor and that his phone was not tapped. The president also wired that the Justice Department, at Judge Davies' request, was "collecting facts as to interference with or failure to comply with the district court's order." The president reminded Faubus that, as governor, he should fully cooperate with the United States district court.

But Faubus remained intransigent and kept the Arkansas National Guard posted around the school. The school board again requested that the federal court suspend the desegregation plan, and the court again refused.

Increasingly, observers were laying some of the blame for the crisis at Eisenhower's door. In Little Rock, Thurgood Marshall told a reporter that the president would have to move soon. When asked if he saw Little Rock as a conflict of authority between the state and federal governments, Marshall replied, "I don't think there's any doubt about that."

But Eisenhower was reluctant to clash with Faubus. He did not want to take sides in the desegregation battle. In July the president had said in a news conference that he could not "imagine any set of circumstances that would ever induce me to send federal troops . . . to enforce the orders of a federal court, because I believe the common sense of Americans will never require it."

"President Eisenhower's position," recalls his attorney general, Herbert Brownell, "was that he was president of all the people. He felt that his role was to stay in a position where, when the showdown came for enforcement, he would be able to talk to both sides and persuade them."

On September 14, President Eisenhower met with Governor Faubus in Newport, Rhode Island, to discuss the crisis in Little Rock.

On September 9, the Justice Department concluded that Governor Faubus had had no concrete evidence that trouble would erupt at Central High if blacks were allowed to enroll; the governor had acted solely as a segregationist—trying to keep blacks out of a white school—when he called out the National Guard. On September 10, at Judge Davies' request, the Justice Department filed a petition for an injunction against Faubus to force his immediate compliance with the desegregation order. The injunction would also require the removal of the National Guard from Central High at once. The hearing on the injunction request would take place on September 20. Meanwhile, Faubus refused to remove the soldiers who were still preventing the black students from entering the school. Faubus later defended his stand, calling federal officials "a bunch of goddamn cowards for not coming in from the beginning and saying, 'Here is a federal court order.'"

On September 14, Faubus met with Eisenhower at the president's summer home in Newport, Rhode Island. Eisenhower told the governor that he did not object to the presence of the Arkansas National Guard at the school, but that they should have been assigned to protect the nine black children, not to scare them away at gunpoint. Faubus appeared amenable to Eisenhower's comments, but then suggested that the president defy the courts by ordering a one-year delay in the desegregation process, ostensibly to allow the governor time to mollify the agitated community. Eisenhower refused, saying that the courts must be obeyed. Faubus seemed to understand, and the president thought he had persuaded the man to allow the youngsters into Central High.

Faubus and the Press

Throughout the Little Rock school crisis, the *Arkansas Gazette* wrote a series of editorials criticizing the actions of Governor Faubus and urging gradual implementation of desegregation under the terms spelled out by the federal courts. The *Gazette* became a target for the governor and the object of an economic boycott run by Faubus' supporters. Despite such opposition, the newspaper received a Pulitzer Prize in 1958 for public service. The newspaper's executive editor, Harry S. Ashmore, won a second Pulitzer for distinguished editorial writing. This editorial originally appeared on October 10, 1957.

Mr. Faubus Is Where He Was

Governor Faubus said at his press conference yesterday that the Little Rock crisis now hinges upon the withdrawal of the nine Negro children who are presently peacefully attending Central High School under federal court order and federal military protection.

This, of course, is one answer.

It happens to be the answer the Citizens Councils have been offering ever since the United States Supreme Court ruled that Negroes could no longer be barred from any school solely on the basis of race. If the Negroes voluntarily choose not to attend white schools then there is no problem. And if they do not voluntarily so choose, but can be coerced or intimidated into withdrawing, there is no problem.

But the federal government has said that these nine children cannot be so coerced or intimidated, and has used the full weight of both the judicial and executive departments to guarantee that they shall not be.

So what Mr. Faubus is saying is that the federal government must abandon its position and let him have his way on his own terms. There is no indication that the federal government will do so.

But still, with all this, the governor contends that all he wants is delay. He says that Negroes cannot attend Central High School peaceably now, but he suggests that they can at some indefinite future date. At one point or another he has suggested that this might be possible next semester or next fall—the last date being, in our judgment, the significant one since it comes after the next gubernatorial election.

But what the governor never explains is why he thinks it will be any easier to carry out the court order then than it was this time around—or any easier, that is, than it would have been had he not recklessly chosen to disrupt the patient and careful work of the responsible local school officials who had every reason to believe that their limited and gradual plan was acceptable to a vast majority of the people.

Could the governor guarantee that no mob would form next semester, or next fall, if the Negro children again presented themselves under court order? He probably could, as a matter of fact, but he has repeatedly indicated that he will not do so—as indeed he cannot do without sacrificing the temporary political advantages he has gained. And so there is no valid reason to assume that delay will resolve the impasse which Mr. Faubus has made.

We doubt that Mr. Faubus can simply wear the federals out—although he is doing a pretty good job of wearing out his own people.

In Little Rock, the black activists hoped to resolve the impasse at the injunction hearing on September 20. But Governor Faubus challenged the jurisdiction of Judge Davies, who was only temporarily assigned to Arkansas; ordinarily he presided in North Dakota. The magistrate rejected the challenge and proceeded with the case, causing the governor's lawyers to protest and storm out of the courtroom. Thurgood Marshall was heard to mumble to his fellow NAACP attorney Wiley Branton, "Now I've seen everything."

Judge Davies immediately ordered Faubus to remove his armed forces from around the high school. That night, Faubus went on television and announced his compliance. He also asked blacks to stay away from the high school until he could arrange for peaceful desegregation. Then, to most everyone's surprise, he left to attend a conference of southern governors in Sea Island, Georgia. While he was there he took in a football game in Atlanta, where, according to *Time* magazine, a fellow governor described him as in a happy mood: "He's really lapping up the glory. There were 33,000 people at the game, and every time they cheered a play, Faubus stood up and bowed."

Reporter Alex Wilson was attacked September 23, the first day the black students entered the school. He was hit on the head with a brick.

On Monday morning, September 23, the Little Rock Nine gathered at Daisy Bates' home to await word from the city police on how they would get to school. Also waiting were four black journalists. The police called shortly after 8 A.M. to tell Bates they would escort the children through a side entrance of the high school, hoping to avoid the angry crowd gathering in front of the building. Bates told the reporters of the plan and advised them to drive to the school.

The black journalists arrived at Central seconds before the students. As the four got out of their car, the 8:45 school bell rang. Suddenly, someone in the throng of hundreds of whites yelled, "Look, here they come!" The reporters had apparently been mistaken for parents escorting their children to school. About twenty whites began to chase the men down the street; others soon followed. Newsman Alex Wilson chose not to flee and was savaged. "Somebody had a brick in his hand," remembers James Hicks, another of the journalists, "and instead of throwing the brick, 'cause he was too close, he hit Alex Wilson up the side of his head . . . Wilson was more than six feet tall, an ex-Marine—he went down like a tree."

Time magazine later reported that "a cop stood on a car bumper to get a better view of the fighting. Faubus henchman James Karam [the state athletic commissioner] . . . cried angrily, 'The nigger started it.'"

Meanwhile, the three boys and six girls under police guard got out of two cars and calmly walked into the school's side entrance. "Look, they're going into the school!" someone shrieked. "Oh, my God, they're in the school!" People screamed, cursed, and wept at the sight.

With the students out of reach, the mob turned its anger on white journalists on the scene. *Life* magazine reporter Paul Welch and two photographers, Grey Villet and Francis Miller, were harassed and beaten. The photographers' equipment was smashed to the ground. The crowd began to chant to the white students now staring out of Central's windows, "Don't stay in there with them."

Before noon the mob had swelled to about a thousand people, and Police Chief Gene Smith felt compelled to quell the rioting by removing the black students from the school.

"I was in my physics class," remembers Ernest Green, the one senior among the nine black students. "A monitor came up from the principal's office [to fetch me] . . . the other eight [black students] were [in his office]. We were told by the principal that we would be sent home for our own safety. The police were having difficulty holding the mob back at the barricade, and they said if they broke through they could not be responsible for our safety." The youngsters were escorted home safely, and Daisy Bates told reporters that they would not return to Central until the president assured them they would be protected.

Still at Sea Island, Governor Faubus said, "The trouble in Little Rock vindicates my good judgment [in sending in the National Guard]." In Washington, President Eisenhower termed the rioting a "disgraceful occurrence." Little Rock Mayor Woodrow Mann, fearing that city police could not contain the crowd if they should return the next day, called the Justice Department. He asked that the president consider sending in federal troops to enforce the court order and keep the peace at Central High. Eisenhower issued an emergency proclamation ordering all Americans to cease and desist from blocking entry to the school and obstructing the federal court order to desegregate Central.

The next morning, as Mann had expected, another restless mob of segregationists outnumbered Little Rock police at the high school. The mayor again telephoned the Justice Department. This time he formally requested the aid of federal troops.

At Eisenhower's orders, that evening more than a thousand members of the 101st Airborne Division flew to Little Rock Air Force Base from Fort Campbell, Kentucky. The Arkansas National Guard was also mobilized, but this time, they were ordered to defend the black students. "President Eisenhower was very loath to intervene," recalls attorney general Brownell. "He wanted so much to have the *Brown* decision enforced without confrontation wherever possible . . . It was really a great struggle in his mind before he reached a decision that he had to intervene in order to carry out his constitutional duty to enforce the Supreme Court's decision."

That night the president went on nationwide television to explain why he was using federal troops, as the segregationists would later put it, against American citizens. "To make this talk," the president began, "I have come to the President's office in the White House. I could have spoken from Rhode Island, where I have been staying recently, but I felt that, in speaking from the house of Lincoln, of Jackson, and of Wilson, my words would better convey both the sadness I feel in the action I was compelled today to take and the firmness with which I intend to pursue this course until the orders at Little Rock can be executed without unlawful interference. In that city, under the leadership of demagogic extremists, disorderly mobs have deliberately prevented the carrying out of proper orders from a federal court . . . This morning the mob again gathered in front of the Central High School of Little Rock, obviously for the purpose of again preventing the carrying out of the court's order relating to the admission of Negro children to that school. Whenever normal agencies prove inadequate to the task . . . the president's responsibility is inescapable . . . I have today issued an executive order directing the use of troops under federal authority to aid in the execution of federal law at Little Rock . . . Our personal opinions about the decision have no bearing on the matter of enforcement . . . Mob rule cannot be allowed to override the decisions of our courts . . . [Most southerners] do not sympathize with mob rule. They, like the rest of our nation, have proved in two great wars their readiness to sacrifice for America. And the foundation of the American way of life is our national respect for law."

The federal troops surrounded Central High School. Little Rock police, who in the past few days had jailed more than forty people on charges of "inciting to riot," continued to arrest small groups of white men near the school. In the city's black neighborhoods, people were unnerved. As one news reporter later described it, "the Negro districts [were] uniformly dark and silent; where a house was lighted, the lights were switched off at the approach of the car." Police watching Daisy Bates' home followed a car that drove slowly past with its lights off. Minutes later an officer returned to the darkened house to report that police had discovered dynamite and firearms in the vehicle.

The next morning, the Little Rock Nine again met at the Bates house, this time to be escorted to school by federal troops. "There was more military hardware than I'd ever seen . . . ," recalls Ernest Green. "The colonel in charge of the

"I have today issued an

executive order

directing the use of

troops . . . at Little Rock."

The First Day at Central High:

An Interview with Melba Pattillo Beals

One of the Little Rock Nine, Melba Pattillo Beals entered Central High as a junior. She attended San Francisco State University and, after receiving a master's degree in journalism from Columbia University, worked for six years as a news reporter for NBC in San Francisco.

There was no thought on my part, on any of our parts, that our going to Central High would trigger this terrible catastrophe. I wanted to go because [students at Central] had more privileges. They had more equipment; they had five floors of opportunity. I understood education before I understood anything else. From the time I was two, my mother said, "You will go to college. Education is your key to survival." I did not have an overwhelming desire to integrate this school and change history. Oh, no, there was none of that.

My getting into Central was almost an accident. I simply raised my hand one day when they said, "Who of you lives in the area of Central High School? Who has good grades?" I had excellent grades. It was an accident of fate. I was sitting in Cincinnati, Ohio, with my mother when Walter Cronkite came on television and said that in late August, Central High School in Little Rock was going to be integrated . . . and these were the children who were going. He mispronounced my name. My mother said, "What did you say?" And that was it . . . Then we came back to Little Rock and I began to be involved in the NAACP's preparations.

The first time, the first day I was able to enter Central High School, what I felt inside was stark raving fear—terrible, wrenching, awful fear. A fear that I cannot explain to you. There are no words for how I felt inside. I had known no pain like that because I did not know what I had done wrong. You see, when you're fifteen years old and someone's going to hit you or hurt you, you want to know what you did wrong. Although I knew the differences between black and white, I didn't know the penalties one paid for being black at that time.

On the first day, the kinds of things that I endured were parents kicking, parents hitting, parents throwing things. You would get tripped; people would just walk up and hit you in the face. And you couldn't hit back. We had been instructed that any attempts to hit back, to respond, to call a name would mean the end of the case.

They separated us. The school officials said to us, "You want integration? We'll give you integration. We will separate you." And so, in a school of 2,500 or so, they sent us nine different ways. My homeroom was, I believe, number 313. That meant I had to go up, by myself, three flights of stairs. The only way I could get up those stairs was to say the Lord's Prayer repeatedly. And that's how I got there. I could not look to my left or my right.

I'd only been in the school a couple of hours and by this time it was apparent that the mob was overrunning the school. Policemen were throwing down their badges and the mob was getting past the wooden sawhorses because the police would no longer fight their own in order to protect us. We were all called into the principal's office and there was great fear that we would not get out of this building . . . Even the adults, the school officials, were panicked. A couple of the black kids who were with me were crying. Someone made a suggestion that if they allowed the mob to hang one kid, then they could get the rest out while they were hanging the one kid. And a gentleman, whom I believed to be the police chief, said, "How are you going to choose? You're going to let them draw straws?" He said, "I'll get them out." And we were taken to the basement of this place and put into two cars, grayish-blue Fords. The drivers were told, "Once you start driving, do not stop." They told us to put our heads down. So the guy revved up the engine and came out of the bowels of this building and as he came up, I could just see hands reaching across this car. I could hear the yelling. I could see guns. The driver didn't hit anybody, but he certainly was forceful and aggressive in the way he exited this driveway because people tried to stop him. He dropped me off at home, and I remember saying, "Thank you for the ride." I should have said, "Thank you for my life."

detail escorting us to school was from South Carolina. He had a very thick southern accent. He went to great pains to assure Mrs. Bates and the other parents that he was there to provide protection . . . It seemed so incongruous that this guy with a deep southern accent was going to provide us with our protection . . . it was going through my head, 'This dude really ain't going to be looking out for me too tough . . . '"

By this time, 350 paratroopers lined two blocks of Park Avenue in front of the school. Major James Meyers spoke to the gathering mob from a sound truck. "Please return to your homes or it will be necessary to disperse you," he barked. One small group called back, "Nigger lover." A man yelled, "They're just bluffing. If you don't want to move, you don't have to." Then, at the Major's order, a dozen paratroopers advanced with their bayonets poised, sending the crowd scurrying.

Inside the school, Major General Edwin A. Walker, commander of the federal forces, spoke to the white students at a special assembly. "What does all this mean to you students?" he asked. "You have often heard it said, no doubt, that the United States is a nation under law, and not under men. This means we are governed by laws . . . and not by the decrees of one man or one class of men . . . I believe that you are well-intentioned, law-abiding citizens who understand the necessity of obeying the law . . . You have nothing to fear from my soldiers and no one will interfere with your coming, going, or your peaceful pursuit of your studies."

The Little Rock Nine were on their way. "The convoy that went from Mrs. Bates' house to the school had a jeep in front, a jeep behind," recalls Ernest Green. "They both had machine gun mounts, [and] there were soldiers with rifles. When we got to the front of the school, the whole school was ringed with paratroopers and helicopters hovering around. We marched up the steps . . . with this circle of soldiers with bayonets drawn . . . Walking up the steps that day was probably one of the biggest feelings I've ever had. I figured I had finally cracked it."

When the black students got inside the school, each was assigned a bodyguard. "The troops were wonderful," remembers Melba Pattillo Beals, then fifteen years old. "They were disciplined, they were attentive, they were caring, they didn't baby us, but they were there."

Eighty white students had left the school after Major General Walker addressed the assembly, but most of those remaining were very friendly to the nine newcomers. At the end of the school day, paratroopers escorted the black students

Daisy Bates watches as the students leave her home for Central High School. They continued to meet at her home each morning before going to school.

From the first day of the school year, the Little Rock Nine were escorted to school by soldiers.

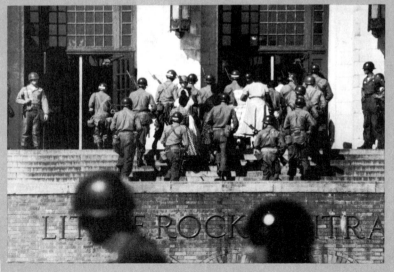

During a televised speech on September 27, Governor Faubus held up a newspaper photograph to illustrate the violence white people suffered at the hands of the federal troops. He failed to mention that the people were part of a mob threatening to attack the black students.

back to the Bates house. One of the youngsters, Minniejean Brown, happily recounted that she had been invited by her white classmates to join the glee club. Some of the students had asked the black kids to eat lunch with them. Reporters from across the nation interviewed white children at the school. The president of the student council told reporter Mike Wallace that if only the white parents would stay away from the school, there would be no violence. Another student commented, "I think it [the opposition to integration] is downright un-American. I think it's the most terrible thing ever seen in America. I mean, I guess I'm sounding too patriotic or something, but I always thought all men were created equal."

On Friday, September 27, with order prevailing in the area of the high school, Governor Faubus spoke on statewide television. "We are now an occupied territory," he said. Displaying newspaper photographs of the troops in action at Central High, he intoned, "Evidence of the naked force of the federal government is here apparent in these unsheathed bayonets in the backs of schoolgirls." Faubus told his audience that a federal soldier had struck one Arkansan in the head with a gunbelt, sending blood streaming down his face. The governor claimed that, if he had been given more time, the situation would have been handled peacefully. He asked, "Does the will of the people—that basic precept of democracy—no longer matter?"

On September 31, the 101st Airborne troops withdrew to Camp Robinson, twelve miles away, leaving the federalized Arkansas National Guard to insure order. By then many of the more segregationist students had returned to Central High School. The initial, relatively calm reception for the nine black students was replaced by tension and harassment.

In October, four of the southern governors who had been at Sea Island with Faubus visited President Eisenhower. They proposed an arrangement that would keep the black children safely enrolled at Central but also get federal troops out of Little Rock. If Faubus would pledge not to interfere, the president said, he would remove the soldiers. Governor Luther Hodges of North Carolina called Faubus, who readily agreed to the deal, saying he would send a telegram to the president outlining his compliance. But the telegram was never sent. "I called him repeatedly," Hodges remembers. "He refused to take the calls. Later . . . he made contact with the president and said that he would give a qualified statement that he would not personally [interfere with the black students]. He did not give assurances from the power of his office, as the state's executive. [White House officials] said they couldn't accept it. I said, 'I don't blame you at all' . . . Faubus just turned completely around. He evidently became a prisoner of the right-wing group . . . that wanted to keep things as they were . . . He was so personally ambitious to move along that he sensed this point of view, of being against integration, . . . was probably the most popular thing that would get him votes." The federalized National Guard remained at Central High.

Faubus received increasing support in Little Rock and all of Arkansas. In early October, he stirred new protests by charging that federal troops had entered the girls' restroom at Central High. Four days later, 600 segregationists gathered at Central Baptist Church to pray for the governor's triumph and the troops' departure.

Other whites, however, lost sympathy for the governor. "I began to change," remembers Craig Rains, a white senior at Central during the 1957-1958 school year, "from being . . . a moderate, who, if I had my way, would have said, 'Let's don't integrate, because it's the state's right to decide.' I changed to someone who felt a real sense of compassion for those students, and felt like they deserved something that I had, and I also developed a real dislike for the people that were out there causing problems."

Jefferson Thomas waits for a bus while white students taunt him from across the street.

At Central High, the presence of the military did not deter adamant segregationists from venting their hostility. Melba Pattillo Beals recalls that at first "there was a feeling of pride and hope that year—yes, this is the United States, yes, there is a reason I salute the flag, and it's going to be okay. These [soldiers will] go with us the first time, [and then it will] be okay. The troops did not, however, mean the end of harassment. It meant the declaration of war." The black youngsters were growing up fast. "I worried about silly things, like keeping my saddle shoes straight, what am I going to wear today—things that a fifteen-year-old girl does worry about," Beals says, "but also which part of the hall to walk in that's the safest. Who's going to hit me with what? Is it going to be hot soup today? Is it going to be so greasy that it ruins the dress my grandmother made for me? How's this day going to go?"

When Minniejean Brown was selected to sing a solo for the glee club, the Mothers' League of Little Rock Central High School protested to school officials that the black students "are not supposed to take part in things like that . . . "

One day in October, Elizabeth Eckford walked into the office of Vice Principal Elizabeth Huckaby, who remembers that the girl was "red-eyed, her handkerchief a damp ball in her hand . . . 'I want to go home,' she said. Her story was one that became too familiar during the rest of the year from all the black children . . . the name-calling, thrown objects, trippings, shovings, kickings . . . It would

Daisy Bates and the Long Fight in Little Rock

Long before desegregation became an issue in Little Rock, Daisy Bates played an active role in the battle for civil rights. In 1941, Bates and her husband, L. C., bought the *Arkansas State Press*, a weekly newspaper with a circulation of 20,000 at its peak. "Our decision was based on the conviction that a newspaper was needed to carry on the fight for Negro rights as nothing else can," Bates wrote later. The *State Press* crusaded against police brutality, slum housing, and injustice in the courts.

I walked out onto the lawn. I heard the deep drone of big planes, and it sounded like music to my ears. I walked around the yard. I saw other women standing in their yards, looking upward, listening. I heard the subdued laughter of children and realized how long it had been since I'd heard that sound. Kept within doors in recent days, they now spilled out onto yards and driveways. From an open kitchen doorway Mrs. Anderson was heard singing. "Nobody knows the trouble I've seen . . ." A fear-paralyzed city had begun to stir.

Around 6 P.M., the long line of trucks, jeeps, and staff cars entered the heart of the city to the wailing sound of sirens and the dramatic flashing of lights from the police cars escorting the caravan to Central High School. The "Battle of Little Rock" was on.

Some of the citizens watching the arrival of the troops cried with relief. Others cursed the federal government for "invading our city." One got the impression that the "Solid South" was no longer solid.

A young white reporter rushed to my house and grabbed me by the hands, swinging me around. "Daisy, they're here! The soldiers are here! Aren't you excited? Aren't you happy?"

"Excited, yes, but not happy," I said after getting myself unwhirled. "Any time it takes eleven thousand five hundred soldiers to assure nine Negro children their constitutional right in a democratic society, I can't be happy."

"I think I understand how you feel," the reporter said. "You're thinking about all the other southern Negro children who'll have to 'hit the line' someday."

"Yes, and I'm sure there will be many."

"What's the next move?" he asked. "Will the children be going back to Central tomorrow?"

I parried the question. I knew the parents would be on tenterhooks waiting to hear from me, and with the same question on their minds. I delayed calling them. I was awaiting a call from Superintendent Blossom. Finally, about 10 P.M., I called all the parents to tell them I had not heard from Mr. Blossom. I assumed that the mob would be at the school the next morning, and therefore decided that the children could not be sent to Central the next day, troops or not.

Shortly after midnight Mr. Blossom telephoned. "Mrs. Bates, I understand you instructed the children that they were not to go to Central in the morning."

"That is correct."

"But General Walker said that he is here to put the children in school. So you must have them at your house by eight thirty in the morning." Major General Edwin A. Walker, chief of the Arkansas Military District, had been put in command of the 101st Airborne

Division and newly federalized Arkansas militia.

"I can't," I said. "I can't reach them. We have an agreement that if I want them, I will call *before* midnight. In order to get some sleep and avoid the harassing calls, they take their phones off the hook after midnight." How I wish I had done the same, I thought wearily, as I listened to the superintendent's urgent tones. "I suppose I could go to each home, but I can't go alone," I said.

"I'll call Hawkins and Christophe and ask them to accompany you," Mr. Blossom said. "You may expect them shortly." Edwin Hawkins was principal of Dunbar Junior High School and L. M. Christophe was principal of Horace Mann High School, both Negro schools.

At about 1 A.M. the three of us set out. Our first stop was some eight blocks away, the home of fifteen-year-old Gloria Ray. We knocked for what seemed ten minutes before we got an answer. The door opened about three inches exposing the muzzle of a shotgun. Behind it stood Gloria's father.

"What do you want now?" was his none-too-cordial greeting, as he looked straight at me. He forgot—I hope that was the reason—to remove his finger from the trigger or at least to lower the gun.

My eyes were fixed on the muzzle, and I could sense that Hawkins and Christophe, standing behind me, were riveted in attention. In my most pleasant, friendliest voice, and trying to look at him instead of the gun, I said that the children were to be at my house by eight thirty the next morning, and that those were the instructions of Superintendent Blossom.

"I don't care if the President of the United States gave you those instructions!" he said irritably. "I won't let Gloria go. She's faced two mobs and that's enough."

Both Mr. Christophe and Mr. Hawkins assured him that with the federal troops there, the children would be safe. We all, of course, added that the decision was up to him. At that point I asked if he wouldn't mind lowering his gun. He did. I told him if he changed his mind to bring Gloria to my house in the morning. Somewhat shakily we made our way to the car.

"Good Lord," sighed Mr. Christophe, "are we going to have to go through this with all nine sets of parents?"

The children's homes were widely scattered over Little Rock, and so our tour took better than three hours. Our encounter with Mr. Ray impressed on our minds the need to identify ourselves immediately upon entering the grounds of each home. But the cautious parents still greeted us with gun in hand, although they were a little more calm than Mr. Ray, and accepted the change in

In 1952, Daisy Bates became president of the Arkansas chapter of the NAACP. Six years later, Bates and the Little Rock Nine received the NAACP's Spingarn Medal for their work in integrating Central High. Bates' book, *The Long Shadow of Little Rock: A Memoir*, published in 1962, is excerpted here.

plans without objection.

At eight twenty-five the next morning, all the children except Gloria had arrived. My phone rang. "What time are we to be there, Mrs. Bates?" It was Gloria.

"They're all here now."

"Wait for me!" she said. "I'll be right over!"

In less than ten minutes, Mr. Ray, shy and smiling, led Gloria into the house. He looked down at his daughter with pride. "Here, Daisy, she's yours. She's determined to go. Take her. You seem to have more influence over her than I have, anyhow."

No sooner had Gloria joined the group than I was called to the telephone. A school official wanted to know whether the children were there. "All nine," I answered. I was told that a convoy for them was on its way.

While we waited, reporters were asking the nine how they felt, and the children, tense and excited, found it difficult to be articulate about the significance of the troops' mission. Half an hour crawled by. Jeff [Jefferson Thomas], standing at the window, called out, "The Army's here! They're here!"

Jeeps were rolling down Twenty-eighth Street. Two passed our house and parked at the end of the block, while two remained at the other end of the block. Paratroopers quickly jumped out and stood across the width of the street at each end of the block—those at the western end standing at attention facing west, and those at the eastern end facing east.

An Army station wagon stopped in front of our house. While photographers, perched precariously on the tops of cars and rooftops, went into action, the paratrooper in charge of the detail leaped out of the station wagon and started up our driveway. As he approached, I heard Minniejean say gleefully, "Oh, look at them, they're so—so soldierly! It gives you goose pimples to look at them!" And then she added solemnly, "For the first time in my life, I feel like an American citizen."

The officer was at the door, and as I opened it, he saluted and said, his voice ringing through the sudden quiet of the livingroom where a number of friends and parents of the nine had gathered to witness this moment in history: "Mrs. Bates, we're ready for the children. We will return them to your home at three thirty o'clock."

I watched them follow him down the sidewalk. Another paratrooper held open the door of the station wagon, and they got in. Turning back into the room, my eyes none too dry, I saw the parents with tears of happiness in their eyes as they watched the group drive off.

not do for the nine to leave. It would make it harder for them to return. It would put pressure on everyone involved, from the president on down . . . I finally persuaded Elizabeth to stay and walked with her to her history class."

The harassment continued through the school year. For several days, anonymous telephone callers to the homes of the black students threatened to shoot the children with acid-filled water pistols. Soon after, a white student pulled out a water gun and sprayed a black girl in the face. She became hysterical, thinking she had been shot with acid, though it was indeed only water.

Shortly before Christmas, one of the Little Rock Nine decided to fight back. "For a couple of weeks there had been a number of white kids following us," recalls Ernest Green, "continuously calling us niggers. 'Nigger, nigger, nigger'— one right after the other. Minniejean Brown was in the lunch line with me, and there was this white kid who was much shorter than Minnie . . . he reminded me of a small dog yelping at somebody's leg.

"Minnie had just picked up her chili, and before I could even say . . . 'Minnie, why don't you tell him to shut up?' Minnie . . . turned around and took that chili and dumped it on the dude's head." For a moment, the cafeteria was dead silent, Green remembers, "and then the help, all black, broke into applause. And the white kids there didn't know what to do. It was the first time that anybody [there] had seen somebody black retaliate."

The incident led to Minniejean's suspension. Then, in February, she was expelled from Central after a white girl called her a "nigger bitch" and she in turn denounced the young woman as "white trash." Minniejean Brown moved to New York City, where she enrolled in another high school. She arrived in New York to the glare of flashbulbs; journalists from throughout the United States and abroad were now tracking the crisis at Little Rock. The *New York Post* editorialized, "Our town has long been a haven for refugees from all over the world. Their numbers will now be increased by one Negro American from Little Rock. Like all the others, Minniejean Brown, expelled from Central High School, will be looking for equality of opportunity . . . The school board, in expelling Minniejean, has put its stamp of approval on the segregationist strategy of terror."

After Brown's departure, segregationist students added a new card to the collection circulating through the school. It read, "One down, eight to go." Craig Rains recalls, "When school was out in May, they still hadn't given up the fight. They came out with a two-color card that said, 'Ike Go Home! Liberation Day, May 29, 1958.'" May 29 was graduation day at Central High.

After Minniejean Brown was expelled, someone at Central High added the "One down . . . eight to go" card to the repertoire of cards such as these that circulated among segregationist students.

Ernest Green became the first black student to graduate from Central High. Police officers and federal troops stood guard as Green and his 601 white class-mates received their diplomas. Green's graduation was a victory, both real and symbolic, for all those who had fought for integration for so long. The seventeen-year-old sensed that, and it made him nervous. "I knew I was walking for the other eight students that were there," Green said years later. "I figured I was making a statement and helping black people's existence in Little Rock . . . I kept telling myself, I just can't trip with all those cameras watching me. But I knew that once I got as far as that principal and received that diploma, I had cracked the wall."

The mostly white audience applauded enthusiastically as one by one the students came up to receive their diplomas. Then came Ernest Green's moment. "When they called my name, there was nothing," he said, "just the name, and then there was eerie silence. Nobody clapped. But I figured they didn't have to . . . because after I got that diploma, that was it. I had accomplished what I had come there for."

On May 29, 1958, Ernest Green became the first black to graduate from Little Rock Central High School.

That summer, Orval Faubus renewed his political posturing against integration. "I stand now and always in opposition to integration by force or at bayonet point," he declared. In July, he won nomination for a third term as governor with an unprecedented sixty-nine percent of the vote. In September, the Supreme Court ruled unanimously that integration must proceed in Little Rock. But Faubus continued to fight, closing down the schools altogether a few days later. He then helped a small group of segregationists set up the Little Rock Private School Corporation, to which he attempted to lease the public schools on a segregated basis. In a Gallup Poll taken in late 1958, Americans selected Faubus as one of their ten most admired men.

During 1958, Little Rock's public schools were closed. Nearly half of the city's white students enrolled in private schools. One third of the students attended schools outside the city, and 643 white students did not attend any school that year. Most of the black high school students, including the Little Rock Nine, did not attend school either.

The Supreme Court ruled that the closing of Little Rock's high schools was unconstitutional and that "evasive schemes" could not be used to circumvent integration. In August 1959, the public high schools were reopened and integrated in accordance with federal requirements.

Also in 1959, the board of directors of the Little Rock Chamber of Commerce issued a formal resolution, stating, "The [*Brown*] decision of the Supreme Court of the United States, however much we dislike it, is the declared law and is binding upon us. We think that the decision was erroneous and that it was a reversal of established law upon an unprecedented basis of psychology and sociology . . . [However] we must in honesty recognize that, because the Supreme Court is the Court of last resort in the country, what it has said must stand until there is a correcting constitutional amendment or until the Court corrects its own error."

The crisis at Little Rock, which threw a state government into direct conflict with the federal government, would have far-reaching repercussions throughout the country and throughout the civil rights movement. And, as it had in Little Rock, the desegregation issue would become a political football for the many southern politicians who were more interested in grandstanding than in fair play.

A Freedom Rider's view through the bus window.

Chapter Five

Down Freedom's Main Line

The Movement's Next Generation

"When I was a boy, Nashville was a divided town . . . One day [my mother and I] were at Kress's, [where they] had these beautiful marble water fountains. One said 'Colored' and one said 'White.' I went over to both fountains and tasted the water and told my mother, 'Tastes the same to me, Mom.' "

Leo Lillard, sit-in participant

Whuhen *Brown v. Board of Education* was decided in 1954, Diane Nash was sixteen years old. When the Montgomery bus boycott ended victoriously, she was eighteen. When Emmett Till was murdered and the trial of his accused killers captured the nation's attention in 1955, John Lewis was fifteen. When Elizabeth Eckford walked through a jeering white mob and into Little Rock's Central High School, Lewis was seventeen. By 1960, Nash and Lewis were in college, members of a generation of blacks who had come of age during the momentous changes of the preceding decade. Youngsters had already played a crucial role in the civil rights movement—Linda Brown and Harry Briggs, Jr., Ernest Green and Elizabeth Eckford. This generation would go on to become even more deeply involved in the fight against racism.

When the *Brown* decision was handed down, black people hoped that the foundation on which Jim Crow had built his house would collapse. But in the years that followed, it became clear that the house would have to be dismantled brick by brick—on the buses, at the lunch counters, in the voting booths.

In the wake of the *Brown* decision and the Montgomery bus boycott, the NAACP had opened several more Youth Council chapters throughout the country. The organization knew that young blacks were eager to get involved in the civil rights movement. The Southern Christian Leadership Conference (SCLC) also began teaching blacks how they might participate in the struggle. As SCLC representatives, Martin Luther King and Ralph Abernathy traveled the South, teaching Christian pacifism. At the same time, they worked to help Montgomery adjust to desegregated buses.

A group called the Fellowship of Reconciliation (FOR) printed several thousand copies of a pamphlet, in comic-book format, entitled *Martin Luther King and the Montgomery Story*. The publication offered instruction in passive resistance and massive nonviolent action against segregation. The FOR distributed these "comic books" throughout the South. Though originally intended for people who didn't usually read books, the pamphlets found their way onto college campuses.

In the fifties, James Lawson was a divinity student at Nashville's Vanderbilt University. A firm believer in pacifism, the young black man had chosen to go to prison during the Korean War rather than take up arms. He was paroled under the recognizance of a group of Methodist ministers, who sent him to India as a missionary. Lawson spent three years there, learning about Mohandas Gandhi's use of nonviolent resistance. On his return to the United States, he enrolled at Oberlin College's theology school in his home state of Ohio. But when he learned of the Montgomery bus boycott and how the people of that city were applying the principles of nonviolence in a mass protest, he traveled to Alabama to meet with the Reverend Martin Luther King, Jr.

For several years, FOR minister Glenn Smiley and civil rights activist Bayard Rustin had been promoting Gandhi's ideas as a tool for blacks in the United States. After listening to James Lawson explain Gandhi's tactics of massive nonviolent resistance, King encouraged the twenty-nine-year-old Lawson to spread the ideals of nonviolence throughout the civil rights movement. Lawson left Oberlin and became southern field secretary for the FOR. This interracial organization had been founded in 1914 as a group devoted to the principles of nonviolence. Lawson was stationed in Nashville, where he resumed his studies at Vanderbilt. At the time, Nashville was sometimes called the Athens of the South and had twelve colleges and universities.

Lawson shared the hopes and frustrations felt by so many blacks in the late fifties. The victories in the Supreme Court were heartening, but after 1956, blacks across the South were anxiously awaiting the next development.

"When people are suffering," says Lawson, looking back on the decade, "they don't want rhetoric and processes which seem to go slowly . . . When they are suffering and they see their people suffering, they want direct participation. They want to be able to say, 'What I'm doing here gives me power and is going to help us change this business.'"

James Lawson, a leader of the sit-in movement.

In 1958, along with Glenn Smiley, a white FOR minister who had helped King with the Montgomery bus boycott, Lawson began offering workshops on non-violence in Nashville and across the South. The men taught students and other activists how to use the tactic of passive resistance. Lawson also traveled to other southern campuses to train students, both black and white. In churches and schools he recruited people for the cause of nonviolence. By 1960, many black campuses in the South had heard of the nonviolence workshops.

The workshops demonstrated that nonviolence was not for the faint of heart. In Nashville, participants had to sit quietly while other students, acting the role of segregationists, jeered, poked, and spit at them. Nonviolence required compassion, commitment, courage, and faith, but most importantly, it required discipline.

Diane Nash, a student at Fisk University in Nashville, was from Chicago. She could not accept the radical segregation of the South and was determined to do something about it. When a friend told her of Jim Lawson's workshops, now held every Tuesday night, she decided to enroll. In the workshops, Nash explains, "Students in Nashville, as well as some of the people who lived in the Nashville

**The
Fellowship of
Reconciliation**

Cover of "comic book"
produced by the
Fellowship of
Reconciliation.

Martin Luther King, Jr., was not the first to champion nonviolent protest in America. The Fellowship of Reconciliation (FOR) has been preaching nonviolence since the early part of the twentieth century. Founded at Cambridge University in 1914 by Henry Hodgkin, an English Quaker, and Friedrich Siegmund-Schultze, pacifist chaplain to the Kaiser, the FOR was established to promote pacifism and international understanding. The organization opened its first American chapter in 1915.

Although the FOR is primarily concerned with the dissemination of intellectual ideas—the majority of its members are students, professors, and ministers—the fellowship does occasionally engage in direct action. The group sponsored the first "Freedom Ride" in 1947. Called "The Journey of Reconciliation," this project sent a biracial group of thirteen on a bus ride through the upper South. Later, the FOR played a key role in the Montgomery bus boycott by sending two of its staffers to serve as consultants: the Reverend Glenn Smiley, FOR national field secretary, and Bayard Rustin, former FOR race relations secretary. Both worked closely with King in planning movement strategy. "The role that I played with Martin," Smiley says, "was one in which I literally lived with him hours and hours and hours at a time, and he pumped me about what nonviolence was." When the boycott ended, Smiley sat next to King on the first integrated bus ride through Montgomery.

The FOR used a $5,000 grant to put out a "comic book" commemorating the event and popularizing the philosophy of nonviolence. The group distributed some 200,000 copies of this ten-cent booklet. Ironically, the publication reached more university students than the semiliterate adults for whom it was originally written.

The FOR and its members have helped create numerous groups that work for social change. These include the American Civil Liberties Union, the National Conference of Christians and Jews, the Workers Defense League, and the Congress of Racial Equality. At present, the FOR has approximately 32,000 members worldwide.

community, were trained and educated in [nonviolent] philosophies and strategies. I remember we used to role-play, and we would do things like pretend we were sitting at lunch counters, in order to prepare ourselves to do that. We would practice things such as how to protect your head from a beating, how to protect each other. If one person was taking a severe beating, we would practice other people putting their bodies in between that person and the violence, so that the violence could be more distributed and hopefully no one would get seriously injured.

"During the workshops," recalls Nash, "we had begun what we called 'testing the lunch counters.' We sent teams of people into department-store restaurants, to attempt to be served. We had anticipated that we'd be refused, and we were. We asked to speak to the manager, and engaged him in a conversation. [We would bring up] the fact that it really was immoral to discriminate against people because of their skin color."

John Lewis, a student at the American Baptist Theological Seminary in Nashville, was encouraged by the Reverend Kelly Miller Smith, president of the Nashville Christian Leadership Conference (the local affiliate of the SCLC), to attend one of the workshops. Lewis had grown up on a farm about fifty miles south of Montgomery, Alabama, and had been deeply moved by the Montgomery bus boycott. Like Diane Nash, he was anxious to participate in the movement. "The workshops became almost like an elective [course] to students like me," he said. "It was the most important thing we were doing. We became a real group of believers."

Lewis, Nash, and a group of other students started an organization they called the Nashville Student Movement. Nash was elected head of the central committee. They hoped to use the tactics they had learned in the nonviolence workshops to abolish segregation in Nashville, starting with department-store lunch counters, where blacks were not served at the time. If Woolworth's was happy to take their money for socks and toothpaste at one counter, the dime store should also take their money at the lunch counter, the students reasoned.

They planned to send a group of kids to sit at a lunch counter, try to order something, and refuse to budge. If these students were arrested, others would take their place. If they were served, they'd go on to the next lunch counter and "sit in" there. When the lunch counters were integrated, they would target segregated movie houses or libraries.

But on February 1, independently of the Nashville activists, four black freshmen from North Carolina Agricultural and Technical College in Greensboro, North

Carolina, staged a sit-in at an F. W. Woolworth Company store. The students had spent the previous night debating what could be done about segregation.

All four had been members of the NAACP Youth Council. At least one of them had read a copy of the FOR "comic book" on nonviolence. They had heard about black people demanding service at whites-only restaurants, and they knew that doing so could land them in jail—no pleasant thought for a black person in the South. But they talked each other into it, and the next day went to the Woolworth's on North Elm Street.

Joseph McNeil bought a tube of toothpaste. His friend Franklin McCain bought some school supplies. Then they, David Richmond, and Ezell Blair, Jr., sat at the lunch counter and ordered coffee from the white waitress. "I'm sorry," she said, "but we don't serve colored here."

"I'm sorry, but we don't

serve colored here."

"I beg your pardon," said McCain. "You just served me at a counter two feet away. Why is it that you serve me at one counter and deny me at another? Why not stop serving me at all the counters?" A black dishwasher walked over. "You know you're not supposed to be here," she said to the young men, calling them "a disgrace to the race."

The four students sat there, without the coffee they had ordered, for over half an hour. At 5:30 P.M., when the store closed, they left. Unsure of what to do next, they sought advice from Dr. George Simpkins, a prominent black dentist. He asked the young men to wait before staging another sit-in, and he wrote to the Congress of Racial Equality (CORE), a group the FOR had helped establish in 1942 to deal with civil rights problems. A week later, CORE's New York office sent a representative, Gordon Carey, who organized more sit-ins by the students. McNeil, McCain, and others targeted Woolworth's and S. H. Kress and Company, another department store. The students politely requested food, remained at the counter when they were refused service, and kept silent.

Soon signs appeared in the stores' windows: "NO TRESPASSING," "We Reserve the Right to Service the Public As We See Fit," and "CLOSED—In the Interest of Public Safety."

The students, meeting with Carey, developed a strategy involving enough students to sustain daily sit-ins until segregation was defeated. The SCLC's Fred Shuttlesworth was in North Carolina the week of the first sit-in in Greensboro. Seeing an opportunity for action, he called Ella Baker, the SCLC's executive director. An energetic woman in her late fifties, Baker was one of the organization's most militant members. She began calling her many colleagues on campuses

Diane Nash, leader of
the Nashville Student
Movement, at age twenty.

The first Greensboro sit-in
participants. From right to
left: David Richmond,
Franklin McCain, Ezell
Blair Jr., and Joseph
McNeil.

and churches in major southern cities. "What are you going to do?" she asked. "It is time to move."

Gordon Carey arranged for activists to begin training students in other cities for more sit-ins. Daisy Bates, in Little Rock, Arkansas, heard of the sit-ins through the movement network and sent people to that city's Philander Smith College to recruit students for training. Students from Alabama State College in Montgomery met at Ralph Abernathy's home to organize sit-ins.

"When the students in Greensboro sat in on February 1," recalls Diane Nash, "we simply made plans to join their effort by sitting in at the same chains . . . We were surprised and delighted to hear reports of other cities joining in the sit-ins. We started feeling the power of the idea whose time had come. We had no inkling that the movement would become so widespread."

As news of the sit-ins spread through the nation's press and students from various colleges shared information by telephone, the sit-in tactic took hold elsewhere. In Tallahassee, whites joined black students from Florida Agricultural and Mechanical University, sharing food at lunch counters to show their disregard for segregated cafeterias. In a span of two weeks, there were sit-ins in eleven cities. But the segregationists also began to turn on the heat. In High Point, North Carolina, the Kress' store removed its lunch-counter stools entirely. In Rock Hill, South Carolina, ammonia was thrown at students during a sit-in. In some communities, hecklers threw "itching powder" on the students and chanted at the black girls, "How about a date when we integrate?" When students in Raleigh, North Carolina, lined up to go into a Woolworth's, they were arrested for trespassing.

Students in northern cities soon adopted the idea of demonstrating. Martin Smolin, a student at Columbia University, led the picketing of Woolworth's in New York. "People have asked me why northerners, especially white people, who have been in the majority in our picketing demonstrations in New York, take an active part in an issue which doesn't concern them," said Smolin. "My answer is that injustice anywhere is everybody's concern."

"It is with a desire to do something that many northern white students look at the sit-in movement of their southern Negro counterparts . . . That the northern response has been almost unanimously favorable is no surprise," wrote Ted Dienstfrey, a student at Columbia. "Of all the current social and political issues—the cold war, disarmament, the draft—the double standard [of] integration is the only one which does not have to be discussed."

Students and the Movement:

An Interview with Diane Nash

Diane Nash left her native Chicago in 1956 to attend Howard University in Washington, D.C. In 1959, Nash transferred to Fisk University in Nashville. The first chairman of the central committee of the Nashville Student Movement, Nash led the campaign to desegregate the lunch counters of Nashville's department stores. She organized sit-ins, trained students, and selected the Nashville contingent for the Freedom Rides.

Because I grew up in Chicago, I didn't have an emotional relationship to segregation. I understood the facts and stories, but there was not an emotional relationship. When I went south and saw the signs that said 'white' and 'colored,' and I actually could not drink out of that water fountain or go to that ladies' room, I had a real emotional reaction. I remember the first time it happened was at the Tennessee State Fair. I had a date with a young man, and I started to go to the ladies' room. And it said 'white' and 'colored,' and I really resented that. I was outraged.

In Chicago, at least, I had had access to public accommodations and lunch counters. So, my response was, "Who's trying to change these things?" I remember getting depressed because I encountered what I thought was so much apathy. At first I couldn't find anyone, and many of the students were saying, "Why are you concerned about that?" They were not interested in trying to effect some kind of change, I thought.

And then I talked to Paul LePrad, who told me about the nonviolent workshops that Jim Lawson was conducting. They were taking place a couple of blocks off campus. Jim had been to India, and he had studied the movement [of] Mohandas Gandhi. He also had been a conscientious objector and had refused to fight in the Korean War. He really is the person that brought Gandhi's philosophy and strategies of nonviolence to this country. He conducted weekly workshops where students in Nashville, as well as some of the people who lived in the Nashville community, were trained and educated in these philosophies and strategies. There were many things I learned in

Diane Nash (second from left) sits with other blacks enjoying a meal at an integrated lunch counter.

those workshops that I have used for the rest of my life.

I remember realizing that with what we were doing, trying to abolish segregation, we were coming up against governors of seven states, judges, politicians, businessmen, and I remember thinking, "I'm only 22 years old. What do I know? What am I doing?" I felt very vulnerable. So when we heard that other cities had demonstrations, it really helped, because there were more of us. And I think we started feeling the power of an idea whose time had come.

The movement had a way of reaching inside me and bringing out things that I never knew were there. Like courage, and love for people. It was a real experience to be seeing a group of people who would put their bodies between you and danger. And to love people that you work with enough that you would

put your body between them and danger. I was afraid of going to jail. I said, "I'll do telephone work, and I'll type, but I'm really afraid to go to jail." But when the time came to go to jail, I was far too busy to be afraid. And we had to go, that's what happened.

I think it's really important that young people today understand that the movement of the sixties was really a people's movement. The media and history seem to record it as Martin Luther King's movement, but young people should realize that it was people just like them, their age, that formulated goals and strategies, and actually developed the movement. When they look around now, and see things that need to be changed, they should say: "What can I do? What can my roommate and I do to effect that change?"

When a reporter asked Congressman Adam Clayton Powell of Harlem if he was advocating that Negroes in New York stay out of national chain stores such as Woolworth's, Powell answered, "Oh, no. I'm advocating that American citizens interested in democracy stay out of these stores."

As northern sympathy for the students grew, southern segregationists insisted that northerners were racists, too, but hid their own bigotry while unfairly painting the South as a repressive, uncivilized region. The *Cincinnati Post and Times Star* acknowledged the truth of these charges and commented, "Discrimination against citizens with darker skin is not a southern problem, alone . . . [in Chicago] Negro college graduates work as redcaps because jobs in which they could use their training are closed to them. It is said, with some justification, that in some respects a Negro is better treated in the South than North. The Southerner, from long association, tends toward a genuine affection for individual Negroes, while resenting Negroes in the abstract. The Northerner on the other hand is inclined to uphold Negro rights, in the abstract, while doing little or nothing to help individual Negroes get an even break."

In general, white southerners viewed the sit-ins skeptically. Bernie Schweid, a sympathetic white businessman in Nashville, says, "Most people did not take the sit-ins too seriously at the beginning, because they felt . . . they are agitators, these are students, some from New York . . . they're not 'our' Negroes. 'Our' Negroes are happy."

White southern segregationists, and even the merchants affected, predicted that this "latest campus fad" would soon pass. CORE had held sit-ins in Chicago in the 1940s, achieving only mild success and prompting little reaction in other cities. In 1958, Kansas and Oklahoma NAACP branches had won some success with sit-ins, but again the tactic faded. Officials in southern cities felt that they had only to wait and this latest problem would go away.

But by the end of February, the *New York Times* wrote in an editorial that ". . . the movement [has] spread from North Carolina, to Virginia, Florida, South Carolina, and Tennessee and involved 15 cities . . . Students of race relations in the area contend that the movement reflects the growing dissatisfaction over the slow pace of desegregation in schools and other public facilities."

By February 18, Nashville's black students had mobilized 200 people for sit-ins at the city's major stores. "The first sit-in we had was really funny," says Diane Nash. "The waitresses were nervous. They must have dropped $2,000 worth of dishes that day . . . It was almost like a cartoon . . . we were sitting there trying not to laugh [but] at the same time we were scared to death."

Nash said people would say "how brave I was for sitting in and marching, [but] I was . . . wall-to-wall terrified. I can remember sitting in class many times [when] I knew we were going to have a demonstration that afternoon. And the palms of my hands would be so sweaty. I was really afraid."

The students' fears were realistic. On Saturday, February 27, a group of white Nashville teens attacked the sit-in students, yanking them off their lunch-counter seats. Paul Laprad, a white Fisk student, described the scene. "Curiously, there were no police inside the store when the white teenagers and others stood in the aisles insulting us, blowing smoke in our faces, grinding out cigarette butts on our backs and finally pulling us off our stools and beating us. Those of us pulled off our seats tried to regain them as soon as possible, but none of us fought back in anger."

When the Nashville police arrived, they arrested not the white teens who had started the fight, but eighty-one of the protestors for "disorderly conduct." Diane Nash recalls, "The police said, 'Okay, all you nigras, get up from the lunch counter or we're going to arrest you.' [Then] they said, 'Everybody's under arrest.' So we all got up and marched to the wagon. Then they turned and looked around at the lunch counter again, and the second wave of students had all taken seats . . . then a third wave. No matter what they did and how many they arrested, there was still a lunch counter full of students there."

"No matter what they did and how many they arrested, there was still a lunch counter full of students there."

Nashville's black adults responded to the arrests by raising nearly $50,000 to bail out the students. The prominent black lawyer Z. Alexander Looby agreed to represent them in court.

The judge literally turned his back as attorney Looby argued that the black students were victims who had been beaten by hooligans and had not caused any disturbance. Looby cut short his argument and then said, staring at the judge's back, "What's the use!"

When the magistrate finally turned to face the court, he pronounced the defendants guilty and fined them $150 plus court costs. But the students did not quit their sit-ins. On March 2, sixty-three were arrested for sitting in at Nashville's Greyhound and Trailways bus terminals. Two weeks later four blacks were finally served at the Greyhound terminal. It was the first sit-in victory in the nation, but it came at a price. The four students who were served were badly beaten as they tried to eat, and the next day two unexploded bombs were discovered at the terminal.

By late March, the police had orders not to arrest the demonstrators because of the national publicity the sit-ins were attracting. "The sit-ins are instigated and

Black and white students conducting sit-ins often met with harassment and violence from angry whites.

planned by and staged for the convenience of the Columbia Broadcasting System [CBS]," said Tennessee governor Buford Ellington.

Nashville's business community was pushing for a settlement. Sales had slumped because whites were afraid to come downtown and blacks were boycotting the stores where the sit-ins were taking place. By early April, an estimated ninety-eight percent of black customers were withholding their business from the stores. Merchant Bernie Schweid remembers those lean times. "The merchants were getting it from both sides, and there was very, very little traffic. One merchant . . . said to me, 'You could roll a bowling ball down Church Street and not hit anybody these days.'"

Business owners proposed a ninety-day trial period, during which they would serve blacks in a portion of the restaurant facilities formerly operated exclusively for white customers. The students refused. "The suggestion of a restricted area involves the same stigma of which we are earnestly trying to rid the community," they wrote in a statement explaining their position. The Nashville sit-ins continued unabated.

1960 was a presidential election year. The Democratic candidate, Senator John F. Kennedy of Massachusetts, had no real experience with civil rights issues. Many civil rights leaders viewed the Republican candidate, Richard Nixon, as more of a supporter of civil rights than the unknown Kennedy. Kennedy saw, however, that President Eisenhower's lack of moral leadership through these turbulent times was a vulnerability to be exploited in the campaign against Nixon, Eisenhower's vice president. Kennedy sought advice from one of his speech writers, Harris Wofford, who recalls the candidate saying, "You know, I'm way behind on this, because I've hardly known any blacks in my life. It isn't an issue that I've thought about a lot . . . I've got to learn a lot, and I've got to catch up fast."

Wofford recalls, "We gave Kennedy a draft of a statement to send to the sit-in students in Atlanta and it [contained words] to the effect of, 'They have shown that the new way for Americans to stand up for their rights is to sit down.' And people were saying, 'That's much too strong. That's really going to bother the white southerners,' and Kennedy said, 'Go with it.'" That statement represented one of the few times that either presidential candidate addressed a civil rights issue during the campaign.

Other white politicians began to wonder whether the older civil rights leaders, who had been seeking change through the courts and Congress, might be losing some of their preeminent status in the movement. Blacks, too, sensed the power shift.

"Negroes all over America knew that the spontaneous and uncorrupted student demonstrations were more than an attack on segregation," wrote journalist Louis Lomax in *Harper's* magazine. "They were proof that the Negro leadership class, epitomized by the NAACP, was no longer the prime mover in the Negro's social revolt. The demonstrations have shifted the desegregation battles from the courtroom to the marketplace."

Privately, some of the older black leaders were lukewarm to the wildcat sit-in movement. It was deflecting press attention away from their own efforts to promote civil rights legislation in Congress. But publicly, the senior leaders praised the students. "The message of this movement is plain and short," said Roy Wilkins, executive secretary of the NAACP, in an April 1960 speech in Cleveland. "Negro youth is finished with racial segregation, not only as a philosophy but as a practice." Martin Luther King, Jr., said of the student activists, "This movement is the eternal refutation of the idea that the colored citizen is satisfied with segregation."

The SCLC's Ella Baker was especially impressed by the burgeoning student movement. "I think it [the movement] spread to a large extent because of the young enthusiasm and the need for action . . . ," she says. "There was a great deal of dissatisfaction among the young with the older leadership. Part of the [reason it] spread was a sister would call her brother at [another] college and ask, 'Why aren't you doing it?'"

But Baker realized that the sit-in movement lacked direction and overall leadership. She appealed to the SCLC to sponsor a meeting of students involved in the sit-ins. The organization agreed, in part because of its desire to stamp the student movement with the SCLC mark. Held on Easter weekend, 1960, the meeting at Shaw University in Raleigh, North Carolina, was dubbed the "Sacrifice for Dignity."

John Lewis and Diane Nash attended, along with northern white students such as Tom Hayden. Ella Baker had hoped to draw about a hundred students. To her amazement, three times that many showed up. "Just as the sit-ins had skyrocketed or escalated without rhyme or reason, so too the response to the concept of a conference escalated beyond our expectations," Baker says.

Several black ministers from the SCLC became concerned as the meeting progressed. The students were not rallying to the idea of becoming a youth arm of the SCLC or joining the youth councils of the local NAACP chapters. In fact,

Baker openly advised the college students to go their own way, avoiding the older groups that had been slow to move for the last few years.

"The ministers from the SCLC, and some others, felt sort of left out," says Baker. "They didn't want to lose them [the students] because this was something new, this was vitality, I suppose. What they didn't know [was] that the young people had already decided they were going to be independent and this was difficult, of course, for someone who had been accustomed to feeling 'these are children of my church' . . . I walked out of the meeting."

"Ella Baker was very important in giving direction to the student movement at that particular point," remembers Diane Nash, "[not in terms of saying] what the students ought to do, but in terms of really seeing how important it was that the students should set the goals and directions and maintain control of the student movement."

Jim Lawson gave a speech at the meeting. He had been expelled from Vanderbilt's divinity school in March for advising the Nashville sit-in students to continue their protest.

"Lawson called this not a silent but a waiting generation," said a student report on the conference. "[Lawson described us] as waiting for the cause, the moment to catapult us into speech, into actualization of our faith . . . The legal question is not central. There has been a failure to implement legal changes [ordered by the Supreme Court] and [segregated] customs remain unchanged. Unless we are prepared to create the climate, the law can never bring victory."

The meeting ended with the formation of a student-run group that would organize the sit-in effort—the Student Nonviolent Coordinating Committee, or SNCC, pronounced "snick." A few months later Ella Baker wrote that the student conference made it "crystal clear that the current sit-in and other demonstrations are concerned with something bigger than a hamburger . . . The Negro and white students, North and South, are seeking to rid America of the scourge of racial segregation and discrimination—not only at the lunch counters but in every aspect of life."

Southern segregationists held a very different view of the upstart students. They saw them as a group hungry for publicity, damaging the South's economy and disturbing its peaceful, if segregated, way of life. "Black supremacy is the goal" of the sit-ins, said Birmingham public safety commissioner Theophilus Eugene "Bull" Connor. He claimed that northern Democrats, the NAACP, and the "Communist front organizations" were behind the students.

Ella Baker, a guiding force for the students, organized the Raleigh Conference that led to the formation of the Student Nonviolent Coordinating Committee (SNCC).

Senator Richard Russell, a Georgia Democrat, accused the sit-ins of robbing the civil rights movement of its "political allure." Russell charged that the students' helter-skelter sit-ins and close cooperation with newspaper and television reporters revealed that "the issue [civil rights] is mostly fictitious . . . it has been phony all the time. It's not really a civil rights issue but a political fight [for power in the South.]"

The Nashville students continued their sit-ins through February and March of 1960. On April 19, Z. Alexander Looby's home was destroyed by dynamite hurled from the window of a passing car at 5:30 A.M. The blast was so powerful that it shattered 147 windows in a building across the street. Looby, Nashville's first black councilman, was the lawyer who had represented the arrested sit-in students. Fortunately, the explosion injured no one.

"Mr. Z. Alexander Looby was a black attorney—conservative politically, a Lincoln Republican of many years—no one could accuse him of being a wild-eyed radical politically," recalls Will Campbell, a white Nashville minister. "And when his house was dynamited, I think it solidified the black community and it enraged a segment of the white community in a fashion that nothing else had."

Nashville mayor Ben West turned his anger from the sit-in students to the perpetrators of the violence. "You all have the power to destroy this city, so let's not have any mobs," he said.

On April 19, 1960, more than 2,000 demonstrators marched silently in Nashville to protest the bombing of Z. Alexander Looby's home.

The bombing of Looby's house jolted the students in Nashville, by far the best organized in the nation. That same day, 2,500 students and community members staged a march on city hall—the movement's first major protest of that kind. It was a silent march, except for the sound of shoes slapping the blacktop. Whites on the street, unaccustomed to such a show of unity by blacks, quizzically watched the orderly yet resolute marchers proceed to city hall. Mayor West was waiting on the building's steps. Diane Nash asked West if he personally believed that it was right for blacks to be sold school supplies and cosmetics at one counter of a store but refused service at its lunch counter.

"We needed him to say, 'Integrate the counters,' to tell Nashville to do what Nashville knows it should have done a long time ago—like about 95 years ago, after the Civil War," Nash said later. Describing her televised confrontation with the mayor, she adds, "So I asked the mayor first of all: 'Mayor West, do *you* feel it is wrong to discriminate against a person solely on the basis of their race or color?'"

West did not hesitate. He nodded and then said yes, he believed that it was wrong.

"They asked me some pretty soul-searching questions," he said later. "And one that was addresssed to me as a man. And I found that I had to answer it frankly and honestly—that I did not agree that it was morally right for someone to sell them merchandise and refuse them service. And I had to answer it just exactly like that . . . It was a moral question—one that a *man* had to answer, not a politician."

The next morning, headlines in the *Nashville Tennesseean* read, "Mayor Says Integrate Counters."

The city's storeowners appeared relieved by West's words. Now they could integrate and point to the mayor as the man who was responsible. "The merchants were afraid to move on their own, were almost looking for an excuse to say, 'Well, if that's what the mayor thinks, then maybe we ought to go ahead,'" said Nashville merchant Bernie Schweid.

SNCC And African Liberation

"Sure we identified with the blacks in Africa, and we were thrilled by what was going on. Here were black people, talking of freedom and liberation and independence, thousands of miles away. We could hardly miss the lesson for ourselves. They were getting their freedom, and we still didn't have ours in what we believed was a free country. We couldn't even get a hamburger and a Coke at the soda fountain. Maybe we were slow in realizing what this meant to us, but then things started moving together. What was happening in Africa, finally, had tremendous influence on us."

—John Lewis of the Student Nonviolent Coordinating Committee

The following countries gained their independence in a single year—between June, 1960 and June, 1961—as the civil rights movement was gathering force.

Zaire	June 30, 1960
Somali	July 1, 1960
Dahomey	August 3, 1960
Ivory Coast	August 8, 1960
Chad	August 11, 1960
Congo Brazzaville	August 15, 1960
Gabon	August 17, 1960
Senegal	August 20, 1960
Mali	September 22, 1960
Nigeria	October 1, 1960
Sierra Leone	April 27, 1961

The day after the march, Martin Luther King came to Nashville to celebrate with the students. King called the Nashville movement "the best organized and the most disciplined in the Southland." He added, "I came to Nashville not to bring inspiration but to gain inspiration from the great movement that has taken place in this community."

Three weeks later, on May 10, six Nashville lunch counters—in stores that had been the prime target of the sit-ins—began serving blacks. The future still held "stand-ins" in Nashville's segregated movie theaters, "sleep-ins" in the lobbies of the city's hotels, and more sit-ins at hard-core segregationist restaurants. But an important and enduring victory had been won.

Nationally, both presidential candidates tried to avoid addressing civil rights issues. To champion segregation openly would mean a loss of the burgeoning black vote and would jeopardize the support of moderate whites. But if a candidate spoke out for the rights of blacks, he risked losing the backing of the white segregationists who controlled southern politics. Nixon faced an additional handicap—he was a Republican. The current Republican president, Dwight D. Eisenhower, had angered Dixie by sending troops to Little Rock.

Kennedy had said that he believed the Supreme Court's "deliberate speed" decision, which in effect allowed southern states to use delaying tactics to avoid school desegregation, was "a satisfactory arrangement." Kennedy was also very closely linked to Alabama governor John Patterson, who had enthusiastically backed the candidate in the primaries and during the Democratic convention. Patterson's support prompted Roy Wilkins of the NAACP to say, "It is very difficult for thoughtful Negro voters to feel at ease about the endorsement of Senator Kennedy by Governor John Patterson . . . Anything with an Alabama odor does not arouse much enthusiasm among Negro citizens." Jackie Robinson, the first black major-league baseball player, campaigned for Nixon.

By October, a month before the election, sit-ins had taken place in 112 southern cities, and many were still going strong. On October 19, a new round of sit-ins began in Atlanta, aimed at the entrenched segregationist practices of the city's major department stores and restaurants. One hundred students from five colleges sat in at eight stores across the city.

Martin Luther King had moved to Atlanta in early 1960 to work more actively as head of the SCLC. He had avoided local civil rights actions because he did not want to interfere with the activities of local movement leaders. But in that city, the students and the older leaders were at odds. The traditional Negro leadership, including King's father, objected to the sit-ins as inappropriate; they

Vice President Richard M. Nixon campaigning in Tennessee.

Massachusetts Senator John F. Kennedy, campaigning in 1960.

felt the battle was in the courts and the voting booths, not on the streets. But the students, whose dedication to nonviolence moved King, appealed to the young leader. He decided to join them for a one-day sit-in, not as a leader but as a participant. As the Ku Klux Klan held counter-demonstrations in the Atlanta streets, Martin Luther King, Jr., was arrested for sitting in the Magnolia Room restaurant of Rich's Department Store.

On October 24, a truce was called by Atlanta's city officials, merchants, and sit-in leaders. The sit-ins would stop, and the protesters would be released from jail.

King, however, was not given his freedom. He had been arrested earlier for driving without a Georgia license, and the sit-in arrest was a violation of his probation. King was sent to a rural jail, Reidsville State Penitentiary, to serve a four-month sentence.

Candidate Richard Nixon privately asked the United States Justice Department to determine if King's constitutional rights had been violated, but he made no public statement on behalf of the jailed leader.

The Kennedy campaign heard of the arrest from Coretta Scott King, who called Harris Wofford, an aide to the candidate. Wofford spoke with Louis Martin, the campaign's top black adviser, who said Kennedy should at least make a gesture of concern for Rev. King. Wofford agreed, but he knew that Kennedy had privately promised the governor of Georgia that he would issue no public statement; the governor, in turn, had indicated he would try to find a way to get King released. Wofford suggested that Kennedy make the limited gesture of telephoning Mrs. King to express his sympathy.

Even that token action was potentially controversial, but aides Wofford and Martin agreed it should be done. Wofford called Sargent Shriver, another Kennedy aide sympathetic to the movement, who was with Kennedy in a hotel near Chicago's O'Hare Airport. Shriver waited until after the departure of other advisers who might counsel Kennedy not to get involved with a potentially explosive issue like civil rights and a controversial character like King. Shriver proposed the telephone call, and Kennedy agreed. He immediately phoned Mrs. King in Atlanta and told her he would keep an eye on her husband's situation.

"[Kennedy] said, 'I'm thinking about you and your husband, and I know this must be a very difficult time for you,'" remembers Coretta Scott King. "'If there's anything I can do to help, I want you to please feel free to call me.'"

Later, Kennedy said of the call, "She is a friend of mine and I was concerned about the situation."

Kennedy's other aides were furious when they heard about the call. They were relieved when no major news stories about it appeared in the white press. Meanwhile, Louis Martin spoke with Robert Kennedy about King's jailing. Later that day, the younger Kennedy called Judge Oscar Mitchell in Atlanta. That story broke in the mainstream press, as did Atlanta mayor William B. Hartsfield's statement that Kennedy campaign aides had called him to ask if he could expedite King's release. The day after John Kennedy's phone call, King was set free on bail.

"It's time for all of us to take off our Nixon button."

"It's time for all of us to take off our Nixon button," said Martin Luther King, Sr., who until then had been favoring the Republicans. White Democrats had long maintained a stranglehold on southern politics, making it essentially a one-party system. That system excluded blacks. Supporting the Democratic candidate was a signif cant and portentous move for the civil rights movement.

The Kennedy campaign printed two million copies of a pamphlet detailing the phone calls. Delivered to black churches and schools, the pamphlet's headline read, "NO COMMENT NIXON vs. A CANDIDATE WITH A HEART—SEN. KENNEDY: The Case Of Martin Luther King, Jr."

"We showed that our candidate was trying to be helpful," says Louis Martin. "As to the political motivation, no doubt about it—we campaigned . . . we were vulnerable to some limited extent in [the] sense that [blacks] regarded all those public officials in the South as Democrats, and we feared the Republicans would use that against us."

According to a post-election Gallup poll, Kennedy received sixty-eight percent of the black vote—seven percent more than the last Democratic candidate, Adlai Stevenson, had garnered against Eisenhower in the 1956 election. In one of the closest presidential elections in American history, Kennedy won by a margin of two-thirds of one percent in the popular vote. Civil rights leaders were quick to stress the importance of Kennedy's support among black voters.

It was a time of high hopes for the civil rights movement. Blacks had helped elect a president. Kennedy was only forty-one years old, and he promised a new vision for the nation. Listening to his inaugural address in January 1961, civil rights leaders and the many student activists who had brought their own energy to the movement took heart at the new president's statement that "the torch has been passed to a new generation of Americans."

But Kennedy introduced no new civil rights legislation. Nor did he fulfill his campaign promise to wipe out housing discrimination in federally funded housing projects "with one stroke of the pen"—that is, with an executive order. Civil

CORE and the Freedom Rides:

An Interview with James Farmer

After receiving a theology degree from Howard University, James Farmer went north to work for the Fellowship of Reconciliation (FOR). He proposed that the FOR establish a new organization to combat racial discrimination with the techniques that Mohandas Gandhi had used in India. Although the fellowship declined to sponsor the project directly, it authorized Farmer to establish the new organization while on the FOR payroll. In 1942, he played an instrumental role in founding the Congress of Racial Equality in Chicago.

CORE's first project was to desegregate a roller-skating rink called White City on the South Side of Chicago. By

The original "Freedom Riders" in 1947 on their "Journey of Reconciliation." James Peck, who also joined the Freedom Rides of 1961, is fourth from left.

1944, CORE chapters
had been formed in New
York, Los Angeles,
Philadelphia, Pittsburgh,
and Detroit. During the
1960s, CORE moved
south to lead the
Freedom Rides.

In 1947, CORE and a sister organization, the Fellowship of Reconciliation, had a kind of Freedom Ride. It was called the "Journey of Reconciliation." The riders, black and white, went through the upper South, not the Deep South, and tested only the seating on buses. This was in response to a Supreme Court decision in the Irene Morgan case in 1946, saying that segregated seating of interstate passengers was unconstitutional. They were unsuccessful in that ride. Some of them were arrested in North Carolina and served on a chain gang as a result.

When I became CORE's national director in 1961, there were letters on my desk from blacks in the Deep South who complained that when they tried to sit on the front seats of buses or to use the bus terminal facilities, they were beaten, or jailed, or thrown out, or all three. This was in spite of the fact that the Supreme Court said they had every right to sit anywhere they wanted to on a bus or to use the bus terminal facilities

without segregation. But those Supreme Court decisions had become merely scraps of paper gathering dust with cobwebs over them. They were not being enforced.

We decided . . . to have an interracial group ride through the South. We wrote letters in advance, following the Gandhian program of advising your adversaries or the people in power of just what you were going to do, when you were going to do it, and how you were going to do it, so that everything would be open and aboveboard. I sent letters to President Kennedy, Robert Kennedy, J. Edgar Hoover, the chairman of the Interstate Commerce Commission, the president of Greyhound Corporation, and the president of Trailways Corporation . . . we got replies from none of those letters.

[After the first lap of the Ride,] Robert Kennedy called Dr. King, who had come into Montgomery to speak at a rally that we were having on behalf of the Freedom Riders. Robert Kennedy

James Farmer leads a line of Freedom Riders arrested in Jackson, Mississippi.

asked Dr. King to intercede, to try to get me to halt the Freedom Ride and have a cooling-off period. After consulting with Diane Nash of SNCC and other Freedom Riders . . . I asked Dr. King to tell Bobby Kennedy that we'd been cooling off for 350 years, and that if we cooled off any more, we'd be in a deep freeze.

I had decided that I was not going to take that ride from Montgomery to Jackson because I was scared. I didn't think the buses would arrive in Jackson safely. I had all kinds of excuses; my father had just died, and two deaths in the same week would have been a bit much for [my] family. Furthermore I had been away from my office for six weeks. None of the students—these were the SNCC students and the few CORE students from Nashville—ever asked me if I was going. They merely assumed I was going because, after all, it was my project. I had started it, and I had gone to Montgomery to join them.

I went down to say goodbye to the students who were going to ride to Jackson. I reached my hand through an open window to shake hands with a young CORE girl from New Orleans, Doris Castle, who was seventeen years old at the time. Her eyes were wide with fear. I said, "Well, Doris, have a safe journey. After the Freedom Ride we'll get together in New Orleans or someplace and we'll have a big bowl of crab gumbo and we'll talk about the next step." She looked at me with total disbelief and said, "But Jim, you're going with us, aren't you?" I said, "Well, no Doris," and went through the whole catalog of reasons. Doris said just two words. In a stage whisper, she said "Jim. *Please*." Well, that was more than I could bear. I said to a CORE aide, "Get my luggage and put it on the bus. I'm going."

rights leaders started a campaign urging people to mail Kennedy pens printed with the words "one stroke of the pen" to remind him of his promise.

"Kennedy attributed that first promise to me and to the civil rights section [of the campaign]," remembers Harris Wofford. "So he said, 'Send them to Wofford,' and the pens piled up—thousands and thousands of pens—in my office."

In December, the month before Kennedy's inauguration, civil rights activists had won a victory in the Supreme Court when the justices ordered integration of bus stations and terminals serving interstate travelers. That court triumph made Kennedy's first few months in office all the more disappointing to blacks. But civil rights leaders still believed that Kennedy was a friend at heart and they knew he owed blacks a political debt. Eisenhower had been reluctant to use federal force after Little Rock. But Kennedy, civil rights leaders hoped, would not back down. Without enforcement from the executive branch, in this case in the form of a ruling from the Interstate Commerce Commission ordering compliance, the Supreme Court ruling would be meaningless. Just how far would Kennedy go to enforce the nation's civil rights laws?

The Congress of Racial Equality (CORE) intended to find out. In 1947 CORE had organized the "Journey of Reconciliation" after the Supreme Court ruled that segregated seating on interstate buses and trains was unconstitutional. Together, black and white CORE workers had traveled by bus throughout the upper South in an attempt to test the ruling. They were harassed and finally arrested in North Carolina for violating the state's segregation laws.

Fourteen years later, CORE planned to confront segregation in transportation once again. James Farmer, the organization's executive director, reasoned that the federal government was not enforcing the law because administration politicians feared losing the support of southern Democrats. "What we had to do," Farmer said, "was to make it more dangerous politically for the federal government *not* to enforce federal law than it would be for them to enforce federal law . . . We decided the way to do it was to have an interracial group ride through the South. This was not civil disobedience really, because we would be merely doing what the Supreme Court said we had a right to do."

The strategy for the "Freedom Ride" was that whites in the group would sit in the back of the bus. Blacks would sit in the front and refuse to move when ordered. At every rest stop, blacks would go into the whites-only waiting rooms and try to use all the facilities. "We felt we could count on the racists of the South to create a crisis so that the federal government would be compelled to enforce the law," Farmer explains.

CORE recruited thirteen people with spotless reputations. The organization wanted to thwart any attempt by segregationists to smear the riders in the press. Among the thirteen were James Farmer; John Lewis, fresh from his experience with the Nashville sit-ins; and forty-six-year-old James Peck, a white CORE member and the only Freedom Rider who had also been on the 1947 Journey of Reconciliation. Their trip began on May 4, 1961, departing Washington, D.C., to travel through Virginia, North Carolina, and South Carolina. They planned to arrive in New Orleans on May 17, the anniversary of the 1954 *Brown* decision.

"We were told that the racists, the segregationists, would go to any extent to hold the line on segregation in interstate travel," remembers James Farmer. "So when we began the ride I think all of us were prepared for as much violence as could be thrown at us. We were prepared for the possibility of death." Several of the Freedom Riders left letters to be delivered to loved ones if they were killed.

The ride began with only occasional scuffles as the riders attempted to use bus terminal restrooms and lunchrooms in Virginia and the Carolinas. On Mother's Day, May 14, the thirteen riders divided into two groups to travel from Atlanta to Birmingham. The only scheduled stop on the way was Anniston, Alabama.

Pulling into the Anniston bus depot, the Greyhound bus carrying the first group of riders was stoned. Its tires were slashed as a swarm of some 200 angry people attacked it. The bus raced away, stopping six miles out of town to fix the flat tires. Here a mob again surrounded the vehicle and someone tossed a firebomb through the rear door. The passengers fled through an emergency exit, and seconds later the bus burst into flames. The next day its burning image covered the front pages of America's newspapers.

Meanwhile, the Trailways bus carrying the other group arrived in Birmingham. At the station a mob of whites was waiting for the Freedom Riders. Public Safety Commissioner Bull Connor later said that he posted no officers at the bus station because of the Mother's Day holiday. Unhindered, the mob assaulted the riders; one of them, William Barbee, was paralyzed for life. It was later learned that an informant had told the FBI in advance that the Freedom Riders would be attacked in Birmingham and that the city police planned to stay away.

At a press conference after the attack, Alabama governor John Patterson told reporters he had no sympathy for the Freedom Riders. "When you go somewhere looking for trouble, you usually find it," he remarked.

In Washington, President Kennedy summoned Justice Department staff members and his brother, Robert, now attorney general, to the White House for an emergency breakfast meeting at 8:30. "The breakfast was in the sitting room outside the president's bedroom in the mansion," remembers Burke Marshall. "The president was still in his pajamas. It was the first time the president had had the problem of serious racial disorders . . . Our recommendation to the president was that he should not use troops unless it was unavoidable." The president and attorney general decided to prepare federal marshals to go to Alabama if necessary. The violence against the Freedom Riders was being given international press coverage and the Kennedys were concerned about their image as they prepared for an upcoming summit with Soviet premier Nikita Khrushchev.

The president placed a call to his former campaign supporter, Alabama governor John Patterson. But the governor would not take the president's calls. His aides said he had gone fishing.

In Birmingham, reporter Robert Shackne interviewed Jim Peck, whose head was heavily bandaged. "Mr. Peck, you have obviously been injured . . . What happened to you?" asked Shackne.

"I was beaten twice yesterday by hoodlums," said Peck. "Once aboard the bus and once in the terminal in Birmingham." When asked how extensive his injuries were, Peck replied, "Well, it is fifty stitches, and that's a lot of stitches."

"And still and all, you are going to continue?" the reporter asked.

"I think it is particularly important at this time when it has become national news that we continue and show that nonviolence can prevail over violence," said Peck.

Attorney General Robert Kennedy has a word with Assistant Attorney General Burke Marshall.

The bus company, however, was reluctant to risk having another of its vehicles bombed, and the company drivers—all white—refused to carry the Freedom Riders. For two days the riders negotiated with the bus company, but finally gave up. They headed for the Birmingham airport, fearing for their safety. Simeon Booker, an *Ebony* reporter, called Robert Kennedy from the airport, and Kennedy later spoke of the "terror" he heard in Booker's voice. The riders made it safely onto the plane and flew to New Orleans.

But the Freedom Ride was not over. A group of students experienced from the sit-ins in Nashville, eight black and two white, decided to go to Birmingham to continue the Freedom Ride.

"If the Freedom Riders had been stopped as a result of violence," said Diane Nash, "I strongly felt that the future of the movement was going to be cut short. The impression would have been that whenever a movement starts, all [you have to do] is attack it with massive violence and the blacks [will] stop."

Nash carefully selected the students who would go to Birmingham and warned them of the violence they might encounter. "We were informed we should be

The second leg of the
Freedom Ride, from
Montgomery to New
Orleans.

Outside of Anniston,
Alabama, the Freedom
Riders' bus was
firebombed.

willing to accept death," said Susan Herman, then a twenty-year-old Fisk University student and one of the ten who went to Birmingham. With the arrival of the Nashville students, the activists re-approached the bus company. Would they let their buses be used by the students? Attorney General Kennedy was now intent on enforcing the Supreme Court's decision mandating racially integrated travel between the states. He was also angered by Governor Patterson's refusal to return the administration's phone calls. Kennedy got on the phone with the Birmingham police and then with the Greyhound bus company.

Kennedy later said that the presence of the Nashville students in Birmingham, waiting to continue the Freedom Ride, seemed to him a "festering sore," an incitement to bloody violence. To Southern segregationists, Kennedy seemed to be working with the Freedom Riders, thumbing his nose at the South instead of telling the activists to stay home and stop causing trouble. Mississippi attorney general Joe Patterson told Kennedy's aides in the Justice Department, "I think they [the Freedom Riders] ought to go home and quit this darned Communist conduct."

The tension escalated when Birmingham police arrested the new Freedom Riders. "The commissioner of public safety, Bull Connor, told us we were being placed in protective custody for our own safety, for our well-being," said Freedom Rider John Lewis. "We went to jail that Wednesday night, May 17, 1961 . . . Thursday night we went on a hunger strike, a fast. We refused to eat anything or drink any water."

On Friday, May 19, at 2 A.M., the students were awakened in their cells by Bull Connor, who flatly announced that he was taking them back to Nashville. The students refused to move. The officers carried them into police cars and drove them to the Tennessee state line, 120 miles from Birmingham, dumping them out beside the highway.

The students called Diane Nash in Nashville, about 100 miles away, and cars were sent to pick them up. The students then went straight back to the Birmingham bus station. When they tried to board a bus for Montgomery, the bus driver said, "I cannot, I will not drive," according to John Lewis. "He said, 'I have only one life to give, and I'm not going to give it to the NAACP or CORE,'" recalls Lewis.

That same day, Governor John Patterson finally returned the White House's phone calls. The president was in a cabinet meeting. Robert Kennedy came out of the meeting to talk to Patterson. It was a brief and unfriendly conversation. Patterson would agree only to meet with John Seigenthaler, a Justice Department aide who had gone to Birmingham to monitor the situation for the Kennedys.

"I went in to see Patterson and he had his whole cabinet sitting around this long table just across from his desk," recalls Seigenthaler, a native of Tennessee. "Patterson said, 'Glad to see you—you're a southerner.'" The governor stood up and gestured to the men seated at the table. "'Now all these people here, they're with me. You go ahead, if you've got a tape recorder on, you go ahead and use it,'" Seigenthaler recalls Patterson saying.

"'Well,' I said, 'I don't have a tape recorder on, Governor, but I'm sure you have one. You feel free to say anything, because anything I'm going to say, I'd feel free to say outside this room and as far as I'm concerned you do the same thing. The thing I'm here to tell you is that there is a strong feeling in the Department of Justice that these people have got to have access to interstate transportation.'"

Patterson eyed Seigenthaler. The other men in the room kept silent. The governor and the president's emissary remained standing.

"I'm going to tell you something," Patterson said, according to Seigenthaler. "The people of this country are so goddamned tired of the mamby-pamby that's in Washington, it's a disgrace. There's nobody in the whole country that's got the spine to stand up to the goddamned niggers except me. And I'll tell you I've got more mail in the drawers of that desk over there congratulating me on the stand that I've taken against Martin Luther King and these rabble-rousers. I'll tell you I believe I'm more popular in this country today than John Kennedy is. I want you to know if the schools in Alabama are integrated, blood's going to flow in the streets and you take that message back to the president and you tell the attorney general that."

Patterson had one more point to make—that if the Kennedys sent in federal marshals, there would be "warfare." Seigenthaler did not flinch; he stuck to his one and only point. "What I'm authorized to say is if you're not going to protect them, the federal government will reluctantly but nonetheless positively move in whatever force is necessary to get these people through. They've got to be given protection and so do other interstate passengers."

Patterson scanned the faces of his cabinet. Seigenthaler remembers him saying next, "Well, let me give you my statement. The state of Alabama is willing and ready and able to protect all people—visitors, tourists, and others on the highways and elsewhere—while they're in the state of Alabama. I'm making that statement to you and Floyd Mann, who is head of the state highway patrol and is sitting on your right."

Alabama governor John Patterson (at head of table) meets with advisers.

Mann pulled Seigenthaler to one side and assured him that the state police would guard the bus from the time it left the city limits of Birmingham until it reached the outer limits of Montgomery, where that city's police would take over.

Seigenthaler was satisfied. Using the governor's telephone, he called Robert Kennedy and told him of Alabama's pledge to protect the Freedom Riders. Kennedy asked whether Seigenthaler believed that Patterson would honor the agreement, and the president's aide said yes. But Kennedy wanted further assurance. Would the governor issue a press release making his promise public? Patterson said that Kennedy could ask the Justice Department to issue a statement. "I'll have my own statement," the governor added, according to Seigenthaler, "but it won't run against what I've already said."

Patterson issued a statement promising protection to any traveler in Alabama. But he added an unexpected final line. It read, "We don't tolerate rabble-rousers and outside agitators."

Robert Kennedy renewed his pressure on the Greyhound Bus Lines. He told George E. Cruit, superintendent of Greyhound's Birmingham terminal, that the federal government's considerable efforts to enable the Freedom Riders to journey from Birmingham to Montgomery would be rendered meaningless if there was no one to drive the bus. "I think you had better get in touch with Mr. Greyhound, or whoever Greyhound is, and somebody better give us an answer to this question," Kennedy said.

On Saturday, May 20, a week after the original buses were bombed and attacked, the new group of riders left Birmingham for Montgomery. The twenty-one Freedom Riders and Alabama officials agreed that the bus would run its normal route, making all stops on its way south to Montgomery. Two Greyhound officials would accompany the riders on the bus. As John Lewis recalls, state police promised "that a private plane would fly over the bus, and there would be a state patrol car every fifteen or twenty miles along the highway between Birmingham and Montgomery—about ninety miles."

All seemed calm as the bus left Birmingham. The Freedom Riders relaxed somewhat—several even napped. But when they reached the city limits of Montgomery, the planes flew away. The patrol cars disappeared as the bus pulled into the quiet Montgomery bus terminal.

"And then, all of a sudden, just like magic, white people everywhere," remembers Freedom Rider Frederick Leonard. "Sticks and bricks. [Cries of] 'Niggers. Kill the niggers.' We were still on the bus. But I think we were deciding—well, maybe we should go off at the back of this bus. Then maybe they wouldn't be

"I think you had better

get in touch with Mr.

Greyhound."

so bad on us. They wanted us to go off the back of the bus. And we decided—no, no—we'll go off the front and take what's coming to us.

"Jim Zwerg was a white fellow from Madison, Wisconsin," Leonard continues. "He had a lot of nerve. And I think what saved me, Bernard Lafayette and Allen Kasen [was that] Jim Zwerg walked off the bus in front of us, and it was like they were possessed—they couldn't believe there was a white man who would help us. And they grabbed him and pulled him into the mob. I mean, it *was* a mob. When we came off the bus, their attention was on him. It was like they didn't see the rest of us, for maybe thirty seconds, they didn't see us at all."

Leonard and two other Freedom Riders fled but were trapped when they reached a railing overlooking a parking lot about fifteen feet below. The three men, one still clinging to a typewriter, had no choice but to jump. They ran from the parking lot and through the back door of a post office. Leonard remembers, "The people in there were carrying on business just like nothing was happening outside. But when we came through there, mail went flying everywhere."

James Peck, one of the Freedom Riders who were attacked in Birmingham, Alabama.

Presidential aide John Seigenthaler, driving a rental car ahead of the bus, had dropped behind after he stopped to buy gas and coffee. Minutes after the bus pulled into the terminal, he drove in front of Montgomery's federal office building, next to the bus station. He heard screams, and when he looked over saw baggage being hurled into the air. Seigenthaler charged his car through an alley and into the middle of the mob.

"The Freedom Riders emerging from the bus were being mauled," he remembers. "It looked like two hundred, three hundred people all over them. There were screams and shouts. As I drove along I saw two young women . . . being pummelled by a woman who was walking behind one of these young women. She had a purse on a strap and was beating [the young woman] over the head and a young, skinny blond teenager in a T-shirt was sort of dancing backwards in front of her [the Freedom Rider], punching her in the face. I bumped the car onto the sidewalk, blew the horn, jumped out of the car, grabbed the one who was being hit, took her back to the car. The other Freedom Rider got into the back seat."

Seigenthaler tried to usher the first young woman into his car, but she resisted, saying, "Mister, this is not your fight. I'm nonviolent. Don't get hurt because of me."

"If she had gotten into the car," says Seigenthaler, "I think I could have gotten away. But that moment of hesitation gave the mob a chance to collect their wits, and one [person] grabbed me by the arm, wheeled me around and said, 'What the hell are you doing?' I said, 'Get back! I'm a federal man.' I turned back to the Freedom Rider, and the lights went out. I [had been] hit with a pipe over one ear. I literally don't remember anything that happened [next]."

Floyd Mann, head of the Alabama State Police, was also in the bus station that morning. He ordered the mob to stop, but they continued to batter the Freedom Riders with fists, baseball bats, and pipes. Mann finally pulled out his gun as one of the activists took a beating right in front of him.

"I just put my pistol to the head of one or two of those folks that was using baseball bats and told them unless they stopped immediately they was going to be hurt," Mann said. "And it did stop the beaters."

Freedom Riders John Lewis (left) and Freddie Leonard.

Mann fired a warning shot into the air, scattering some of the ruffians. He ordered state troopers to the scene, but by the time they arrived, Jim Zwerg and Seigenthaler had been knocked unconscious and the mob had set several cars aflame. Mann telephoned the governor, who declared martial law in Montgomery.

The next day Jim Zwerg spoke to a television reporter from his hospital bed. Zwerg said that "segregation must be stopped. It must be broken down. Those of us who are on the Freedom Rides will continue. I'm not sure if I'll be able to, but we are going on to New Orleans no matter what happens. We are dedicated to this. We will take hitting. We'll take beatings. We're willing to accept death. But we are going to keep coming until we can ride [from] anywhere in the South to anyplace else in the South, as Americans, without anyone making any comment."

News of the vicious attack quickly reached Washington. Robert Kennedy realized that Governor Patterson had broken his promise. Not only had the Freedom Riders been savagely beaten, but the president's representative had been knocked unconscious and left lying in the street for nearly half an hour. Kennedy now believed he was justified in sending federal marshals to Alabama, even though it would mean a showdown between the state of Alabama and the federal government.

Seigenthaler recalls that when Robert Kennedy called him in the hospital, Kennedy jokingly asked, "How's my popularity down there?" Seigenthaler replied, "If you're planning on running for public office, don't do it in Alabama."

Kennedy sent 600 federal marshals to Maxwell Air Force Base outside Montgomery, prompting Governor Patterson to say, "We regret such federal interference. It is unwarranted, unneeded . . . I think the federal position has been one which has encouraged these outside agitators to come into our state and this encouragement has helped to create this problem we have here. Now the

John Lewis and Jim
Zwerg, after being
assaulted with other
Freedom Riders in
Montgomery, Alabama.

Attorney General Robert
Kennedy speaks with
John Seigenthaler, a
Justice Department
official beaten by the
mob when the Freedom
Riders arrived in
Montgomery.

federal government comes in here and illegally interferes in a domestic situation they themselves helped to create."

About 200 of the officers were sent into the city to protect the hospital and the Freedom Riders. As the crisis intensified, Martin Luther King, Jr., flew to Montgomery. The next evening, King addressed a rally in support of the Freedom Riders. Protected by a ring of federal marshals, the mass meeting was held at Ralph Abernathy's First Baptist Church as night fell.

With the darkness came a mob of several thousand whites, who surrounded the church. They threatened and cursed the blacks inside, who became more frightened by the minute.

"Now we've got an ugly mob outside," King told the crowd overflowing the church pews. "They have injured some of the federal marshals. They've burned some automobiles. But we are not giving in, . . . and maybe it takes something like this for the federal government to see that Alabama is not going to place any limit on itself—it must be imposed from without."

Since the bus boycott, racial tension had intensified in Montgomery. The city had recently closed all its public parks and its zoo rather than allow blacks to visit them. The pent-up hatred toward the civil rights activists was now welling up. Around 3:00 A.M., still trapped inside the church, King telephoned Robert Kennedy. The civil rights leader angrily asked the attorney general if there was law and order in the United States.

Kennedy later related that he replied "that our people were down there, and that as long as he was in the church he might say a prayer for us. [King] didn't think that was very humorous. He rather berated me for what was happening to him at the time. I said that I didn't think that he'd be alive if it hadn't been for us, that we were going to keep him alive and that the marshals would keep the church from burning down."

Kennedy then called Governor Patterson. Patterson lashed out at him for sending the marshals to Montgomery in the first place, and for ordering them to encircle the First Baptist Church that night without first consulting the governor. "Patterson was making a political oration against Negroes and the federal government and the Supreme Court and the system of federal law and the Civil War and everything," says Burke Marshall, who listened as Kennedy spoke with Patterson.

Kennedy let the governor vent his fury, but then broke in, saying, "You're making political speeches at me, John. You don't have to make political speeches at me over the telephone."

Outside the church, the federal marshals clashed with the angry crowd. The mob threw bottles, and the marshals threw tear gas, which drifted into the church, choking the people inside.

"The first thing we must do here tonight," King said above the sounds of rioting in the streets outside, "is to decide we are not going to become panicky. That we are going to be calm, and that we are going to continue to stand up for what we know is right . . . Alabama will have to face the fact that we are determined to be free. The main thing I want to say to you is fear not, we've come too far to turn back . . . We are not afraid and we shall overcome."

The Reverend Fred Shuttlesworth, an adviser of the Freedom Riders, took to the pulpit in an attempt to calm the crowd, still coughing as tear gas drifted in. "It is a sin and a shame before God," he said, "that these people who govern us would let things come to such a sad state. But God is not dead. The most guilty man in this state tonight is Governor John Patterson."

After his talk with Kennedy, Patterson declared martial law in the state, ordering the state police and the Alabama National Guard to disperse the crowd. The state troopers escorted King and the other people out of the church.

Robert Kennedy now called for a cooling-off period, a chance to ease the tension that threatened to erupt anew at anytime. Later, reflecting on his talks with his brother during the crisis, he said, "I think the president was fed up with John Patterson . . . he was [also] fed up with the Freedom Riders who went down there after [the initial bombing], when it didn't do any good to go down there."

As the administration had feared, their intervention had wrought political damage in the South. "If this were a labor dispute, the President would be silent and his little brother wouldn't be sitting at that big desk barking orders over the phone and looking like Mickey Rooney just in from a touch football game," wrote the *Montgomery Advertiser*.

The Freedom Riders were determined to continue their journey. On May 24, two days after the church siege, twenty-seven Freedom Riders left Montgomery in two buses. Martin Luther King, Jr., still on probation after his arrest during the Atlanta sit-ins, decided not to join the rides. Several of the riders resented his decision not to share the danger as well as the publicity their ride had drawn.

But the immediate concern was the fate of the riders. "We got to the border between Alabama and Mississippi and saw that famous sign, 'Welcome to the Magnolia State,' and our hearts jumped into our mouths," remembers CORE's James Farmer. "There were Mississippi National Guard flanking the highways with their guns pointed toward the forest on both sides of the road . . . [when]

we got to the suburbs of Jackson, one of the Freedom Riders broke into song
. . . the words went something like this:

> I'm taking a ride on the Greyhound bus line.
> I'm riding the front seat to Jackson this time.
> Hallelujah, I'm traveling;
> Hallelujah, ain't it fine?
> Hallelujah, I'm traveling
> Down Freedom's main line."

When the Freedom Riders arrived in Jackson, no mob greeted them at the terminal.
As they got off the buses and entered the whites-only waiting room, they were
accompanied only by the police. Recalls rider Frederick Leonard, "As we walked
through, the police just said, 'Keep moving' and let us go through the white side.
We never got stopped. They just said, 'Keep moving,' and they passed us right
on through the white terminal into the paddy wagon and into jail. There was no
violence in Mississippi."

Robert Kennedy had made a deal with Mississippi's United States senator
James O. Eastland, a rabid segregationist. Kennedy had pledged not to use federal
force to carry out United States civil rights laws guaranteeing integrated bus
terminal facilities to interstate bus riders. Eastland had promised that there would
be no mob violence. Kennedy, like his brother the president, wanted an end to
the headlines and television pictures of mob violence.

Once they were arrested for violating state laws and placed in local jails, the
Freedom Riders were beyond Robert Kennedy's reach. The Mississippi courts
would have their way with the much-loathed Freedom Riders.

On May 25, the day after they were arrested, the Freedom Riders were tried.
"The prosecution got up, accused us of trespassing, took his seat," remembers
Frederick Leonard. "Our attorney, Jack Young, got up to defend us as human
beings. While he was defending us the judge turned his back [and] looked at the
wall. When [Young] finished, the judge turned around. *Bam*—sixty days in the
state penitentiary, and there we were, on the road to Parchman [State Penitentiary],
maximum security."

But as that group was sent to jail, more Freedom Riders arrived in Jackson,
where they were arrested for trying to integrate the bus terminal. Others followed.
Throughout the summer, more than 300 Freedom Riders traveled through the
Deep South in an effort to integrate according to the Supreme Court ruling. Robert

Kennedy petitioned the Interstate Commerce Commission to give greater focus to the Court's mandate against segregation in interstate bus terminals, asking for specific regulations governing all such facilities. But this ruling did not take shape until September; for now, it was jail for the Freedom Riders.

As news of the jailings spread across the nation, Robert Kennedy became frustrated. He wanted to placate blacks, but he also wanted to please the Democratic party's southern wing. Kennedy decided to try to redirect the movement and deflect it from getting involved in violent confrontations requiring the administration's intervention. He began to stress the need for more black voter registration. The power of the ballot box, he reasoned, would force southern politicians to be more responsive to black needs in housing, education, and public accommodations.

"If they register[ed] and participated in elections, even half of them or a third of them . . . " he said later. "If you get it [black voter registration] up over fifteen percent of the whole voter population, they [blacks] could have major impact.

"During the Freedom Rides," he added, "I had a number of meetings with these various civil rights groups, and I said that it [voter registration] wasn't going to be as dramatic. There wasn't going to be as much publicity about it, but I thought that's where they should go and that's what they should do. I had some conversations with Martin Luther King along those lines. I think [King and the other civil rights leaders] rather resented it."

The leaders of SNCC, the student organization, thought that the Kennedys were simply trying to undercut the mounting civil rights movement. The NAACP worried that its own voter-registration efforts would now become secondary, that their leadership role in that area would be forgotten.

The Kennedys urged large philanthropic foundations to contribute to what would become the Voter Education Project, headquartered in Atlanta. With the influx of money, civil rights leaders came to agree that swelling the ranks of black voters could only help to ensure that blacks would win their civil rights in America. The press responded positively to the idea of more blacks registering to vote. Such a quest for enfranchisement was in the American tradition, editorials said. There was widespread relief that the violence was over.

For several years after the Freedom Rides, civil rights workers in the deepest South, from Louisiana bayous to the Florida Keys, would be asked by local blacks, "Are you one of them Freedom Riders?" The answer might be, "No, ma'am, we're working for voter registration," or "No, sir, we're doing legal research for the NAACP," or "No, son, we're here to teach folks how to read."

But if the workers were seen as part of the civil rights movement, the people called them Freedom Riders. The courage and tenacity of those pioneers had captured the imagination and awe of blacks throughout the Southland.

A black protester arrested in Birmingham.

Chapter Six

Freedom in the Air

The Lessons of Albany and Birmingham

"Charlie Jones looked at me and said, 'Bernice, sing a song.' And I started 'Over My Head I See Trouble in the Air.' By the time it got to where 'trouble' was supposed to be, I didn't see any trouble, so I put 'freedom' in there. That was the first time I had the awareness that these songs were mine and I could use them for what I needed."

Bernice Johnson Reagon
of the Freedom Singers

In the spring of 1961, there was little to indicate that the small southwest-Georgia city of Albany would become the setting for one of the next major acts in the civil rights drama. It was not a busy urban center, but a farming capital of 56,000 people, forty percent of them black. Peanuts, pecans, and corn had replaced the once-ubiquitous cotton on the farms surrounding the city.

The black neighborhoods, with their unpaved streets, were home to people who enjoyed some opportunities that their counterparts throughout the South did not. The farms offered plenty of work, as did the nightclubs and resorts that attracted swells from Atlanta and as far away as Tallahassee, Florida's capital. Blacks in Albany owned liquor stores, billiard parlors, taxi companies, and beauty shops, and their grown children attended Albany State College.

But Albany was no different from any other southern town in its entrenched segregationist practices. Despite the *Brown* decision, white schools did not admit black students. And despite the great number of blacks in Albany, few had been allowed to register to vote.

At all-black Albany State, students were beginning to resist this institutionalized bigotry. Many, such as Bernice Johnson, were members of the NAACP's Youth Council, and earlier that year they had staged a rally to protest the harassment of women students—white men sometimes sneaked into the dormitories or threw eggs at students on campus.

After the rally, members of the student government were suspended. This made the black college students more eager than ever to get involved with the civil rights movement. They had all heard about the sit-ins and the Freedom Rides. "We didn't belong to Albany, Georgia, as a people," recalls Bernice Johnson. "We belonged to black people. Nationally, black people were doing something, and we would say, 'When is it going to happen [here]?'"

In the summer of 1961, field representatives of the recently formed Student Nonviolent Coordinating Committee (SNCC) had arrived in Albany to help organize against segregation. Albany was one of their first attempts at mobilizing an entire community. But they had already encountered a fearful reception from rural blacks in surrounding counties, and had made little progress. Few blacks were willing to risk white reprisals by trying to register to vote, even if accompanied by a SNCC organizer.

SNCC differed from the more established Southern Christian Leadership Conference (SCLC) in its approach to organizing a black community. Whereas the SCLC generally worked with such leaders as ministers, attorneys, teachers, and other black professionals, the student-run SNCC was a grassroots organization.

SNCC representatives talked with high school and college kids, visited churches, and met with the young and the old. They looked for natural leaders, not necessarily those with credentials, and tried to help people build a solidarity that would last long after SNCC had left town.

On November 1, 1961, a ruling by the Interstate Commerce Commission went into effect that backed up the Supreme Court's 1960 decision prohibiting segregation in interstate bus and train stations. Twenty-two-year-old Charles Sherrod and his fellow SNCC worker Cordell Reagon decided to "test" the ruling at Albany's Trailways bus terminal. Along with a group of black students, they sat down in the whites-only waiting room and refused to leave. Within minutes the Albany police arrived, ordering them out. The students left without resistance, but they had made their point to local blacks: no one with dark skin yet had equal access to those facilities.

"We ran into all kinds of obstacles," Cordell Reagon recalls. "The NAACP was saying we were taking their members and other people were saying we were Communists . . . even Negroes were saying this."

Bernice Johnson didn't care that the two young men were from SNCC; she cared only that "they were for freedom." Johnson remembers that in early November she went to the NAACP district meeting in Atlanta as the secretary of the Albany NAACP Youth Council. At the meeting, she was warned that SNCC workers "'come in and get you stirred up and leave you in jail and the NAACP has to pay the bills.' I was real upset. I didn't know what was happening . . . The NAACP might have been a different group but it should have had the same [goals] from where I stood. I said, 'We're working for the same things, aren't we?' What an answer I got. The regional NAACP came down to a meeting of our chapter—Vernon Jordan, Ruby Hurley . . . and blasted SNCC. These people thought it was important enough to stop SNCC that they came down to Albany to tell us how SNCC would lead us wrong."

Charles Sherrod fanned the flames when he called a meeting of the NAACP Youth Council without the knowledge of Thomas Chatmon, the organization's adviser, and E. D. Hamilton, the Albany branch president. Hamilton had flatly told the SNCC students to get out of town. At the meeting, Sherrod denounced whites for keeping the bus terminal segregated in defiance of federal law, and told the youths that they needed new leadership.

The squabbling among the civil rights groups threatened to tear them apart. But on November 17 several local adult groups formed the Albany Movement, an umbrella organization that would attempt to coordinate the activists. The

Dr. William Anderson, an osteopath, was elected president of the Albany Movement in November, 1961.

In the early 1960s, Charles Sherrod (far right) and Cordell Reagon (not pictured here) traveled the countryside around Albany, Georgia, encouraging black residents to register to vote.

Albany Movement included the Ministerial Alliance, the Negro Voters League, and the Criterion Club, a group of black professionals. The movement's leader, chosen because he did almost no business with whites and was therefore less subject to economic reprisal, was Dr. William Anderson, an osteopath and drugstore owner. Slater King was elected vice president.

Despite the new partnership, the Albany NAACP planned to recapture the initiative from SNCC. They hoped to have one of their members arrested in the illegally segregated bus terminal. The NAACP could then bail that person out and go to court asking that the federal government's desegregation ruling be enforced.

But Sherrod, Reagon, and Charles Jones, another SNCC worker, had other ideas. On November 22, both NAACP and SNCC people sat in at the Albany bus terminal and were arrested. The NAACP bailed out its representatives, but the SNCC protesters, two students from Albany State, chose to remain in jail. Although the arrests violated federal law, Albany Police Chief Laurie Pritchett declared that the protesters "were not arrested on a federal charge, they were arrested on a city ordinance of failing to obey the orders of a law enforcement officer . . . It had nothing to do with interstate commerce."

The arrest of the protesters galvanized Albany's blacks. Their shared indignation at the arrogance of the city's white officials mended the rift between SNCC and the NAACP, at least for the moment.

Three days later, the Albany Movement held its first mass meeting, in a church. The people sang "We Shall Overcome" and listened to speeches by the students who had been arrested in the bus station. On November 27 the five students went on trial, and movement members held a mass rally. Blacks kneeled on the sidewalk to pray for the students' release. Four hundred people signed a petition asking that the students, expelled from Albany State for their arrests, be allowed to return to school.

On December 10, ten Freedom Riders, five white and five black, rode into Albany on an integrated train from Atlanta. At Albany's Central Railway Terminal, the blacks walked into the white section and the whites entered the black section. Eight of them were arrested for trespassing.

The arrests brought the national press to town. At a crowded church rally the day after the incident, James Forman, one of the SNCC Freedom Riders, called for more protest marches. The next day 267 students from Albany's black high school and from Albany State marched on the train station. They were arrested after they disregarded police orders to end the march. Most of them, true to the SNCC philosophy, refused to be bailed out of jail.

On Wednesday, December 13, Slater King, who had been elected vice president of the newly formed Albany Movement, led 200 protesters to city hall. At the courthouse steps they stopped to pray for the students' release. As SNCC had hoped, people were drawing on their own strengths, notably their passionate religious commitment, to rally under the civil rights banner. By the end of the march, Slater King and his 200 marchers were on their way to jail. Police Chief Laurie Pritchett arrested them for parading without a permit. "We can't tolerate the NAACP or the SNCC or any other nigger organization [taking] over this town with mass demonstrations," Pritchett said in a news conference.

By mid-December, Chief Pritchett and his officers had arrested more than 500 demonstrators. Albany's mayor, Asa Kelley, agreed to negotiate the possible integration of the bus and train stations as well as conditions for the release of the protesters now packing city jails.

The Albany Movement had not anticipated so many arrests, especially of homemakers, cooks, maids, and laborers. Recognizing the need for outside help, movement president William Anderson decided to call an old college classmate in Atlanta—Martin Luther King, Jr. He asked the minister to come to Albany to speak at a movement rally.

That Friday night the Shiloh Baptist Church overflowed with people who had come to hear Rev. King. Loudspeakers were set up outside for those who couldn't get in. "I woke up this morning with my mind stayed on freedom," they sang. "Martin Luther King says freedom—Let the white man say freedom."

"I can say nothing to you but to continue on in your determination to be free," King told them. He urged the audience not to be swayed by those who claimed that time, not activism, would bring integration. "Maybe you can't legislate morality," he said, "but you can regulate behavior." King entreated the crowd to embrace nonviolence: "They can put you in a dungeon and transform you to glory. If they try to kill you, develop a willingness to die . . . We will win with the power of your capacity to endure."

King had driven in from Atlanta with Ralph Abernathy and Wyatt T. Walker, executive director of the SCLC. The three men expected to make only one appearance, at the rally. But Anderson, in an emotional benediction after King's speech, announced a mass march on city hall the next day and then, before the tearful audience, asked King to lead it. King agreed.

The next afternoon, King and about 250 demonstrators were arrested at city hall. Ralph Abernathy and Dr. Anderson were among them. Chief of police Laurie Pritchett, sensing that any harm done to King would only fuel the anger of Albany's blacks, posted several officers and a detective with a submachine gun to guard the minister. Rather than being sent straight to jail, King, Abernathy, and Anderson were held in Pritchett's office until that night to ensure their safety. Pritchett's cautious handling of King that day was only the first of many countertactics the police chief would employ.

"I did research," the chief said later. "I found his method was nonviolence . . . to fill the jails, same as Gandhi in India. And once they filled the jails, we'd have no capacity to arrest and then we'd have to give in to his demands. I sat down and took a map. How many jails was in a fifteen-mile radius, how many was in a thirty-mile radius? And I contacted those authorities. They assured us that we could use their [jails]."

King, Abernathy, and Dr. W. C. Anderson being arrested by Police Chief Laurie Pritchett.

King vowed to stay in jail until the city agreed to desegregate. As the demonstrations continued, the Albany Movement watched Pritchett with the grudging admiration of a chicken farmer for a sly fox. The word for him, said the SCLC's Wyatt Walker, was "slick." Recalls Walker, "He did have enough intelligence to read Dr. King's book [on the Montgomery bus boycott] and he culled from that a way to avoid confrontation . . . by being nonbrutal [in handling the protest]."

After refusing bond, King told reporters he wanted thousands to come to Albany and join him in jail. Meanwhile, Wyatt Walker pledged to devote the SCLC's money and people to the cause. His offer rankled local black leaders. Marion Page, a retired postal worker and secretary of the Albany Movement, announced that "as of now we need no help."

Black journalist Louis Lomax quoted blacks in Albany as saying, "Dr. Walker can't come to Albany and take over," and "We can bake our own cake—all we need from the Atlanta boys is more flour and sugar." The internecine conflicts among black activists surfaced again. SNCC workers were angry that Walker and King, whom they derisively called "De Lawd" for what they considered his "royal" treatment by the press, would try to take over the movement they had been developing for many weeks. Lomax quoted one student as saying, "Why didn't Walker stay the hell in Atlanta, send us more money, let us have Martin to speak and walk with the marchers! If he had done that, we could have won. No. He had to come running into town . . . he's just found a new world to conquer."

Walker, however, saw himself and the SCLC staff as "firefighters" who had come to the rescue of the inexperienced Albany activists. "I'll try to say this as charitably as I can," he said. "SNCC was in over its head. They wanted the international and national attention that Martin Luther King's presence would generate. But they did not want the input of his organization."

Whites in Albany heard about the divisions among the black leadership. The *Albany Herald*'s segregationist publisher James Gray ran an editorial saying that blacks and whites in Albany would have solved their problems if King had "not come in from the outside."

Police Chief Pritchett held a press conference to announce that "outside agitation by people with criminal records is largely responsible for the trouble here." He stressed that the Freedom Riders arrested in the terminal for violating the segregation laws had police records. He failed to mention that the arrests were for other nonviolent protests.

Although King had spoken of the "strange illusion [among whites] that [local] Negroes don't want to be free," he was now in jail and could not counter this latest offensive from segregationist leaders. In his absence, the movement failed to develop further strategy. Dr. Anderson, the Albany Movement's leader, had never before been directly involved in civil rights activism.

Playing to local blacks' desire to retain control of the movement, city officials offered a deal to Marion Page, the Albany Movement's secretary, that would provide for the demonstrators' release and for desegregation of the bus and train terminals. The authorities also said the local leaders could bring any further demands before a meeting of the city commissioners. In return, the Albany Movement had to promise to end its demonstrations. On December 18, Page, Anderson, and other Albany leaders agreed orally to the deal, and King, along with other protesters, was released from jail on property bonds offered by local residents. King, who had not been party to the negotiations, said he was leaving jail because he did "not want to stand in the way of peaceful negotiations." The civil rights leader then left Albany. But a few weeks later, as the city failed to integrate the terminals or meet with the blacks, King told reporters, "I'm sorry I was bailed out. I didn't understand at the time what was happening. We thought that the victory had been won. When we got out we discovered it was all a hoax."

Police Chief Pritchett was jubilant. "We met nonviolence with nonviolence and we are indeed proud of the outcome," he said. Newspapers around the country jumped on the story. New York's *Herald Tribune* called Albany "one of the most stunning defeats of King's career." King told reporters that, in the future, he would demand written agreements.

Despite this setback, the Albany activists were relentless as the new year began. On January 12, 1962, eighteen-year-old Ola Mae Quarterman sat down in the front section of an Albany bus. The white driver asked her if she knew that blacks were supposed to sit in the rear. "I paid my damn twenty cents and I can sit where I want to," she retorted. Quarterman was arrested and found guilty of using "vulgar language." The police and the prosecution carefully avoided any mention of the issue of segregated seating on Albany's buses. SNCC workers launched a bus boycott in support of Quarterman, and in three weeks the Montgomery-style strike had closed down the bus system. SNCC also sent students to the whites-only Carnegie Library, where they applied for library cards. The police escorted them out. Charles Sherrod was arrested for sitting in the white section of the Trailways bus terminal lunchroom. He was charged only with loitering; again the issue of segregation was not broached in court. "We don't allow people to go in there and just make it their home," said Chief Pritchett.

In February, Martin Luther King, Jr., returned to Albany to stand trial for his December arrest. He was found guilty of marching without a permit, but the judge, requesting a transcript of the trial, delayed sentencing until July.

Meanwhile, at the trial of the ten Freedom Riders who had come to Albany in December, SNCC's Sherrod tried to take a seat in the front of the courtroom. Before he could do so, a court guard knocked him down and dragged him to the back of the room—where blacks were supposed to sit. When white SNCC activists Bob Zellner, Tom and Casey Hayden, and Per Laursen accompanied Sherrod to the black section, guards dragged them all out of the courtroom. The judge, looking on, simply commented, "The officers are enforcing the rules of the court."

At the sentencing of King and Abernathy in July, the men were ordered to pay $78 in fines or serve forty-five days in jail. Both leaders chose jail. The national press returned; King told reporters he would be sent to a work gang. President Kennedy, alarmed by the news, asked the Justice Department for a report on Albany. Burke Marshall, the assistant attorney general for civil rights, began talks with Pritchett and other Albany officials. He also spoke with Coretta Scott King, telling her the federal government was seeking her husband's release. SCLC staffers rushed back to Albany, and a mass rally was scheduled for the next night.

But just three days after the sentencing, King and Abernathy were released under peculiar circumstances. At the time, Chief Pritchett claimed that an unidentified black man had paid their fines. Pritchett has since admitted that he arranged for the payment to be made, but to this day, he refuses to divulge the full story.

"I know what happened," Pritchett said, "but frankly, you know, it was a matter of strategy. I knew that if he [King] stayed in jail, we'd continue to have problems. So, I talked to some people. I said, 'We've got to get him out and once we do I think he'll leave here . . . ' Yes, it was done at my request. And it sort of surprised Dr. King. This was the only time I've ever seen when [it] seemed he didn't know which way to go."

King called the move a "cunning tactic." At a rally that night, Abernathy said, "I've been thrown out of a lot of places in my day but I've never been thrown out of jail." He added, "I fought in France and in Germany for America. Now I wanted to fight on the streets of Albany for America. But, mysteriously, somebody paid the fine with hopes that they would get us out of jail. The chief broke my heart when he said that [we were going to leave town]. Of course, we are going to stay in Albany."

Local officials still refused to negotiate with black leaders. State and national politicians began to enter the arena. One of them, avid segregationist Marvin Griffin, promised during a campaign speech to put "Martin Luther King so far back in the jail you will have to pump air to him."

President Kennedy, in a nationally televised news conference, said, "I find it wholly inexplicable why the city of Albany will not sit down with the citizens of Albany, who may be Negroes, and attempt to secure for them, in a peaceful way, their rights. The U.S. government is involved in sitting down at Geneva with the Soviet Union. I can't understand why the . . . city council of Albany . . . can't do the same for American citizens."

Albany mayor Asa Kelley, who until now had favored offering concessions to blacks, said Kennedy had spoken "inappropriately" and could spark trouble by siding with the blacks. Kelley now refused to negotiate. Georgia senator Richard Russell declared, "The stamp of approval upon the constant violation of city laws from the highest source in our land is certain to encourage the importation of many other professionals and notoriety seekers and worsen an already bad situation."

The NAACP's chief Washington lobbyist, Clarence Mitchell, met with Attorney General Robert Kennedy and proposed that the government begin backing up the president's words by withdrawing federal assistance from the Albany area, particularly from Turner Air Force Base. A group of 100 ministers asked that the president address the civil rights crisis on national television—that he issue a modern version of the Emancipation Proclamation, the document that freed the slaves in 1863.

As the situation in Albany became a national issue, King decided to take a more militant stance. After leaving jail he went to Atlanta, vowing to return in a week to lead "protests that will turn Albany upside down."

But before King could act, Federal District Judge J. Robert Elliott, a Kennedy appointee, issued a temporary restraining order to stop the demonstrations that had disrupted the city for eight months. King and other protest leaders were specifically ordered not to march. King, now back in Albany, said he would abide by the court order even though it took away the Albany Movement's strongest weapon—public protest. "The federal courts have given us our greatest victories, and I cannot in good conscience declare war on them," said King, talking to reporters in the yard of William Anderson's home. But the minister added, "We regret to say that recent events have revealed to us that there are some federal judges in the South who are engaged in a conspiracy with state and political leaders to maintain the evil system of segregation."

"It is a fact," said Burke Marshall, assistant attorney general for civil rights, "that the federal judge in that district [Elliott] . . . turned out to be a terrible judge. He was a terrible mistake." John F. Kennedy was a pragmatic politician. Seeking to maintain southern ties, he made a point of listening to southern senators when making judicial appointments. Several such appointments on Kennedy's part generated controversy among civil rights workers.

Rev. Sam Wells, a long-time Albany activist, went to Shiloh Baptist Church the night after the court handed down its order and said he would march anyway. Wells waved the court document in the air, SNCC's Sherrod recalls, and said, "I see Dr. King's name. And I see Dr. Anderson's name. And I see Charles Sherrod . . . But I don't see Samuel Wells and I don't see Miss Sue Samples and I don't see Mrs. Rufus Grant. Now where are those names?" "And with that," Sherrod says, "he marched about [160] folks out of the church that night and went to jail."

Two days later, Mrs. Slater King, wife of the Albany Movement's vice president, took some food to arrested friends in the Camilla jail. The guards there ordered her away. "All you niggers away from the fence," barked one officer. Mrs. King, who was pregnant, was carrying one child in her arms and had two more walking along beside her. She did not move quickly enough for the guards, and a sheriff's deputy cursed at her. She told him to arrest her if he wanted to. The man knocked her down and kicked her until she lost consciousness. Mrs. King soon miscarried.

"I've been thrown out of a lot of places in my day but I've never been thrown out of jail."

On July 24, four days after Judge Elliott issued the restraining order barring all demonstrations, Appeals Court Judge Elbert P. Tuttle, an Eisenhower appointee, set aside the order. The next day the black community, enraged at Mrs. King's beating, marched through the streets two-thousand strong. For the first time, protesters in Albany clashed violently with police. The demonstrators, many of them teenagers, threw bricks, rocks, and bottles at the police, who backed off without fighting back. Chief Pritchett, taking full advantage of the lapse by Martin Luther King's followers, asked reporters, "Did you see them nonviolent rocks?"

Pritchett's statement sparked a crisis among the demonstrators, who had always portrayed themselves as nonviolent warriors in the fight against segregation. King had been ready to exert still more pressure on the city commission, but he called it off, asking for a "Day of Penance" among blacks to atone for the violence. SNCC's Sherrod and other protesters, anxious to renew the Albany campaign, now criticized King. They maintained that nonviolence was a tactic, not the movement's goal—the goal was desegregation of public facilities. Halting the marches now could jeopardize the movement's progress. But King would not change his mind. With Sherrod and Abernathy he toured Albany's pool halls and bars, asking that there be no more violence. Two white detectives, sent by Pritchett for King's protection, came along. So did television crews.

Police Chief Laurie Pritchett arresting King in Albany on July 27, 1962.

"I hate to hold up your pool game," King said at one stop. "I used to be a pool shark myself." Then, over the clicking of pool balls, he said, "We are in the midst of a great movement . . . We have had our demonstrations saying we will no longer accept segregation. One thing about this movement is that it is nonviolent. As you know there was some violence last night. Nothing could hurt our movement more. It's exactly what our opposition likes to see . . . we don't need guns—just the power of souls."

Ralph Abernathy told the poolroom crowd that King's words were not an appeal to "stop resisting the evil system of segregation. Nonviolence is the way for the strong, not the weak . . . those little guns that Negroes have for family protection are nothing to the arsenal the police have. But we have soul force. As they call for state troopers, we call God to send his heavenly angels . . . "

Two days later, King led a prayer meeting in front of city hall. He wanted to meet with the city commissioners, who had refused to discuss the blacks' demands. King and Abernathy waited outside with ten other people. Around 2 P.M., Abernathy kneeled on the ground and began to pray. "Can't you see you're causing a disturbance?" asked Chief Pritchett. Abernathy ignored him, praying even louder as reporters crowded around. Pritchett yanked the minister to his feet and arrested him. By 4 P.M., however, another group of demonstrators was at city hall; eighteen students and SNCC workers knelt down to pray and they too were arrested.

One of the students, William Hansen, a white SNCC worker from Cincinnati, was placed in the whites-only section of the Dougherty Jail. A deputy sheriff told the other white prisoners, "This is one of those guys who came down here to straighten us out." A prisoner replied, "Well, I'll straighten *him* out." Hansen was beaten unconscious, his lip split open, his jaw broken.

Black lawyer C. B. King heard of the beating and went to the jail to check on Hansen. After waiting anxiously outside Sheriff Cull Campbell's office, King loudly insisted that every prisoner was entitled to medical treatment. Getting no response, he walked into the sheriff's office. Campbell stood and said, "Nigger, haven't I told you to wait out there?"

Rev. James C. Harris, who had accompanied King to the jail, recalls that the sheriff then "picked up a walking stick out of a basket . . . and hit Mr. King over the head, breaking the cane. Mr. King escaped the office, and I did as well." Later the *New York Times* reported that Sheriff Campbell admitted to the beating. "He didn't get out, so God-damn it, I put him out." Campbell told another newspaper reporter, "Yeah, I knocked the hell out of him, and I'll do it again. I let him know he's a damn nigger. I'm a white man, and he's a damn nigger."

Meanwhile, Chief Pritchett was seeking a permanent restraining order to stop further demonstrations. He told Judge Elliott that Martin Luther King's presence in Albany had "raised community tension to the kindling point." Mayor Kelley, in a press conference, said that he and the city commissioners were "anxious to discuss problems with local Negroes"—after King left town. He declared that he would "never negotiate with outside agitators whose avowed purpose was to create turmoil."

On August 4 the city commissioners boasted in a statement to reporters that "firm but fair law enforcement [had] broken the back of the Albany Movement." That movement had never been more than an invasion by a group of civil rights professionals, they added.

Martin Luther King, Jr., was freed on August 10 after two weeks in jail. He told reporters he would return to Atlanta to allow local blacks to negotiate with white officials. But even after he had left, city fathers refused to meet with the movement's local leaders. The segregationists claimed they wanted a "new and responsible voice for the colored citizens of Albany." On August 15, King returned to Albany, and local black leaders finally managed to meet with the mayor. They

Protesters in Albany not only sang and marched but also prayed. Typically, the police would arrest the protesters for being a "public nuisance."

Freedom Singing:

An Interview with Bernice Johnson Reagon

The protests in Albany, Georgia lasted from 1961 to 1965. One of the things that kept people fighting all that time was music. Albany was a deeply spiritual community and its music transformed not only the singer, but the movement as well. In 1962, SNCC established the Freedom Singers, a chorus that traveled throughout the country providing inspiration and raising funds for the civil rights movement. Bernice Johnson was one of the original Freedom Singers.

The Freedom Singers. From left to right: Charles Neblett, Bernice Johnson, Cordell Reagon, Rutha Mae Harris.

My father is a minister and I grew up in a church. We didn't get a piano in that church until I was eleven, so my early music was *a cappella* and my first instruments were hands and feet. To this day, that's the only way I can deal comfortably with creating music. But church was not the only place that music occurred because the same thing happened at school, on the playground. I went to a seven-grade, one-room school house. At noontime, my teacher would come outside and teach us games and songs.

I ended up being arrested in the second wave of arrests in Albany. And when we got to jail, Slater King, who was already in jail, said, "Bernice, is that you?" And I said yes. And he said, "Sing a song."

The singing tradition in Albany was congregational. There were no soloists; there were song leaders. If Slater said, "Bernice, sing a song," he wasn't asking for a solo, he was asking me to plant a seed. The minute you start the song, the song is created by everybody there. There is really almost a musical explosion.

The mass meetings always started with these freedom songs. Most of the meeting was singing. Songs were the bed of everything, and I'd never seen or felt songs do that [before]. I'd had songs in college and high school and church, but in the movement, all the words sounded different. "This Little Light of Mine, I'm Going to Let it Shine," which I'd sung all my life, said something very different. We varied the verses: "All in the street, I'm going to let it shine, All in the jailhouse, I'm going to let it shine."

The voice I have now I got the first time I sang in a movement meeting, after I got out of jail. I did the song, "Over My Head I See Freedom in the Air," but I had never heard that voice before. I had never been that me before. And once I became that me, I have never let that me go . . . a transformation took place inside of the people. The singing was just the echo of that.

They could not stop our sound. They would have to kill us to stop us from singing. Sometimes the police would plead and say, "Please stop singing." And you would just know that your word was being heard, and you felt joy. There is a way in which those songs kept us from being touched by people who would want us not to be who we were becoming. There was a woman at Shiloh Baptist Church who would sing one song, "Come and Go With Me To That Land," for an hour. It was not a song anymore. People are clapping, the feet are going and you could hear her three blocks away. Your ears are not enough, your eyes are not enough, your body is not enough, and you can't block it. The only way you survive the singing is to open up and let go and be moved by it to another space.

won no concessions, however, and King's only recourse was to hold a news conference and rail against the stubborn segregationists. A few days later, King left Albany.

That Labor Day weekend, seventy-five protesters from the North, including ministers, laymen, and rabbis, drove to Albany to show their support for the activists. There they followed in King's footsteps, stopping to pray on the steps of city hall. Chief Pritchett treated them no better than he had King, sending them to jail. "You have come to aid and abet the violators of this city and country," he said. "If you come as violators, you will be treated as such. Go back to your homes. Clear your own cities of sin and lawlessness."

The mass meetings in Albany continued for six more years. In that sense, SNCC could claim Albany as a victory. Albany also provided SNCC with valuable lessons on organizing a community, lessons they would use in Mississippi during the Freedom Summer.

For Bernice Johnson, who later married SNCC worker Cordell Reagon, the Albany Movement had meant personal growth. "I had grown up in a society where there were very clear lines," she says. "The civil rights movement gave me the power to challenge any line that limits me . . . [the] movement said that if something puts you down, you have to fight against it."

Dr. William Anderson, the Albany Movement's president, called it "an overwhelming success, in that there was a change in the attitude of the people involved. They had [decided] that they would never accept that segregated society as it was anymore. There was [also] a change in the attitude of the kids who saw their parents step into the forefront and lead the demonstrations. They were determined that they would never go through what their parents went through to get the recognition that they should have as citizens."

For many of Albany's citizens, the movement was a moral victory. But Albany's schools remained segregated. The city had closed its parks rather than integrate them. The library was integrated only after all the chairs were removed.

Even so, the SCLC learned many valuable lessons from Albany. The national press attention King's presence brought to the city did not resolve the confrontation. Garnering public support did not always mean that the federal government would step in to defend civil rights.

King's sense of his own leadership was wavering. He told reporters that the Albany Movement's purpose had been "so vague that we got nothing and the people were left depressed and in despair."

"The civil rights

movement gave me

the power to

challenge any line

that limits me."

"When Martin left Albany he was very depressed," recalls Andrew Young, an SCLC staff member at that time. "He knew what had happened . . . It was a federal judge that called off that movement. [King] had a very emotional exchange with Burke Marshall [of the Justice Department] over that, because he felt as though the Kennedy administration had helped to undercut the possibility of continuing in Albany."

King later told the press, "One of the greatest problems we face with the FBI in the South is that the agents are white southerners who have been influenced by the mores of their community. To maintain their status, they have to be friendly with the local police and people who are promoting segregation. Every time I saw FBI men in Albany, they were with the local police force." This statement enraged FBI director J. Edgar Hoover, who was already convinced that the civil rights movement was infiltrated by Communists. Later, it would be learned that Marion Page, the Albany Movement's secretary, had spoken with police chief Pritchett almost nightly and had been in regular contact with the FBI.

Black journalist Louis Lomax wrote of King, "[In] The next town he visits to inspire those who are ready to suffer for their rights, he will find people saying 'Remember Albany.'"

The Reverend Fred Shuttlesworth wanted that town to be Birmingham. "Dr. King's image at this time was slightly on the wane because he had not projected [a victory in Albany]," recalls Shuttlesworth. "I said, 'I assure you, if you come to Birmingham, this movement can not only gain prestige, it can really shake the country.'" As head of a Birmingham-based group called the Alabama Christian Movement for Human Rights, Shuttlesworth was the leader of black activists in that city. He convinced the SCLC to make Birmingham the target of its next offensive.

Birmingham was infamous for the Mother's Day, 1961, mob attack on the Freedom Riders, when police failed to intervene. Even local papers, usually supportive of Birmingham police commissioner Bull Connor, were outraged by that incident. One editorial asked, "Where were the police?" Trezzvant W. Anderson wrote in the *Pittsburgh Courier*, a national black weekly, that black leaders condemned Birmingham as the "worst big city in the U.S.A." Between 1957 and 1963, eighteen unsolved bombings in black neighborhoods earned the city its nickname of "Bombingham." Bull Connor sent his men to break up black political meetings, and since 1956 the NAACP had been kept out of Alabama. In 1962 the city closed sixty-eight parks, thirty-eight playgrounds, six swimming pools

Birmingham, Alabama. As King described it, "Birmingham is probably the most thoroughly segregated city in the United States."

The Reverend Fred Shuttlesworth, spiritual leader of Birmingham's black community.

and four golf courses to avoid complying with a federal court order to desegregate public facilities.

Rev. Shuttlesworth's home had been bombed to ruins in 1956. "Were there any arrests?" asked columnist Anderson in his article. "You can bet your life there were not . . . The Reverend Mr. Shuttlesworth himself was chain whipped on a public street by a white mob at Phillips High School when he took his children there in 1957 to seek to enroll them [in the white school]. His wife was stabbed during the same incident with white cops present. Has anybody been convicted? No indeed."

With a population of 350,000, Birmingham was in 1960 Alabama's largest city. A steel town, it was one of the region's major business centers. Blacks accounted for forty percent of the city's population, but were three times less likely than white residents to hold a high-school diploma. Only one of every six black employees was a skilled or trained worker, as opposed to three-quarters of whites. The median annual income for blacks was $3,000, less than half of that for white people. Singer Nat King Cole had been beaten on stage during a 1956 Birmingham performance, and on Labor Day, 1957, a carload of drunken whites had grabbed a black man off a street corner, taken him to a country shack, and castrated him.

The ravaging of the Freedom Riders in May, 1961, and President Kennedy's decision to send in federal marshals had drawn unwelcome national publicity to Birmingham. Economic development had begun to lag as the city's reputation tarnished. A group of whites, headed by Chamber of Commerce president Sidney Smyer, proposed a change in the structure of the city government. Under the existing system, a tightknit group of three segregationist city commissioners ran Birmingham. One was Commissioner of Public Safety Bull Connor. Smyer's group wanted the city to switch to a mayor-council form of government, giving the new chief executive officer direct control over the police department and putting Bull Connor out of office.

On November 6, 1962, Birmingham voters approved the new form of government—a mayor and nine council members. The next step was a mayoral election. Connor, undaunted, declared his candidacy, as did Albert Boutwell, former lieutenant governor of Alabama and a moderate segregationist.

In January, 1963, the SCLC held a three-day retreat in Dorchester, Georgia. King, working with Ralph Abernathy, Wyatt Walker and Rev. Shuttlesworth, carved out a careful plan of attack on segregation in Birmingham. King believed that the failure in Albany had stemmed from a complete lack of strategy. The civil rights leaders vowed that Birmingham would be different. They called their plan Project "C"—for "confrontation." It would be launched in March, 1963, with Birmingham's downtown businesses as its primary focus.

Two weeks after the retreat, King began a national tour in preparation for the Birmingham offensive. He delivered twenty-eight speeches in sixteen cities, telling his listeners, "As Birmingham goes, so goes the South." He asked for volunteers and donations everywhere he went, including a private party at the home of singer Harry Belafonte that was attended by seventy-five eastern liberals. After a similar gathering in Hollywood, King had collected nearly $75,000 in bail money for the anticipated arrests.

Walker and Shuttlesworth handled the preparations in Birmingham. They studied the city's laws and regulations to learn what constituted grounds for arrest. In Albany, the SCLC had not realized that they needed a parade permit to demonstrate.

"Since the Sixteenth Street Baptist Church was going to be our headquarters," Walker said, "I had it timed as to how long it took a youngster to walk [from there to the stores targeted for the protest], how long it took an older person, how long it would take a middle-aged person. And I picked out the best routes. Under some subterfuge I visited all three of [the targeted] stores and counted the stools, the tables, the chairs, and [figured out] the best method for ingress and egress."

The year before, some Birmingham merchants had tried to integrate lunch counters, restrooms, and drinking fountains and even hired some black clerks after a student-led boycott deprived them of about eighty percent of black patronage. A handful of businessmen agreed to remove their Colored Only signs. In response, Public Safety Commissioner Connor sent inspectors to cite the stores for building-code violations. The businesses returned their Colored Only signs. As summer emptied the schools and black students became unavailable, the boycott faded.

Now, a year later, news of the impending demonstrations leaked to Birmingham's business community. With the lucrative Easter shopping season approaching, merchants did not want another boycott. Vincent Townsend, editor of the *Birmingham News*, called Burke Marshall at the Justice Department. He asked Marshall to have a representative of the Kennedy administration call Martin Luther King and request that he cancel the Birmingham protests.

On April 2, Marshall called King and entreated him to leave Birmingham. Bull Connor had been defeated by the moderate white segregationist Albert Boutwell that very day in a special mayoral election (the first election produced no clear victor). Marshall asked King to give the new mayor a chance to resolve black grievances. But King said no; much had happened since his exit from Albany.

Shortly after King left the city, the Ku Klux Klan had bombed four black churches outside Albany. In October, 1962, King had learned of the riots at Ole Miss as James Meredith enrolled as the university's first black student. Two people were killed and 375 injured. In January, 1963, King had listened to Alabama's new governor, George Wallace, give his inauguration speech and work the crowd into cheers as he cried, "Segregation now! Segregation tomorrow! Segregation forever!"

"Segregation now!

Segregation tomorrow!

Segregation forever!"

February had brought another setback: the Kennedy administration refused King's requests to issue a modern emancipation proclamation to outlaw segregation on the 100th anniversary of the original document's signing. The administration was preoccupied with the cold war. Just a few months before, the Cuban missile crisis had placed the nation in unprecedented danger; compared with that, the civil rights movement was simply a local disturbance. Kennedy did send a civil rights bill to Congress, but it languished in committee and was forgotten.

At a press conference, reporters aggressively questioned King about what he hoped to accomplish in Birmingham, given his difficulties in Albany. King snapped back, "The Negro has enough buying power in Birmingham to make the difference between profit and loss in any business. This was not true in Albany, Georgia."

Albert Boutwell had beaten Bull Connor by 8,000 votes in the mayoral election. The headline in the *Birmingham News* ran, "A New Day Dawns for Birmingham." But the SCLC was convinced that Boutwell was "just a dignified Bull Connor," as King put it. As a state senator, Boutwell had authored legislation thwarting the *Brown* decision. He may have been a moderate segregationist compared to Bull Connor, but in the eyes of the SCLC he was still a segregationist.

On the first day of the protests, hours after Boutwell's victory, twenty blacks were arrested for trespassing as they picketed a downtown store. Rev. Shuttlesworth had tried to get a city permit for the demonstration, but Bull Connor brashly told him, "You will get a permit in Birmingham to picket—I will picket you over to the city jail."

City merchants were not pleased. "I was upset with Dr. King," remembers David Vann, a white Birmingham lawyer representing the downtown stores, "because he wouldn't give us a chance to prove what we could do through the political processes. A year and a day after Connor had been reelected with the largest vote in history, a majority of the people in this city voted to terminate his office. And when he ran for mayor, we rejected him."

Some members of the black community were also less than enthusiastic about the new protests. One of them was A. G. Gaston, a millionaire who, despite his misgivings, made his Gaston Motel available to the SCLC and provided financing as well.

After the election, Connor immediately went to court asking that he and the two other commissioners be allowed to complete the terms of office they had earlier been elected to serve, before the voters had decided to do away with the commission form of government. While waiting for the dispute to be settled, the citizens of Birmingham found themselves with two city governments. As David Vann remembers, "On Tuesdays, the [old] Commission met . . . and proceeded to govern the city, and when they finished, they would march out and [the] nine [new] Council members would march in, and they would proceed to adopt laws and spend money and conduct the affairs of the city." Municipal employees found their paychecks signed by both Boutwell and Connor.

During this governmental turmoil, the SCLC accelerated its demonstrations. On Saturday, April 6, Shuttlesworth led thirty protesters to city hall and the entire group was sent to jail. The next day, Palm Sunday, A. D. King, the younger brother of Martin Luther King, headed a prayer march through the downtown streets. Police using dogs and nightsticks clashed violently with the demonstrators.

Bull Connor, still in control of the police, sought a court injunction banning further picketing. On Wednesday, April 10, Alabama Circuit Court Judge W. A. Jenkins, Jr., issued an order naming 133 civil rights leaders whom he forbade to take part in or encourage any sit-ins, picketing, or other demonstrations. The list included King, Abernathy, and Shuttlesworth. In Albany, King's refusal to defy the court injunction and the subsequent lapse in the demonstrations had irrevocably hampered the movement's momentum. Furthermore, Project "C" called for King to subject himself to arrest in Birmingham on April 12, Good Friday. If the minister obeyed the court order, the movement would lose a carefully planned chance to attract the attention of television and newspapers.

On Friday morning, King met with his staff at the Gaston Motel. "We already had [many] people in jail," remembers Andrew Young, "but all the money was gone, and we couldn't get people out . . . the black business community and some of the clergy [were] pressuring us to call off the demonstrations and just get out of town. We didn't know what to do. [King] sat there in Room 30 in the

Theophilus Eugene "Bull" Connor, Birmingham's commissioner of public safety.

Bull Connor ordered his police department to use police dogs to break up the demonstrations.

Gaston Motel and didn't say anything. He listened to people talking for about two hours.'

King then left the suite's living room and went into the bedroom. When he emerged, he told his staff, "Look, I don't know what to do. I just know that something has got to change in Birmingham. I don't know whether I can raise money to get people out of jail. I do know that I can go into jail with them."

As King turned to go, he looked toward Ralph Abernathy, his constant adviser and companion. According to Andrew Young, Rev. Abernathy said he didn't want to go to jail; he needed to be in his church pulpit on Easter Sunday. King turned to his best friend and said, "Ralph, you've always been with me, but I'm going [regardless]." Abernathy followed.

"Not knowing how it was going to work out, he walked out of the room and went down to the church and led a demonstration and went to jail," recalls Young. "That was, I think, the beginning of his true leadership."

A half mile into a march toward downtown Birmingham, King and Abernathy were arrested along with fifty other demonstrators. Media cameras were there to capture the symbolism as Martin Luther King was loaded into Bull Connor's windowless police van on that Good Friday.

King was placed in solitary confinement in Birmingham's jail. Demonstrators gathered on the steps of the Sixteenth Street Baptist Church and sang in brave jubilation. Afterwards, some of them moved across the street to the city's Kelly Ingram Park. The police moved in, and brief fights broke out, but the protests ended peacefully. Later, a full-page ad taken out by members of the local white clergy appeared in the *Birmingham News*, calling King a troublemaker. From his cell, King responded to the ministers' letter by writing in the margins of the newspaper and on scraps of toilet paper.

"I have yet to engage in a direct action campaign that was well-timed in the view of those who have not suffered unduly from the disease of segregation," he wrote in what was later published as the essay, "Letter from a Birmingham Jail." "For years now, I have heard the word 'Wait.' It rings in the ears of every Negro with piercing familiarity. This 'Wait' has almost always meant 'Never.' We must come to see with one of our distinguished jurists that 'justice too long delayed is justice denied.'" The letter went on to explain, to the clergy and to the world, why the fight against racism must not be delayed.

Coretta Scott King heard nothing from her jailed husband all weekend. Fearing for his safety, on Easter Sunday she sought advice from Wyatt Walker, executive

Letter from a Birmingham Jail

Written in April, 1963, Martin Luther King, Jr.'s letter from jail stands as one of the most important documents of nonviolent protest in the civil rights movement. King began the letter by writing notes in the margins of the *Birmingham News*, which printed an open letter from eight clergymen who attacked King's role in Birmingham. King's letter was first published as a pamphlet by the American Friends Service Committee, a Quaker group. It was reprinted in dozens of periodicals and soon, with over a million copies in circulation, it became a classic of protest literature. Excerpts from the 6,500-word letter follow.

April 16, 1963
Birmingham, Alabama

My Dear Fellow Clergymen:

While confined here in the Birmingham city jail, I came across your recent statement calling my present activities "unwise and untimely." Seldom do I pause to answer criticism of my work and ideas . . . but since I feel that you are men of genuine good will and that your criticisms are sincerely set forth, I want to try to answer your statement in what I hope will be patient and reasonable terms.

. . . You may well ask, "Why direct action? Why sit-ins, marches, and so forth? Isn't negotiation a better path?" You are quite right in calling for negotiations. Indeed, this is the very purpose of direct action. Nonviolent direct action seeks to create such a crisis and foster such a tension that a community which has constantly refused to negotiate is forced to confront the issue. It seeks so to dramatize the issue that it can no longer be ignored. My citing the creation of tension as part of the work of the nonviolent-resister may sound rather shocking. But I must confess that I am not afraid of the word "tension." I have earnestly opposed violent tension, but there is a type of constructive, nonviolent tension which is necessary for growth. Just as Socrates felt that it was necessary to create a tension in the mind so that individuals could rise from the bondage of myths and half-truths to the unfettered realm of creative analysis and objective appraisal, so must we see the need for nonviolent gadflies to create the kind of tension in society that will help men rise from the dark depths of prejudice and racism to the majestic heights of understanding and brotherhood.

The purpose of our direct-action program is to create a situation so crisis-packed that it will inevitably open the door to negotiation. I therefore concur with you in your call for negotiation. Too long has our beloved Southland been bogged down in a tragic effort to live in monologue rather than dialogue.

. . . One of the basic points in your statement is that the action that I and my associates have taken in Birmingham is untimely. Some have asked: "Why didn't you give the new city administration time to act?" The only answer that I can give to this query is that the new Birmingham administration must be prodded about as much as the outgoing one, before it will act. We are sadly mistaken if we feel that the election of Albert Boutwell as mayor will bring the millennium to Birmingham. While Mr. Boutwell is a much more gentle person than Mr. Connor, they are both segregationists, dedicated to maintenance of the status quo. I have hoped that Mr. Boutwell will be reasonable enough to see the futility of massive resistance . . . My friends, I must say to you that we have not made a single gain in civil rights without determined legal and nonviolent pressure. Lamentably, it is an historical fact that privileged groups seldom give up their privileges voluntarily. Individuals may see the moral light and voluntarily give up their unjust posture, but, as Reinhold Niebuhr has reminded us, groups tend to be more immoral than individuals.

We know through painful experience that freedom is never voluntarily given by the oppressor; it must be demanded by the oppressed. . . Frankly, I have yet to engage in a direct-action campaign that was "well-timed" in view of those who have not suffered unduly from the disease of segregation. For years now I have heard the word "Wait!" It rings in the ear of every Negro with piercing familiarity. This "Wait" has almost always meant "Never." We must come to see, with one of our distinguished jurists, that "justice too long delayed is justice denied." We have waited for more than 340 years for our constitutional and God-given rights. The nations of Asia and Africa are moving with jetlike speed toward gaining political independence, but we still creep at horse-and-buggy pace toward gaining a cup of coffee at a lunch counter. Perhaps it is easy for those who have never felt the stinging darts of segregation to say, "Wait." But when you have seen vicious mobs lynch your mothers and fathers at will and drown your sisters and brothers at whim; when you have seen hate-filled policemen curse, kick, and even kill your black brothers and sisters; when you see the vast majority of your twenty million Negro brothers smothering in an airtight cage of poverty in the midst of an affluent society;

director of the SCLC. He suggested she call the president. On Monday, Kennedy returned her phone call.

"He said, 'I want you to know that we are doing everything we can, and Dr. King is safe,'" Mrs. King recalls, "and Martin said after that [phone call] the treatment changed markedly."

The demonstrations began to lose supporters as King's incarceration dragged on. Finally, on April 20, King and Abernathy accepted release on bond. They went straight to the Gaston Motel to plan the next phase of Project "C." James Bevel, a veteran of the student sit-ins in Nashville, had devised a strategy. He wanted to use Birmingham's black children as demonstrators. Bevel argued that while many adults might be reluctant to march—afraid of going to jail at the cost of their jobs—children would be less fearful. Also, he told King, the sight of when you suddenly find your tongue twisted and your speech stammering as you seek to explain to your six-year-old daughter why she can't go to the public amusement park that has just been advertised on television, and see tears welling up in her eyes when she is told that Funtown is closed to colored children, and see ominous clouds of inferiority beginning to form in her little mental sky, and see her beginning to distort her personality by developing an unconscious bitterness toward white people; when you have to concoct an answer for a five-year-old son who is asking, "Daddy, why do white people treat colored people so mean?"; when you take a cross-country drive and find it necessary to sleep night after night in the uncomfortable corners of your automobile because no motel will accept you; when you are humiliated day in and day out by nagging signs reading "white" and "colored"; when your first name becomes "nigger," your middle name becomes "boy" (however old you are) and your last name becomes "John," and your wife and mother are never given the respected title "Mrs."; when you are harried by day and haunted by night by the fact that you are a Negro, living constantly at tiptoe stance, never quite knowing what to expect next, and are plagued with inner fears and outer resentments; when you are forever fighting a degenerating sense of "nobodiness"—then you will understand why we find it difficult to wait. There comes a time when the cup of endurance runs over, and men are no longer willing to be plunged into the abyss of despair. I hope, sirs, you can understand our legitimate and unavoidable impatience . . .

young children being hauled off to jail would dramatically stir the nation's conscience.

"Most adults have bills to pay—house notes, rents, car notes, utility bills," argued Bevel, "but the young people . . . are not hooked with all those responsibilities. A boy from high school has the same effect in terms of being in jail, in terms of putting pressure on the city, as his father, and yet there's no economic threat to the family, because the father is still on the job."

While King went to court on April 22 to be tried in connection with the Good Friday protest, SCLC workers Bevel, Andrew Young, Dorothy Cotton, and Bernard Lee recruited black schoolchildren from all over Birmingham. They asked the students to go to their local churches and see a film, *The Nashville Story*, about a student sit-in movement. King was found guilty of civil contempt but remained free pending appeal. On Thursday, May 2, the children began their demonstrations in Birmingham. King addressed a gathering of them at the Sixteenth Street Baptist Church. They ranged in age from six to eighteen. He told the youngsters he was proud of them, that they were fighting for their parents and for the future of America. Groups of children began to march toward downtown.

Police moved in to arrest them, at first herding them into paddy wagons. For four hours they continued to march from the church, singing songs of freedom. As their numbers increased, Bull Connor brought in school buses to haul them away. By the end of the day, 959 children had been taken to Birmingham jails. From Washington, Robert Kennedy called King to argue that the children could be seriously hurt by Connor's police tactics.

The next day, more than a thousand children stayed out of school, gathering at the church to march. Bull Connor, hoping to abort the demonstrations before they began, brought out the city's police dogs. He also ordered firefighters to turn their hoses on the youngsters. With 100 pounds of pressure per square inch, the water hit with enough force to rip the bark off trees. Children were knocked down by the streams, slammed into curbs and over parked cars. Several demonstrators were attacked by dogs.

As Connor lashed the demonstrators with water, black businessman A. G. Gaston, from his office across the street, was on the phone with attorney David Vann. Gaston "was expressing a great deal of resentment about King coming in and messing up things just when we [through the city government] were getting a new start," Vann recalls. "And then he said to me, 'But Lawyer Vann, they've turned the fire hoses on a black girl. They're rolling that little girl right down the middle of the street. I can't talk to you no more.'"

Vann would later say that it was then, when Connor's troopers attacked the children, that "in the twinkling of an eye the whole black community instantaneously consolidated . . . behind Dr. King."

Birmingham's blacks were raging with anger. At a demonstration the next day, some brandished guns and knives. James Bevel, fearing a riot that would be blamed on the movement, announced through a policeman's bullhorn, "Okay, get off the streets now. We're not going to have violence. If you're not going to respect policemen, you're not going to be in the movement." Tension mounted; the SCLC had created a protest it could not control.

The marches grew in size. By Monday, May 6, more than two thousand demonstrators had been jailed, some in Birmingham, others in a temporary prison camp at the Alabama state fairgrounds. The next day, the confrontation moved into the downtown area, and Bull Connor once again summoned his firemen and ordered the hoses turned on. When the public safety commissioner was told that Rev. Shuttlesworth had been injured by the hurtling water and taken to the hospital by ambulance, he broke into a smile and said, "I'm sorry I missed it. I wish they'd carried him away in a hearse."

Across the nation people watched television pictures of children being blasted with water hoses and chased by police dogs. Newspapers and magazines at home and abroad were filled with reports and photographs. The news coverage shocked the American public. In Washington, the Kennedy administration also watched.

As demonstrators filled the jails, the city had to establish temporary prison camps.

"There were pictures throughout the nation, throughout the world," recalls Burke Marshall, then head of the Justice Department's Civil Rights Division. "It was a matter of great concern to the president, because it was a hopeless situation in terms of any lawful resolution." The federal government worried about America's image abroad.

But President Kennedy, according to Marshall, could exercise no executive power in Birmingham. "There was no legal remedy," Marshall said. "That was clear from the start. We discussed it with the president so he understood, but most of the country did not. You know, they wanted him to send in troops, do this and that . . . "

As Kennedy considered his options, the situation worsened. Alabama governor George Wallace sent in 500 state troopers. Television and newspaper reporters intensified their coverage. As King and the SCLC had hoped, the press had drawn the whole world's attention to Birmingham.

"It was a masterpiece [in] the use of media to explain a cause to the general public," says David Vann. "In those days, we had fifteen minutes of national news and fifteen minutes of local news, and in marching only one block they could get enough news film to fill all of the newscasts of all the television stations in the United States."

Governor Wallace did not share the president's concern over America's image. "It seems to me that other parts of the world ought to be concerned about what we are thinking of them instead of what they think of us," Wallace said. "After all, we're feeding most of them. And whenever they start rejecting twenty-five cents of each dollar of foreign-aid money that we send them, then I'll be concerned about their attitude toward us. But until they reject that twenty-five cents . . . that southerners pay for foreign aid to these countries, I will never be concerned

The Birmingham Fire
Department turned their
hoses on the young
demonstrators. The force
of the water tore bark off
trees.

about their attitude. In the first place, the average man in Africa or Asia doesn't even know where he is, much less where Alabama is."

Kennedy, seeking a quick settlement, had sent Burke Marshall to Birmingham on May 4 to encourage negotiations between King and the city's business leaders. Marshall learned that most of Birmingham's white leaders were not speaking to blacks, and that the white business community was not speaking to Bull Connor and his police department. Some blacks would not talk to blacks whom they considered too radical, while others refused to speak to fellow blacks they thought of as "Uncle Toms." And except for lawyer David Vann, whites were not speaking to King. "Anything that Martin Luther King wanted was poison to them [whites]," said Marshall.

The federal aide asked King what concessions he wanted from the whites of Birmingham. Marshall recalls that King said he really was not sure now that the protests had escalated uncontrollably; the campaign's original goal, desegregation of downtown stores, now seemed too small an issue. Blacks wanted integration in every aspect of the city's life, King said. But at Marshall's insistence, King agreed that the bottom line remained the desegregation of lunch counters in downtown stores.

With the dispute over the new city government's legitimacy still pending in court, it was up to the private sector to work out a settlement. Marshall approached the city's leading business owners and presented King's demands. A mercantile group called the Senior Citizens Committee represented about seventy percent of Birmingham's businesses and employed about eighty percent of the city's workers.

The demonstrations were now reaching the proportions that James Bevel had worried about on Saturday. Fearing damage to downtown stores, the business leaders hastened the negotiations. After both sides declared a day of truce, clearing the streets, the merchants agreed to desegregate lunch counters and hire black workers in clerical and sales positions. Joseph Rauh, a lawyer for the United Auto Workers union and a long-time civil rights activist, arranged for the UAW and other labor unions to create a bail fund to secure the release of the 800 black people still in jail.

On Monday, May 10, at two separate news conferences, the accord was announced to the public. Bull Connor fumed. He demanded to know the names of the businessmen who had secretly negotiated the truce. Connor's fellow commissioners, still seeking to retain control of the city, joined him in condemning the deal as "capitulation by certain weak-kneed white people under threat of violence by the rabble-rousing Negro, King." On a local radio broadcast, Connor urged whites to boycott the downtown stores that had agreed to integrate.

The night after the accord was announced, the Ku Klux Klan rallied outside the city. Robert Shelton, Grand Dragon of the white supremacist group, said, "We would like to state at this time that any concessions that Martin Luther King or any other group of Negro leaders in Birmingham have received are not worth the paper they're written on or the bag that's holding the water. No business people in Birmingham or any other city have the authority to attempt any type of negotiations when it deals with governmental affairs with municipalities. Martin Luther King's epitaph, in my opinion, can be written here in Birmingham."

After the Klan meeting, bombs exploded at the home of Martin Luther King's brother and at the Gaston Motel, where King had been staying. Crowds of blacks assembled at both sites. Over the objections of Jefferson County sheriff Mel Bailey, state troopers moved in, as did Connor's police. As rioting erupted, the lawmen pummeled blacks with clubs and rifles. Thirty-five blacks and five whites were injured. Seven stores were set ablaze. Attorney General Robert Kennedy, fearing that the violence might trigger rioting nationwide, convinced his brother to send in federal troops. The president dispatched soldiers to Fort McClellan, thirty miles outside of Birmingham, hoping that the threat of federal intervention would induce state and local authorities to restore the peace. Kennedy said he would not allow the agreement between the businessmen and the SCLC to be "sabotaged by a few extremists."

"This government," the president announced, "will do whatever must be done to preserve order, protect the lives of its citizens, and uphold the law of the land . . . those who labored so hard to achieve the peaceful, constructive settlement of last week can feel nothing but dismay at the efforts of those who would replace conciliation and good will with violence and hate."

Kennedy's tactic quieted the city. The conflict ended altogether when the Alabama Supreme Court recognized Mayor Albert Boutwell and the new council as the legitimate government of Birmingham. The new mayor honored the negotiated settlement.

Connor, however, had not finished his assault on the civil rights movement. When a federal court ordered the University of Alabama to admit black students, Connor joined forces with Governor George Wallace. The governor sent Connor to a meeting of the segregationist Citizens' Council in Tuscaloosa to ask them to stay away from the university. "Leave it alone," he entreated the white supremacists. "Those Kennedys up there in Washington, that little old Bobby-soxer and his brother the president, they'd give anything in the world if we had some trouble here." The crowd cheered as Connor ended with, "If we don't have any trouble, we can beat 'em at their own game."

On June 11, Wallace literally stood in the doorway of a university building, blocking the entrance of James Hood and Vivian Malone, two black students trying to register. "It is important that the people of this state and nation understand," he intoned, "that this action is in violation of rights reserved for the state by the Constitution of the United States and the Constitution of the state of Alabama." With television cameras recording the confrontation, Deputy Attorney General Nicholas Katzenbach asked Wallace if he intended to act on his defiance. When Wallace failed to reply, the marshals and lawyers accompanied the black students to their dormitories.

Newly elected Governor George Wallace blocking the entrance to the University of Alabama as a representative from the U.S. Justice Department, Nicholas Katzenbach, informs him of the federal government's intent to integrate the school.

Later that day, Alabama National Guard General Henry Graham, backed by federal marshals, asked the governor to step aside. Wallace left the campus, and the black students walked through the door, breaking the color barrier at the university.

That night President Kennedy spoke on national television. The civil rights issue dominated his agenda. "The fires of frustration and discord are busy in every city," the president said. "Redress is sought in the street, in demonstrations, parades and protests which create tensions and threaten violence. We face, therefore, a moral crisis as a country and as a people.

"I am therefore asking the Congress to enact legislation giving all Americans the right to be served in facilities which are open to the public—hotels, restaurants, theatres, retail stores and similar establishments. This seems to me to be an elementary right. Its denial is an arbitrary indignity that no American in 1963 should have to endure . . . "

Kennedy delivered a new civil rights bill to Congress on June 19. Stronger than the bill that had died in Congress at the beginning of the year, the new bill would outlaw segregation in all interstate public accommodations, allow the attorney general to initiate suits for school integration, and give the attorney general the important power to shut off funds to any federal programs in which discrimination occurred. It also contained a provision that helped ensure the right to vote by declaring that a person who had a sixth-grade education would be presumed to be literate.

King, the SCLC, CORE, the NAACP, SNCC, and other civil rights groups had no intention of allowing this bill to die in Congress. To demonstrate the strength of public demand for this legislation, they would march on Washington.

The March on Washington

August 28, 1963

In 1963, A. Philip Randolph was the civil rights movement's elder statesman. The seventy-four-year-old leader's closely cropped gray hair and stentorian voice reinforced his commanding presence. Randolph was the founder of the Brotherhood of Sleeping Car Porters (BSCP), a union of black porters who worked on the country's trains. When Randolph founded the BSCP in 1925, there were no railway unions open to blacks. For many years, BSCP members acted as "civil rights missionaries on wheels." Traveling from station to station throughout the country, the porters organized not only for labor, but for civil rights as well.

For half a century Randolph was at the forefront of grass roots efforts to improve the lives of black Americans. In 1941, as the country prepared for World War II, he planned a mass march on Washington to demand more jobs for blacks in the defense industries. The war had ended the depression for millions of unemployed whites, but thousands of black workers remained out of work. Shortly before the day of the march, President Franklin Delano Roosevelt met with Randolph and agreed to issue an executive order declaring that "there shall be no discrimination in the employment of workers in defense industries or government because of race, creed, color or national origin." Executive Order 8802 represented the federal government's strongest civil rights action since the post-Civil War Reconstruction era. Roosevelt also agreed to establish the Fair Employment Practices Committee. In return, Randolph called off the protest march.

In 1963, finding a decent job was still very difficult for blacks in America. Black unemployment stood at eleven percent, while for whites the figure was just five percent. And whereas a white family earned, on average, about $6,500 a year, a black family earned $3,500 a year. Randolph again decided to organize a national march on Washington to show that black citizens were tired of waiting for fair treatment and equal opportunity. After the violent attacks on the Birmingham demonstrators earlier in 1963, the march took on a broader meaning.

In the nine years since the Supreme Court's *Brown* decision, America had witnessed intense racial turmoil. Media pictures of Bull Connor and his men turning attack dogs and firehoses on demonstrators had shocked the nation.

Some of the march organizers worried that only a few thousand people would participate in the march. In fact, more than 250,000 demonstrators came to march on Washington.

The Southern Regional Council, a biracial information and research group, estimated that, in the wake of Birmingham, nearly 15,000 persons—mostly black—were arrested during various protest demonstrations throughout the nation. Louis Martin, the Kennedy administration's leading black adviser, wrote in a memo to White House officials, "Events in Birmingham have seemed to electrify Negro concerns all across the country. As this is written, demonstrations and marches are being planned . . . The accelerated tempo of Negro restiveness and the rivalries of some leaders for top billing, coupled with the resistance of segregationists, may soon create the most critical state of race relations since the Civil War."

A. Philip Randolph (right), the senior civil rights leader who first planned a march on Washington in 1941, with Bayard Rustin, deputy director of the 1963 march.

Randolph and his colleague Bayard Rustin met with labor and civil rights leaders to plan the August 28 march. They agreed to expand the goals of the march to include demands for passage of the Civil Rights Act; integration of public schools by year's end; enactment of a fair employment practices bill prohibiting job discrimination; and the original demand for job training and placement.

President Kennedy tried to persuade the civil rights leaders to call off the march, arguing that violence was likely. The president also felt that, to ensure passage of the civil rights bill, it was important for blacks to stay off the streets and portray themselves as unthreatening. On learning of the leaders' determination to carry through with the march, however, Kennedy reluctantly endorsed the cause.

"The fact that he took that attitude rather than the attitude of almost everyone else in the Senate and Congress . . . made a difference to the character of the march," remembers Burke Marshall, the assistant attorney general for the Justice Department's civil rights division, "because if he had opposed it, it would have been more of a rebellious type of march."

The march's themes became unity, racial harmony, and, especially, a cry to "Pass the Bill." The March on Washington Committee appointed Bayard Rustin deputy director of the event. It was his job to work out the logistics. The organizers hoped that 100,000 marchers would participate. As Rustin later remembered, "We wanted to get everybody, from the whole country, into Washington by nine o'clock in the morning and out of Washington by sundown. This required all kinds of things that you had to think through. You had to think how many toilets you

needed, where they should be. Where is your line of march? We had to consult doctors on exactly what people should bring to eat so that they wouldn't get sick . . . We had to arrange for drinking water. We had to arrange what we would do if there was a terrible thunderstorm that day. We had to think of the sound system."

People learned of the march through local civil rights and church groups all across the country. "Freedom buses" and "freedom trains" brought marchers from all across the country, north and south. In all, more than thirty special trains and 2,000 chartered buses delivered people to Washington, in numbers unimagined by the organizers— over a quarter of a million people, as many as 60,000 of them white. It was, at that time, the largest demonstration for human rights in the history of the republic.

The march represented a coalition of civil rights workers, church groups, and labor leaders. Some of the march organizers can be seen here leading the crowd.

It was a hot day in August, but the marchers refreshed themselves by cooling their feet in the reflecting pool.

Marchers came from across the country, black and white, young and old.

Musicians entertained the vast throng waiting for the speeches t begin. The performers included folksingers Josh White, Odetta, Mahali Jackson, Joan Baez, Bob Dylan, and the trio Peter, Paul and Mary.

A. Philip Randolph opened the program. "Fellow Americans," h said to the sea of faces in front of the Lincoln Memorial, "we ar gathered here in the largest demonstration in the history of this nation Let the nation and the world know the meaning of our numbers. W are not a pressure group, we are not an organization or a group o organizations, we are not a mob. We are the advance guard of a massiv moral revolution for jobs and freedom."

SNCC's John Lewis, one of the scheduled speakers, had planned t deliver a fiery speech denouncing the civil rights bill as too little to late. He wanted to warn the country that blacks would not wait for th president or Congress to end racial discrimination, but would soon "tak matters into our own hands and create a source of power outside of any national structure . . . we will march through the South, through the heart of Dixie, the way Sherman did, leaving a scorched earth with our nonviolence."

The march organizers received the text of all the speeches the night before the event, and copies were also delivered to the press. After reading Lewis' speech, the organizers asked him to soften his attack on the government. Word came that Cardinal Patrick O'Boyle had threatened to withdraw from the march if Lewis were permitted to deliver his speech unchanged. The March on Washington's fragile coalition of white liberals, church leaders, labor representatives, and black activists was in jeopardy.

Martin Luther King, Jr., Rustin, and others each spoke with Lewis, but the young leader would not compromise—not until A. Philip Randolph discussed the matter with him. In deference to Randolph's position, Lewis finally agreed to modify his stance. He and fellow SNCC leaders James Forman and Courtland Cox rewrote the material, working furiously at a portable typewriter set up behind Lincoln's Statue. They finished only minutes before Lewis stood to give his oration.

Even with modifications, Lewis' speech was the most hard-hitting of the day. "By the force of our demands, our determination and our numbers," he said, "we shall splinter the segregated South into a thousand pieces, and put them back together in the image of God and democracy." He went on to say that SNCC supported the civil rights bill "with reservations."

Then Martin Luther King, Jr., stood to speak. King, the most popular of all the civil rights leaders, delivered a speech that would be heard on television stations across the land. It was a speech of hope and determination, epitomizing the day's message of racial harmony, love, unity, and a belief that blacks and whites could live together in peace.

The event was a resounding success, extensively covered by the media. There were no major disturbances. Many Americans witnessed for the first time black people and white united, marching and celebrating side by side.

As Bayard Rustin remembered, "The March on Washington took place because the Negro needed allies . . . The March was not a Negro

James Forman (standing, wearing a suit) joins other SNCC workers in song. While SNCC participated in the march, the group doubted the effectiveness of such demonstrations.

Only eighteen days after the celebrated march, four young girls were killed when someone threw dynamite into a church in Birmingham, Alabama.

action. It was an action by Negroes and whites together. Not just the leaders of the Negro organizations, but leading Catholic, Protestant, and Jewish spokesmen called the people into the street. And Catholics, Protestants, and Jews, white and black, responded."

There is no way of knowing whether the March on Washington boosted the progress of the Civil Rights Act through Congress. For many months afterward, the legislators resisted the bill. But America witnessed an unprecedented spectacle that day. The march brought joy and a sense of possibility to people throughout the nation who perhaps had not understood the civil rights movement before or who had felt threatened by it.

But ardent segregationists remained unmoved. In Birmingham, Alabama, just eighteen days after the march, dynamite exploded in the Sixteenth Street Baptist Church, where children were attending a Bible school class. Four of the youngsters were killed—Denise McNair, age eleven, and Cynthia Wesley, Carole Robertson, and Addie Mae Collins, all age fourteen. On that same Sunday, Birmingham police killed a black youth in the street, and another young black man riding a bicycle in that city was attacked and murdered by a group of whites.

To many outside observers, the March on Washington became almost synonymous with the civil rights movement itself. But the hard truth, brought home so soon by the Birmingham murders, was that it was only one day in the long and continuing fight for equality.

"I Have a Dream"

August 28, 1963
Lincoln Memorial, Washington, D.C.

I'm happy to join with you today in what will go down in history as the greatest demonstration for freedom in the history of our nation.

Fivescore years ago, a great American, in whose symbolic shadow we stand today, signed the Emancipation Proclamation. This momentous decree came as a great beacon light of hope to millions of Negro slaves who had been seared in the flames of withering injustice. It came as a joyous daybreak to end the long night of their captivity.

But one hundred years later, the Negro still is not free; one hundred years later, the life of the Negro is still sadly crippled by the manacles of segregation and the chains of discrimination; one hundred years later, the Negro lives on a lonely island of poverty in the midst of a vast ocean of material prosperity; one hundred years later, the Negro is still languished in the corners of American society and finds himself in exile in his own land . . .

Nineteen sixty-three is not an end, but a beginning. And those who hope that the Negro needed to blow off steam and will now be content, will have a rude awakening if the nation returns to business as usual. There will be neither rest nor tranquility in America until the Negro is granted his citizenship rights. The whirlwinds of the revolt will continue to shake the foundations of our nation until the bright day of justice emerges . . .

There are those who are asking the devotees of Civil Rights, "When will you be satisfied?" We can never be satisfied as long as the Negro is the victim of the unspeakable horrors of police brutality; we can never be satisifed as long as our bodies, heavy with the fatigue of travel, cannot gain lodging in the motels of the highways and the hotels of the cities; we cannot be satisfied as long as the Negro's basic mobility is from a smaller ghetto to a larger one; we can never be satisfied as long as our children are stripped of their selfhood and robbed of their dignity by signs stating "For Whites Only"; we cannot be satisfied as long as the Negro in Mississippi cannot vote and a Negro in New York believes he has nothing for which to vote. No! No, we are not satisfied, and we will not be satisfied until "justice rolls down like waters and righteousness like a mighty stream."

I am not unmindful that some of you have come here out of great trials and tribulations. Some of you have come fresh from narrow jail cells. Some of you have come from areas where your quest for freedom left you battered by the storms of persecution and staggered by the winds of police brutality. You have been the veterans of creative suffering. Continue to work with the faith that unearned suffering is redemptive. Go back to Mississippi. Go back to Alabama. Go back to South Carolina. Go back to Georgia. Go back to Louisiana. Go back to the slums and ghettos of our northern cities, knowing that somehow the situation can and will be changed. Let us not wallow in the valley of despair.

I say to you today, my friends, so even though we face the difficulties of today and tomorrow, I still have a dream. It is a dream deeply rooted in the American meaning of its creed, "We hold these truths to be self-evident, that all men are created equal." I have a dream that one day on the red hills of Georgia, sons of former slaves and the sons of former slave owners will be able to sit down together at the table of brotherhood. I have a dream that one day even the state of Mississippi, a state sweltering with the heat of injustice, sweltering with the heat of oppression, will be transformed into an oasis of freedom and justice. I have a dream that my four little children will one day live in a nation where they will not be judged by the color of their skin, but the content of their character.

I have a dream today!

I have a dream that one day down in Alabama—with its vicious racists, with its governor having his lips dripping with the words of interposition and nullification—one day right there in Alabama, little black boys and black girls will be able to join hands with little white boys and white girls as sisters and brothers.

I have a dream today!

I have a dream that one day "every valley shall be exalted and every hill and mountain shall be made low. The rough places will be made plain and the crooked places will be made straight, and the glory of the Lord shall be revealed, and all flesh shall see it together."

This is our hope. This is the faith that I go back to the South with. With this faith we shall be able to transform the jangling discords of our nation into a beautiful symphony of brotherhood. With this faith we will be able to work together, to pray together, to struggle together, to go to jail together, to stand up for freedom together, knowing that we will be free one day. And this will be the day. This will be the day when all of God's children will be able to sing with new meaning, "My country 'tis of thee, sweet land of liberty, of thee I sing. Land where my fathers died, land of the pilgrim's pride, from every mountainside, let freedom ring." And if America is to be a great nation, this must become true . . .

So let freedom ring from the prodigious hilltops of New Hampshire, let freedom ring from the mighty mountains of New York, let freedom ring from the heightening Alleghenies of Pennsylvania; let freedom ring from the snow-capped Rockies of Colorado; let freedom ring from the curvaceous slopes of California. But not only that. Let freedom ring from Stone Mountain of Georgia; let freedom ring from Lookout Mountain of Tennessee; let freedom ring from every hill and molehill of Mississippi. From every mountainside, let freedom ring.

And when this happens and when we allow freedom to ring, when we let it ring from every village and every hamlet, from every state and every city, we will be able to speed up that day when all God's children, black men and white men, Jews and gentiles, Protestants and Catholics, will be able to join hands and sing in the words of the old Negro spiritual: "Free at last. Free at last. Thank God Almighty, we are free at last."

In Mississippi, several civil rights groups joined under the organizational name of COFO (Council of Federated Organizations) to work for voting rights.

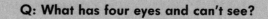

Chapter Seven

Mississippi

Freedom Has Never Been Free

Q: What has four eyes and can't see?

A: Mississippi.

—a children's riddle

In the 1950s, trying to organize for civil rights in Mississippi was like trying to pick a plantation's entire cotton crop singlehandedly—one boll at a time, in the middle of the night, with a gun pointed at your head. Forty-five percent of Mississippi's people were black, a higher percentage than in any other state. Mississippi also led the nation in beatings, lynchings, and mysterious disappearances. Only five percent of black Mississippians were registered to vote, the lowest rate in the United States. With majorities in many counties, blacks might well have controlled local politics through the ballot box. But segregationists were not about to let blacks vote; many would sooner kill them.

Between 1950 and 1960, more than 315,000 blacks migrated from the Magnolia State, the poorest one in the nation, and seventy-five percent of the state's college graduates, almost all of them white, also left. Mississippi had fewer doctors, accountants, nurses, and lawyers per capita than any other state in the nation. In 1959, the NAACP counted only one black dentist, five black lawyers, and sixty black doctors in the entire state.

Blacks in Mississippi had little chance of landing a good job and plenty of chances to get into trouble. They came to grief if they tried to register to vote or if they didn't ride in the back of the bus. Children could not enter all-white public schools, and eating at a white restaurant or lunch counter was out of the question. The population of Jackson, the state's capital and its largest community, was approximately 100,000, but Jackson's only bookstore was a Baptist-run religious shop. Most of Mississippi's counties had no bookstores at all. One-third of the counties had no public library.

When Medgar Evers came home from World War II, his brother Charlie talked him into trying to vote in their hometown of Decatur. The Evers brothers and four other blacks registered at the courthouse, but when they tried to vote on election day, they were met by a mob of whites wielding guns and knives. Years later, Medgar Evers described the experience to a reporter. "We had all seen a lot of dead people in the war," he said. "I had been on Omaha Beach. All we wanted to be was ordinary citizens. We fought during the war for America, Mississippi included. Now, after the Germans and the Japanese hadn't killed us, it looked as though the white Mississippians would . . . We knew we weren't going to get by this mob." The blacks left without even seeing the voting booth.

Upon his graduation from Alcorn Agricultural and Mechanical College, Evers became an insurance agent, though he dreamed of being a lawyer. In 1954 he applied to the law school at the University of Mississippi in Oxford. While he waited for a response from the all-white institution, the United States Supreme

Court ruled that racially segregated schools were unconstitutional. White southerners responded angrily, some of them forming white Citizens' Councils to resist integration. Mississippi attorney general James P. Coleman, who later became governor of the state, invited Evers to Jackson to discuss his desire to enroll at "Ole Miss."

"They asked me was I sincere," Evers wrote later. "I told them yes. They asked me was I prompted by the NAACP, and I told them no. They asked me where I would stay, and I answered, 'On the campus, sir. I'm very hygienic, I bathe every day, and I assure you this brown won't rub off.'" Evers was rejected, ostensibly because he supplied no recommendations from Mississippi whites.

Unable to attend law school, Evers went to work that December for the NAACP. He was the association's first field director in Mississippi. Many white Mississippians equated the NAACP with the Communist party. At play, white children chanted that its initials stood for "Niggers, Apes, Alligators, Coons, and Possums."

In preparation for his new job, the thirty-year-old Evers bought an Oldsmobile with a powerful V-8 engine. The car was big enough to resist being forced off the road, roomy enough for sleeping in when Evers could find no motel that allowed blacks, and powerful enough to ensure fast escape from threatening situations. Over the next eight years, Evers logged thousands of miles on that Oldsmobile.

In rural Mississippi, the NAACP's activities extended beyond the pursuit of integration through the courts. Often the organization investigated the murders of blacks because local police generally dismissed such killings as "accidents." During his first year with the NAACP, Evers traveled to the town of Money in search of evidence and witnesses for the trial of the two men accused of the kidnapping and murder of fourteen-year-old Emmett Till. That same year, Evers also visited the town of Belzoni, along with Ruby Hurley, the NAACP's regional director based in Birmingham, Alabama. In Belzoni the two searched for people who might have witnessed the murder of the Reverend George Lee, a local black minister who had helped organize a branch of the NAACP and had also dared to register to vote.

As an NAACP organizer, Evers was an obvious target for white terrorism. Friends who rang his doorbell might hear the sounds of someone barricading the door with furniture. The window blinds were always drawn, and Evers kept several guns in the house and one in the Oldsmobile. He coached his children on what to do if shooting ever broke out: they were to lie flat on the floor or, if possible, hide in the bathtub.

The Evers family received daily death threats over the telephone. Evers always listened, sometimes trying to persuade the callers that they had no reason to be so angry. His wife Myrlie once answered the phone and heard a woman's voice say, "What are you trying to do? That nigger husband of yours is going to get himself killed if he doesn't watch his step!" Mrs. Evers retorted, "You must be a fool . . . Hate like that will build up inside you until it poisons you." The caller began to curse.

"Then I heard Medgar's voice on the [extension] telephone," Myrlie Evers recalls. He asked his wife to hang up.

Evers waited as the caller attacked him and blacks in general. Then the woman's husband got on the line and continued the tirade. Eventually, the conversation cooled off, and Evers said goodbye in a friendly voice. He then turned to his wife.

"Myrlie," he said, "don't ever do what you did. If you can't take it, just put the phone down . . . You can sometimes win them over if you are just patient enough."

Medgar Evers (left), the first full-time field secretary for the NAACP in Mississippi, sits next to NAACP officials Ruby Hurley and Gloster Current.

"Through the telephone calls and threats, as well as editorials in the newspapers," Mrs. Evers said years later, whites "were saying that this was simply not a time for this kind of organization—that it was going to do more harm to blacks than good. Blacks, on the other hand, were afraid for the most part—afraid of losing jobs, afraid of being hurt, afraid of being killed. So for [Medgar or] any one person trying to organize it was a very difficult task, because you were dealing with almost insurmountable odds against eliminating the fear from black people's hearts and getting them to become actively involved. I think of how even some of our classmates would see Medgar coming and cross the street . . . We would go door to door to some of the teachers' homes, and talk to them about joining the NAACP, and they'd say, 'No way, I'll lose my job.' The only black newspaper [in Jackson] was very negative about Medgar. He was called a young upstart, wet behind the ears, and someone who would never be able to pull together black people because they had better sense than being involved with an organization like the NAACP."

After the Supreme Court's *Brown* decision in 1954, white segregationists in Mississippi hardened their stance. Not only did they refuse to integrate the schools, they also altered the state constitution to permit Mississippi officials to close schools to avoid desegregation. The state legislature also outlawed common-law marriage. That meant that many black children were suddenly considered illegitimate in the eyes of the state and therefore, under another Mississippi law, ineligible to attend public school. To avoid the NAACP lawsuit on school integration, the legislature banned "barratry," which is the offense of frequently stirring up lawsuits and legal quarrels.

Many of the state's prominent bankers, lawyers, doctors, and politicians joined the white Citizens' Council. "There was concern about inter-racial dating, to be perfectly frank," said William Simmons, then editor of the organization's newspaper. "The Citizens' Councils were formed in the summer of 1954 following the *Brown v. Board of Education* decision, for the reason that it dealt directly with education and parents were very concerned about their children, about the effect it would have on them . . . The strategy of the Citizens' Council during the year following the U.S. Supreme Court decision was to delay, to delay, to delay . . ."

In support of the white Citizens' Council, the state legislatue created the Sovereignty Commission, whose sole purpose was to preserve Mississippi's "sovereign right" to maintain a segregated society. It was later revealed that, each month, the commission funneled $5,000 in taxpayers' money into the aggressively racist Citizens' Council.

Medgar Evers worked with local leaders of the NAACP, including Amzie Moore, Rev. George Lee, Gus Courts, C. C. Bryant, and Aaron Henry. But violence stymied their progress. Lee was killed in 1955, and Courts was shot shortly thereafter and later driven out of the state.

In July 1960, Robert Parris Moses, a twenty-six-year-old teacher from New York, was traveling through Mississippi for the Student Nonviolent Coordinating Committee, recruiting people for a SNCC conference that October. During the trip, Moses met Amzie Moore, a respected black businessman and local NAACP leader who was frustrated by the association's lack of success. The student sit-ins in the South had begun just a few months earlier, and both men were intrigued by SNCC's direct-action techniques. Moore encouraged Moses to bring more SNCC workers to Mississippi.

The following summer, Moses returned to the Magnolia State with a team of SNCC workers. C. C. Bryant, head of the NAACP in the town of McComb, invited SNCC to begin a month-long campaign to register blacks there. Bryant's overture to the student-run group was in keeping with the attitude of several local NAACP chapters, which often welcomed help from others. But the association's national office in New York was less enthusiastic. The various civil rights organizations often found themselves competing for the limited funds available from supporters. They also vied frequently for the attention of the national media. The NAACP sought to make Mississippi *its* project, and the organization did not welcome the participation of other groups. Medgar Evers was pleased to accept assistance with the NAACP's voter registration efforts, but he had to do so quietly.

Thus the NAACP, an organization dedicated to ending discrimination through the legal and political systems, hoped to become the leading civil rights group in a state that recognized neither the authority of the law nor the sanctity of the courts. A further irony was that the association, whose members were mainly middle-class blacks, would find few such people to work with in Mississippi, the nation's poorest state.

"The strategy of the Citizens' Council was to delay, to delay, to delay..."

SNCC's Bob Moses, together with C. C. Bryant and NAACP member Webb Owens, planned a voter registration education program in McComb. They offered a weekly class teaching black people how to register. To ensure that the project was financially self-supporting, they accepted no money from SNCC. Instead they solicited small donations—often just five or ten dollars each—from local supporters. To save money, SNCC workers from out of state stayed with local NAACP members, and people volunteered their cars and their time.

By early August, other SNCC workers had arrived in McComb. Reginald Robinson and John Hardy walked door to door, trying to convince black residents to take the registration test. Many of the region's black people, eager to participate in the movement, asked the McComb activists to help them set up voter registration schools. As enthusiasm for the project grew, still more SNCC workers arrived, sent by the organization's headquarters in Atlanta.

But as the voter registration project burgeoned, so did white resistance. Bob Moses was arrested as he tried to accompany three people to the registrar's office in Liberty, the county seat. A week later he was beaten up by Billy Jack Caston, a cousin of the local sheriff.

In nearby Amite County, Moses met with NAACP leader E. W. Steptoe, whose tarpaper shack served as the movement's base of operations there. Steptoe's neighbor, farmer Herbert Lee, was a father of nine but prosperous enough to own a car. Lee agreed to drive Moses and Steptoe around the county during their door-to-door campaign.

On August 18, SNCC worker Marion Barry arrived in McComb. A strong proponent of direct action, Barry set up a workshop for black teenagers to teach them nonviolent protest methods. Some of the youngsters had been helping Moses with the voter registration drive and felt frustrated that they themselves were too young to vote. Through Barry's workshop, they now saw another way to participate. Two of the teenagers, Curtis Hayes and Hollis Watkins, staged a sit-in at the town's whites-only Woolworth's lunch counter—an unprecedented act in that rural county. The boys were arrested and sentenced to thirty days in jail.

A few weeks later, fifteen-year-old Brenda Travis and five older high-school students held another sit-in. Travis was expelled from Burgland High School and sentenced to a year in a state school for delinquents. The older students were sentenced to eight months in jail.

Then, on September 25, Herbert Lee, the man who had driven Moses and Steptoe around Amite County, was killed by a bullet wound to the head. Ten days later, Moses and other SNCC workers marched with more than a hundred black high-school students through the streets of McComb, protesting the brutal killing and the release of the white man accused of his murder. When the marchers stopped to pray on the steps of city hall, they were arrested. Upon their release on bond, Bob Moses and SNCC organizer Chuck McDew started what they called Nonviolent High School, offering classes for the children who had been expelled from Burgland High after the protests. Within a few weeks the SNCC workers were arrested on charges of contributing to the delinquency of minors and sentenced to four months in jail.

C. C. Bryant, the local NAACP head who had initiated the SNCC voter registration project, had not anticipated murder, mayhem, and the arrests of children. In October, he asked the NAACP's national headquarters in New York to "condemn the SNCC operation and have it moved out." Medgar Evers also thought that the McComb organizers had overextended themselves. By going beyond voting rights and staging sit-ins and protest demonstrations, SNCC had started a battle it could not win, at least not in 1961.

After their release from jail, in December, the SNCC organizers left McComb. While they had been in prison, others from SNCC had launched the Albany, Georgia, campaign. The young organization's experiences in both communities would provide them with the skills they needed to launch a major offensive in Mississippi two years later.

While the McComb project was developing, Medgar Evers and NAACP attorney Constance Baker Motley were trying to help James Meredith break down racial barriers at the all-white University of Mississippi—the same institution whose law school had rejected Evers seven years earlier.

Meredith had approached Evers in January 1961. Then a sophomore at all-black Jackson State, Meredith wanted to transfer to Ole Miss. Evers suggested he write to Thurgood Marshall, the head of the NAACP Legal Defense Fund. Meredith did so, explaining that he was a Mississippi native with nine years of military service (he had been a staff sergeant in the U.S. Air Force) and twelve college courses to his credit. Marshall told Evers he was interested in the case, but wanted more information from Meredith. He didn't want to invest the NAACP's time and money if the young man's academic record wasn't strong enough to qualify him for admission.

As they worked on the Meredith case, Evers and the NAACP also targeted other strongholds of segregation in Mississippi. In Leake County, they sought integration of the elementary and secondary schools. In Jackson, Evers had called the Chamber of Commerce in December 1960 to request that blacks be hired as clerks and cashiers in the downtown stores. When his request was denied, he immediately launched a consumer boycott of the city's shopping district. The strike faltered, however, when Evers was reluctant to back it up with picketing. He lacked the bail money he would need if protesters were arrested, and there were no black bail bondsmen in the state. White bondsmen, he knew, would not help get black civil rights activists out of jail.

Evers also won a lawsuit to desegregate Jackson's privately owned buses, and was pursuing a suit seeking integration of the city's parks.

James Meredith, attempting to register at the University of Mississippi, is stopped by Lieutenant Governor Paul Johnson. Though ordered by a federal court to admit Meredith, the government of the state of Mississippi refused.

Meanwhile, white supremacists continued to strike back. A black soldier was beaten unconscious when he demanded service in a Meridian, Mississippi, restaurant. In Taylorsville, another black soldier refused to sit in the back of a bus and was dragged from the vehicle and pummeled to death by the town policeman. In court the accused officer claimed self-defense, alleging that the man had tried to strike him. The grand jury did not indict him.

But of all the civil rights efforts then underway in Mississippi, James Meredith's case attracted the most attention. For whites, Ole Miss was a preserve of traditional southern life—a life that excluded blacks. Located in the town of Oxford, it was a social beehive, the home of the state's premier football team and twenty-five fraternities and sororities. In four years the institution had produced two Miss Americas, two Miss Mississippis and one Miss Dixie. Whites would no sooner allow a black youngster to attend the university than they would let a black woman enter one of those beauty pageants. The school's mascot was "Colonel Reb," a caricature of a Confederate Army general.

On September 3, 1962, a federal district court ordered the University of Mississippi to admit James Meredith. Governor Ross Barnett, an ardent segregationist, went on statewide television to make his stand against the ruling. At the time, the governor's popularity was sagging; the crowd had jeered him at an Ole Miss football game the year before, after a scandal involving gold-plated faucets in the bathrooms of the governor's mansion. Now Barnett intended to seize on a political issue that could galvanize every segregationist in the state.

The governor began his television speech by terming the time at hand "a solemn hour . . . the moment of our greatest crisis since the War Between the States." The crisis, he said, resulted from "an ambitious federal government employing naked and arbitrary power." He appealed to white racial pride and fear, arguing, "There is no case in history where the Caucasian race has survived social integration . . . We must either submit to the unlawful dictate of the federal government or stand up like men and tell them, 'Never.'"

The next day, a headline in the *Jackson Daily News* declared, "Ross Risks Jail to Halt Mixing." Mississippi's United States Senator James O. Eastland vowed, "I certainly support him to the limit." But James Meredith told Evers and others not to worry. He believed he had widespread support among white Mississippians who felt the state had gone too far.

While state politicians generally cheered Barnett, Congressman Frank Smith accused the governor of leading the state "down another blind alley . . . Whether we like it or not the question of state vs. federal law was settled one hundred years ago." In the university town of Oxford, eight ministers issued a statement urging that "the entire population act in a manner consistent with Christian teaching concerning the value and dignity of man." The university's Episcopal rector, Duncan M. Gray, Jr., asked that politicians and students exercise "the leadership necessary to assure the peaceful admission of James Meredith to the university."

On Saturday, September 29, 1962, at an Ole Miss football game in Jackson, Governor Barnett addressed the crowd at halftime. The "Rebels" were leading Kentucky by a score of 7-0. The audience waved thousands of Confederate flags. "I love Mississippi," said the governor. "I love her people, her customs! And I love and respect her heritage." At each pause in his speech, the crowd chanted. "Never, Never, Never, Never, N-o-o-o Never." "Ross's standing like Gibraltar. He shall never falter." "Ask us what we say, it's to hell with Bobby K." "Never shall our emblem go, from Colonel Reb to Old Black Joe."

Despite his hardcore public stance, Barnett was privately negotiating with the Kennedys. The federal government was determined to see James Meredith enrolled at Ole Miss. On Sunday, September 30, the governor called the White House and suggested that the Army troops slated to escort Meredith to the university draw their guns and "force" the state to allow the young man to register. Barnett could thus save face with the segregationists and shift the political blame onto the Kennedys. The president refused. He threatened to reveal that Barnett had been negotiating with his administration. The governor begged the president not to do that, and Kennedy then proposed bringing Meredith to the campus that very night. Kennedy would announce on television that Meredith was already at Ole Miss, in hopes of defusing the situation. Kennedy had already authorized the use of federal troops if necessary, and the Mississippi National Guard was at the ready. By 4 P.M., 123 deputy marshals, 316 border patrolmen, and 97 federal prison guards had moved into place at the Lyceum, the campus administration building.

Around 6 P.M., the plane carrying James Meredith landed at Oxford's airport. He was secretly escorted to a room in Baxter Hall on the campus, where he closed the door and picked up a newspaper to read. Twenty-four federal agents guarded the hallway outside. Meanwhile, a rowdy crowd, unaware of Meredith's presence, aimed their fury at the marshals blocking the front door of the Lyceum. They shouted racial slurs and chanted, "Two-four-six-eight, we ain't gonna integrate. We hate Kennedy!"

By 7 P.M., mayhem reigned. A white youth attacked a black military truck driver, spraying him in the face with a fire extinguisher. The rabble threw rocks and bottles and began to overturn cars and smash windows. As the violence escalated, the Mississippi state highway patrolmen drove away. Federal officials anxiously called Governor Barnett, asking him to get the troopers back on the scene. Barnett said he would, but the troopers did not return.

The governor had promised the Kennedys that he would make a televised announcement of the state's compliance with Meredith's enrollment. As the campus violence raged, Barnett faced the cameras. "As governor of the State of Mississippi, I have just been informed by the attorney general of the United States that Meredith has today been placed on the campus of the University of Mississippi . . . ," he said. "I urge all Mississippians and instruct every state official under my command to do everything in their power to preserve peace and to avoid violence in any form."

The governor then added, "Surrounded on all sides by the armed forces and oppressive power of the U.S.A., my courage and commitment do not waver . . . To the officials of the federal government I say, 'Gentlemen, you are trampling on the sovereignty of this great state . . . You are destroying the Constitution of this great nation . . . May God have mercy on your souls . . . '"

Unaware of the governor's words, President Kennedy prepared to make his own television speech to the nation. As he did so, the federal marshals on campus began firing tear gas. "Americans are free . . . to disagree with the law, but not to disobey it," the president said. "For in any government of laws and not of men, no man, however prominent and powerful, and no matter however unruly and boisterous, is entitled to defy a court of law . . . You have a new opportunity to show that you are men of patriotism and integrity. For the most effective means of upholding the law is not the state policemen or the marshals or the National Guard. It is you."

On campus, the rioting was out of control. Shortly after the president finished his speech, the body of French reporter Paul Guihard was discovered. Guihard had been shot in the back at close range. Ray Gunter, an Oxford resident who was watching the mayhem, was shot dead at about 11 P.M. John McLaurin, Barnett's representative at Ole Miss, recalled that night. "If Governor Barnett had gotten on the radio and asked for people to come to Oxford to defend the state of Mississippi," he said, "I felt like the road wouldn't have carried all the people that would've come in through Mississippi, Alabama, Arkansas, Tennessee, and Louisiana."

Governor Ross Barnett on the campus of Ole Miss.

Around 10 P.M., Deputy Attorney General Nicholas Katzenbach called the White House from Oxford to say that federal troops would be needed to squelch the rioting. Army Secretary Cyrus Vance ordered troops at an air station in Tennessee to move in. At 11:45, the president called Barnett again to demand that the highway patrolmen return to the scene. Barnett agreed, but by midnight the order had not been issued. The governor went on the radio and declared, "I call on Mississippi to keep the faith and courage. We will never surrender."

Hours had passed by the time the army troops finally landed at Oxford from Memphis. At 3:55 A.M. the president ordered them to move immediately to Ole Miss. In his message to the Army commander, Kennedy termed the incident "the worst thing" he had seen in his nearly 45 years. It was 4:30 A.M. before the president, assured that the savagery was over, went to bed. A force of several hundred federal personnel was in Oxford. One-hundred-sixty marshals had been injured and twenty-eight had been shot. Two men were dead. Two hundred people had been arrested, less than a quarter of them University of Mississippi students.

At 7:55 A.M., just hours after the violence had been quelled, James Meredith walked across the now-quiet campus to the Lyceum and registered as a student. He met with no resistance. At 9 A.M. he began his first class, Colonial American History.

Meredith's ordeal did not end that morning. Federal marshals stayed on campus to guard him. Often he met with harassment, as when a group of angry whites surrounded him in the dining hall. But he also met with support. On one occasion, seven white students defiantly sat down at his table to share a meal with him. Medgar Evers visited Meredith on weekends to assess the situation for the NAACP. In the summer of 1963, James Meredith graduated from the University of Mississippi with a bachelor's degree in political science. Pinned to his gown he wore a "Never" button—turned upside down.

The NAACP, particularly Medgar Evers and Constance Baker Motley, had won the esteem of many black Mississippians. John Salter, a civil rights leader with the NAACP's Youth Council in Jackson, wrote later that "almost every black in Mississippi knew that James Meredith was in the University of Mississippi, that Ross Barnett and the Citizens' Council had lost a major round, that the federal government would, in some instances at least, constructively involve itself all the way, even down in Mississippi. For the first time in their lives, Mississippi blacks had seen a very tangible civil rights victory for one of their own, and if there was fear within themselves, there was no longer quite as much apathy. There was a new interest in the battle against segregation and discrimination, especially among youth."

By the end of 1962, the civil rights climate in Mississippi had changed dramatically. The NAACP's success at the University of Mississippi added to an emerging sense of hope and possibility among blacks.

Each October, the Mississippi State Fair was held in Jackson. Traditionally, the first week of the fair was for whites only, after which blacks were allowed in for only three days. Before the 1962 fair, though, Evers and Salter's NAACP Youth Council organized a boycott, hoping that Meredith's success at Ole Miss would embolden blacks to participate. The story of the impending strike became front-page news. Police surrounded the fairgrounds, anticipating violence, but none came. As usual, marching bands of black high-school students heralded the opening day of the blacks-only part of the event. But instead of marching onto the grounds, they remained outside, bolstering the boycott participants. Evers later estimated that the boycott was sixty percent effective, an impressive measure for rural Mississippi.

At Christmas dinner, 1962, Medgar Evers told a group of friends that he believed Mississippi was ready for a large-scale civil rights movement of its own, much like the one in Albany, Georgia. But his optimism was tempered by the certainty that a hard fight lay ahead. "The white man won't change easily," he said. "Some of these people are going to fight hard. And more of our people could get killed."

In the spring of 1963, Evers revived his campaign against segregation in the city of Jackson. In letters to the governor, to Jackson's mayor, Allen C. Thompson, and to the city's Chamber of Commerce, he wrote that "the NAACP is determined to put an end to all forms of racial discrimination in Jackson . . . We shall use all legal means of protest—picketing, marches, mass meetings, litigation . . . We call upon President John F. Kennedy and on other national leaders who share our love of freedom to use their good offices in helping to get these discussions started."

In reaction to the letter, Mayor Thompson told store owners, "Nobody is going to come here and tell our businessmen what to do." He said he would not talk, much less negotiate, with "any member of the NAACP, CORE, or any other racial agitators." On May 12, the mayor made a televised appeal to Jackson's black citizens not to cooperate with Evers. "You live in a beautiful city . . . ," he said. "You have twenty-four-hour protection by the police department . . . or suppose you need the fire department? . . . You live in a city where you can work, where you can make a comfortable living . . . Now with these privileges that you have come certain responsibilities . . . Do not listen to false rumors which will stir you, worry you and upset you. Refuse to pay attention to these outside agitators who are only interested in getting money out of you, using you for their own purposes and who will advocate destroying everything that you and the white people working side by side [with you] have built up over the last hundred years . . . There will be no meetings with the NAACP or any other such group."

A week later, with the help of the Federal Communications Commission, Evers made a televised response to the mayor. "I speak as a native Mississippian," he said. "I was educated in Mississippi schools and served overseas in our nation's armed forces in the war against Hitlerism and fascism . . . Most southern people . . . usually think of the NAACP as a 'northern outside group' . . . Now the mayor says that if the so-called outside agitators would leave us alone everything would be all right. This has always been the position of those who would deny Negro citizens their constitutional rights . . . never in its history has the South as a region, without outside pressure, granted the Negro his citizenship rights . . . Tonight the Negro knows from his radio and television . . . about the new free nation in Africa and knows that a Congo native can be a locomotive engineer, but in Jackson he cannot even drive a garbage truck. Then he looks about his home community and what does he see, to quote our mayor, in this 'progressive, beautiful, friendly, prosperous city with an exciting future?' He sees a city where Negro citizens are refused admittance to the city auditorium and the coliseum;

"Tonight the Negro . . . knows about the new free nation in Africa and know that a Congo native can be a locomotive engineer, but in Jackson he cannot even drive a garbage truck."

his children refused a ticket to a good movie in a downtown theater; his wife and children refused service at a lunch counter in a downtown store where they trade . . . He sees a city of over 150,000, of which forty percent is Negro, in which there is not a single Negro policeman or policewoman, school crossing guard, fireman, clerk, stenographer . . . He sees local hospitals which segregate Negro patients . . . The mayor spoke of the twenty-four-hour police protection we have . . . There are questions in the minds of many Negroes whether we have twenty-four hours of protection or twenty-four hours of harassment . . . "

Evers' impassioned speech stirred both blacks and whites in Jackson. "You could sense it in the smiles of white people on the street," Myrlie Evers wrote later, "the reports of unusual politeness in the shops and stores, in the sudden, quiet removal of racial signs at the bus depot and train station. Most impressive of all were the telephone calls, some from callers who admitted they were white, nearly all commending the speech . . . Few whites dared give their names."

On May 28, the NAACP began sit-ins at the Woolworth's store downtown. Evers himself did not take part; his associates feared that he was too vulnerable a target for segregationist retaliation. At the lunch counter, thugs attacked the sit-in participants, including John Salter and Tougaloo College student Anne Moody, throwing pepper in their eyes and spraying them with paint.[*] The incident drew national television coverage, prompting Mayor Thompson to negotiate with a group of black ministers. He agreed to hire some black policemen and school-crossing guards. Blacks would also be allowed to use the city's all-white parks and libraries, and school desegregation, he pledged, would begin soon. But by nightfall the white Citizens' Council and members of the state legislature had successfully pressured the mayor to renounce the deal. Over the radio, he denied ever making any settlement with Jackson's black community, but he promised to work with them.

That night, someone threw a Molotov cocktail at Medgar Evers' home. As tensions grew, SNCC workers came to town to offer training sessions on how to conduct sit-ins. Two days after the bombing, some students at Lanier High School began to sing movement songs on the school lawn during their lunch break. Hundreds of other students soon joined them. Police officers with attack dogs arrived and began to beat the students with clubs. Evers called the United States Justice Department to complain. Later that week, students conducting a protest march downtown were clubbed, arrested, and taken to the state fairground, which had been transformed into an open-air jail.

*see photograph on p. 134.

Evers wanted to respond to the arrests by mounting massive protest demonstrations, but the NAACP warned him that it could not afford to supply bail money indefinitely. The board of directors in New York wanted to concentrate on court suits; they told Field Secretary Evers to stick to voter registration and membership drives. Frustrated, Evers canceled his plans for stepped-up demonstrations. He decided to try to raise money on his own, through rallies and concerts. Singer Lena Horne agreed to give a benefit performance in Jackson.

On June 7, Horne addressed an NAACP rally in Jackson and sang in concert later that night for an audience of 3,500. Then Evers spoke to the crowd. "It's not enough just to sit here tonight and voice your approval and clap your hands and shed your tears and sing and then go out and do nothing about this struggle," he said. "Freedom has never been free . . . I love my children and I love my wife with all my heart. And I would die, and die gladly, if that would make a better life for them."

Five days later, on June 12, Myrlie Evers sat at home watching President Kennedy on television. Her husband was still at work. She had spoken to him on the phone three times that day and been struck by the way he insisted in each conversation, "I want you to know how much I love you."

On television, the president said, "The forces of frustration and discord are burning in every city, North and South . . . Where legal remedies are not at hand, redress is sought in the streets in demonstrations, parades, and protests which create tensions—and threaten lives. We face therefore a moral crisis as a country and a people. It is time to act in the Congress, in your state and local legislative body, and, above all, in your daily lives."

After the president's speech, Mrs. Evers lay down and dozed off. She didn't hear her husband's car until just after midnight. As the car door slammed, the sound of gunfire pierced the air. Myrlie Evers screamed, and neighbors came out. Medgar Evers had been shot.

Neighbors laid Evers on a mattress and drove him to the hospital. He died later that night. A black doctor who was a friend of the family came to tell Mrs. Evers that he had stayed with her husband until the end. When a white nurse in the emergency room had moved slowly, the doctor had shouted at her, "This man is Medgar Evers, field secretary of the NAACP!" The doctor assured Mrs. Evers that everything possible had been done to try to save her husband.

The next night, Mrs. Evers spoke at a movement rally in Jackson. "Nothing can bring Medgar back, but the cause can live on," she told the crowd. "It was

The Assassination of Medgar Evers:

An Interview with Myrlie Evers

To be born black and to live in Mississippi was to say that your life wasn't worth much. Medgar knew full well when he assumed the position of field director for the NAACP that there were going to be threats and that his life would possibly be taken from him. During the period when the economic boycotts were so successful and we were having rallies every day and every night, it became evident that Medgar was a target because he was the leader. The whole mood of white Mississippi was that if Medgar Evers were eliminated, the problem would be solved. Our home was firebombed, we received threats on almost an hourly basis at home, he received threats through the mail. It was a life of never knowing when that bullet was going to hit. It was something that Medgar knew, but as he said to me and to his followers in the mass meetings, we can't let that stop us. There was a job to be done.

. . . In the early years, it was something I really fought. I could not give full support to Medgar's work because I wanted him for us, I wanted our lives to go on for a long period of time. But I realized his total commitment to the cause, I realized that he would not be happy unless he were giving his all, unless he were leading the movement. And we came to realize, in those last few days, last few months, that our time was short; it was simply in the air. You knew that something was going to happen, and the logical person for it to happen to was Medgar. It certainly brought us closer during that time. As

Myrlie Evers bids farewell to her slain husband.

a matter of fact, we didn't talk; we didn't have to. We communicated without words. It was a touch, it was a look, it was holding each other, it was music playing—and I used to try to reassure him and tell him, "Nothing is going to happen to you. The FBI is here. Everybody knows you. You're in the press; they wouldn't dare do anything to you." Medgar's approach was a much more realistic one, and he would say, "Honey, you've got to be strong. I want you to take care of my children. It probably won't be too long."

. . . Medgar was an absolutely marvelous father. He could talk to the children and tell them what was happening, and he devised a game with them where they decided what was the safest place in the house to hide if something hap-

pened. The children made a decision with their father that the bathtub was safest. They could not understand everything, but they were well aware that their father's life was in danger. At their young ages—three, eight, and nine—they worried constantly about that.

I recall the last day that we had together. Medgar told the children how much he loved them. He turned to me and said, "I'm so tired, I don't know if I can go on, but I have to." And I rushed toward him and hugged him and told him, "It's going to be all right." We clung to each other. He walked out the door, and he came back in and said, "I love you. I'll call you." During that day, he called two or three times, which was a little unusual with all of the activity that was going on.

Late that night, he came home. The children were still up. I was asleep across the bed and we heard the motor of the car coming in and pulling into the driveway. We heard him get out of the car and the car door slam, and in that same instant, we heard the loud gunfire. The children fell to the floor, as he had taught them to, and I made a run for the front door, turned on the light, and there he was. The bullet had pushed him forward, as I understand, and the strong man that he was, he had his keys in his hand, and had pulled his body around the rest of the way, to the door. There he lay. I screamed, and people came out. Our next door neighbor fired a gun, as he said, to try to frighten anyone away, and I knew then that that was it.

. . . People from the neighborhood began to gather, and there were some whose color happened to be white. I don't think I have ever hated as much in my life as I did at that moment. I can recall wanting to have a machine gun in my hands and to stand there and mow them all down. I can't explain the depth of my hatred at that point . . . Medgar's influence has directed me in terms of dealing with that hate. He told me that hate was not a healthy thing.

. . . Two trials were held for the accused assassin of Medgar. Both ended in hung juries. The whole case was very interesting insofar as the way the ac-cused killer was treated. He had a large cell that was open for him to come and go as he wanted to. He had television sets, he had typewriters, he had almost all the comforts of home. This man was also accorded a major parade along the route of the highway on his way home. People had banners that were waved, welcoming the hero home. The accused killer also made a statement to the press that he was glad to have gotten rid of "varmints." The governor, Ross Barnett, actually made a visit to the accused during the first trial. He walked in the door when I was on the witness stand—stood, looked at me, and went over to the accused killer, sat down, shook his hand.

I had mixed emotions about it all . . . a white man had been brought to trial for the murder of a black. That was a step forward, a very small one, but a step forward. However, the fact that there were two trials, that this man was treated as a hero, and that everything was dropped, still said to me that black is black. Even today, the justice that is accorded other ethnic groups in the United States is still not accorded blacks in Mississippi. We're still fighting for first-class citizenship.

his wish that this movement be one of the most successful that this nation has ever known. We cannot let his death be in vain."

At Evers' funeral, about a thousand black youths spontaneously marched down Capitol Street, the main downtown business route. They were soon joined by many of their elders. Police ordered the crowd to disperse. Instead, rocks and bottles flew. "We want the killer!" people shouted. Police dogs were brought onto the scene as the demonstration became a riot. Then a white man grabbed a police bullhorn and barked, "You're not gonna win anything with bottles and bricks. Hold it . . . My name is John Doar. I'm from the Justice Department and anyone around here knows I stand for what is right . . . Go on home . . . Let's not have a riot here." Dave Dennis, CORE staff member, helped Doar calm the crowd, which eventually dispersed.

Medgar Evers was buried at Arlington National Cemetery. The following day, his family went to the White House to see President Kennedy. Myrlie Evers wanted to tell Kennedy that she was devastated. She meant to tell the president that her husband had fought in a war for his nation and had returned home a second-class citizen. She wanted to express her anger that he had been killed for trying to defend the constitutional rights of his people. But when Kennedy asked her, "How are you doing?" she could only reply, "Fine, thank you, Mr. President." Kennedy then gave two of the Evers children small gifts—a PT-109 tie clip for Darrell and a medallion with the presidential seal for Rena. He told them they should be proud of their father and their heritage.

Meanwhile, police had arrested a suspect in the shooting: Byron de la Beckwith, a member of the white Citizens' Council in the town of Greenwood, eighty miles from Jackson. The murder weapon belonged to him and his fingerprints were found on the gun's sight, which police had found separately. Officials had also learned from cab drivers that Beckwith had asked for directions to Evers' house.

Despite the compelling evidence, the charges against Beckwith were dropped after two trials ended in hung juries. The acquitted man later ran as a Democratic candidate for the post of lieutenant governor.

After Evers' death, his brother Charles took over his job as field secretary for the NAACP in Jackson. The organization's headquarters made it clear to him that the NAACP worked through the courts and the political system. That meant registering voters.

For years, the authorities had used many devious means to keep blacks from exercising their right to vote. Until 1954, the Mississippi state constitution stipulated that to qualify to vote, a person had to be able to "read or interpret" that

After Evers' funeral, police and demonstrators clashed in the streets of Jackson, Mississippi.

document. Because more and more blacks had been learning to read, however, the state legislature changed the requirement from "read or interpret" to "read *and* interpret." That provision allowed white registrars to judge arbitrarily whether a black person met the test. Most often, of course, blacks "failed"—even some people with doctoral degrees.

Segregationists often insisted that they were not opposed to blacks voting, but were concerned that poorly educated blacks might be exploited by unscrupulous politicians. Southern blacks, maintained William Simmons of the Citizens' Council, were often "not asked to vote as Americans but as blacks. Now, there has been some history in the South of black 'block voting.' Most often it has been connected with political machines of generally a corrupt nature. I can mention two: the E. H. Crump machine in Memphis, Tennessee, and the [Huey] Long Machine in Louisiana . . . And part of their power was a manipulable black block vote. One could see this coming about . . . "

On November 22, 1963, President John F. Kennedy was assassinated in Dallas.

On November 22, l963, President Kennedy was assassinated. Five days later, Lyndon Baines Johnson addressed a joint session of Congress as the nation's thirty-sixth president. "No memorial or eulogy could more eloquently honor President Kennedy's memory than the earliest possible passage of the civil rights bill for which he fought," said the new president. "We have talked for one hundred years or more. Yes, it is time now to write the next chapter—and to write it in books of law." The Civil Rights Act that Kennedy had sent to Congress shortly before the march on Washington was the most comprehensive piece of legislation addressing discrimination since Reconstruction. Even with Johnson's support, it seemed unlikely that the bill would make it through both houses of Congress without substantial compromises.

The Kennedy administration and the Justice Department had crafted the bill to outlaw racial segregation and discrimination in all publicly or privately owned facilities that were open to the general public. But the legislation barely addressed the issue that many black leaders considered most crucial—the right to vote.

For years the NAACP had been working to help black Mississippians exercise their right to vote, with little success. In early 1962, SNCC had sought funding for a voter registration campaign from the Voter Education Project. "We have people strategically located in each of the five Congressional districts [in Mississippi]," SNCC's application read. "The field workers . . . are going to live with the people, develop their own leaders and teach them the process of registration and the effective use of the franchise." SNCC received a grant of $5,000 from the Voter Education Project.

Amzie Moore (second from right) had the original idea of bringing activists from outside Mississippi to help organize that state. With Bob Moses (far left), Moore helped organize the volunteers' activities. Julian Bond stands next to Moses; next to Moore are Hollis Watkins (left) and E. W. Steptoe.

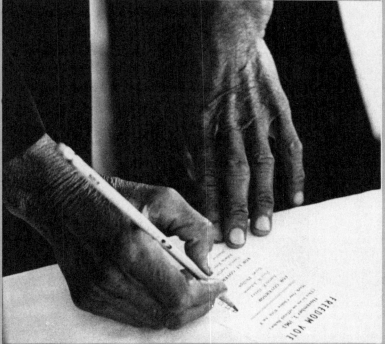

As a demonstration of interest (and a rehearsal for the real thing), COFO launched the Freedom Vote in the fall of 1963.

Also in 1962, several local civil rights groups in Mississippi joined forces with SNCC, CORE, the NAACP, and the SCLC, forming an umbrella group called the Council of Federated Organizations (COFO). COFO's first major move was to launch a project it dubbed the Freedom Vote, during the fall of 1963. The project had two goals: to demonstrate to Mississippi whites and the federal government that, despite segregationist claims to the contrary, blacks were indeed interested in voting, and to provide practice in casting the ballot to people denied that right all their lives. As in most southern states, virtually all political power in Mississippi rested with Democrats. Blacks, excluded from the political process, could not vote in the state's gubernatorial election that November. Instead, SNCC offered blacks the Freedom Vote, a mock election in which unofficial "Freedom Party" candidates challenged the Democratic and Republican hopefuls. The Freedom Party was open to all citizens, regardless of race. For governor, the Freedom Party candidate was Aaron Henry, a black pharmacist from Clarksdale who was the chairman of COFO and the state president of the NAACP. The Reverend Edwin King, a white chaplain at all-black Tougaloo College, was Henry's running mate for lieutenant governor.

To help get out the Freedom Vote, Bob Moses, the project's chief field organizer, and Allard Lowenstein, who developed the idea, brought in sixty white students from Yale and Stanford universities for two weeks of campaigning. The young northerners walked door to door in black neighborhoods, spreading word of the practice election. Despite many arrests and beatings, the workers carried on. "What we have discovered is that the people who run Mississippi today can only do so by force," said Lowenstein. "They cannot allow free elections in Mississippi, because if they did, they wouldn't run Mississippi." On the day of the mock election, 93,000 people cast their "votes" at tables set up on the sidewalks and in barbershops and beauty parlors. Henry and King won handily.

The Freedom Vote had proved an effective consciousness-raising tool, but it was only the beginning. "Eventually, black people were going to be electing people to office—black people to office," said Bob Moses. "But it wasn't a thought in their mind at that time. So what you had to do was . . . use the voter registration drive as a way of preparing them for what was coming next . . . the actual election of people to these offices."

On the heels of this successful project, COFO decided to launch an even more ambitious voting rights project the following summer. Inviting hundreds of students from across the nation to participate, SNCC workers planned a massive registration drive throughout Mississippi. Some SNCC staffers opposed the idea, arguing that bringing in so many white outsiders would only undermine the power of the local blacks. But some black Mississippians felt differently. Fannie Lou Hamer, a sharecropper on a cotton plantation who had become deeply involved in the Freedom Vote, heartily endorsed the idea of inviting energetic, idealistic young people back to Mississippi. "The people, by and large, wanted the students to come back . . . ," remembers SNCC's Bob Moses, "so we were at loggerheads . . . and I guess what I felt was that . . . there were larger things happening in the country, there was the 1964 Civil Rights Act. Mississippi was reacting to that, and we were feeling the backlash . . . growing in Mississippi against gains [for blacks] that were made nationally but which were not having any immediate effect in Mississippi . . . burning churches, murder . . . I felt in that context I had to step in . . . between the staff and the people we were working with. And so that's how the decision was made to actually invite the students down for the summer of '64."

"We are going to

Mississippi in force."

The project became known as "Freedom Summer." Unlike the Freedom Vote of the previous fall and winter, the new project sought to educate and register black voters for the real elections of 1964—a presidential election year. In February 1964, Bob Moses went to Stanford University to recruit students for Freedom Summer. Its goals, he told them, were to expand black voter registration in the state; to organize a legally constituted "Freedom Democratic Party" that would challenge the whites-only Mississippi Democratic party; to establish "freedom schools" to teach reading and math to black children in a state where there was no mandatory attendance law and black children more often worked in the fields than went to school; and finally, to open community centers where indigent blacks could obtain legal and medical assistance.

Civil rights activists looked forward to the summer with great anticipation. "Nineteen-sixty-four could really be the year for Mississippi," said John Lewis, the national chairman of SNCC. "Before the Negro people get the right to vote, there will have to be a massive confrontation . . . We are going to Mississippi in force." The segregationists, however, were also preparing. "This is it," said Jackson mayor Allen Thompson. "They are not bluffing, and we are not bluffing. We are going to be ready for them . . . They won't have a chance."

The mayor expanded the city's police force from 200 to more than 300 officers. He purchased 250 shotguns and a 13,000-pound armored personnel carrier called "Thompson's tank," which had steel walls and bulletproof windshields. He had oversized paddy wagons built, brought in two-and-a-half-ton searchlight trucks, and arranged to use the fairgrounds as a makeshift prison. The state legislature approved a request from the governor to hire 700 additional state highway patrolmen. The lawmakers also made it a felony to distribute flyers calling for boycotts and made it illegal to operate a school without a county government permit, outlawing the planned freedom schools.

The state seemed to be girding for war, and indeed the Jackson newspapers viewed the upcoming Freedom Summer project as an "invasion." Charles J. Brenner of the National States Rights Party wrote to SNCC's James Forman, "You are right about one thing. This is going to be a long, hot summer. But the 'heat' will be applied to the race-mixing trash by the decent people . . . When your Communist-oriented goons get to Mississippi, I hope they get their just dues . . ."

Forman, executive director of SNCC, went to Oxford, Ohio, where the students selected for the summer project were attending a week-long orientation session at Western College for Women. Three-quarters of the 800 students were white, and about 300 of them were women. Their average age was twenty-one. Each volunteer was required to bring $500 for bail, plus enough cash to cover living expenses, any medical bills they might incur, and transportation home at the end of the summer. Most came from well-off families and were the sons and daughters of professional people. Most hailed from the Northeast, the largest contingent coming from New York State.

Forman warned the volunteers, "I may be killed. You may be killed. The whole staff may go." R. Jess Brown, a black lawyer from Mississippi, told the students, "If you're riding down somewhere, and a cop stops you and starts to put you under arrest, even though you haven't committed any crime, go to jail. Mississippi is not the place to start conducting constitutional law classes for the policemen, many of whom don't have a fifth-grade education."

FBI chief J. Edgar Hoover, on a visit to Mississippi, made it clear that he did not intend to use his agency to "wet-nurse" the students in Mississippi. The FBI, he argued, was an investigative organization, not a protection force. Hoover did not plan to intercede between the COFO people and those who might try to thwart them.

On Saturday, June 20, the first wave of recruits—200 of them—left for Mississippi from Oxford, Ohio. The next day, three civil rights workers, including one of the summer volunteers, were reported missing. The volunteer was Andrew Goodman, a twenty-year-old Queens College student from New York City. He had arrived in the town of Meridian with twenty-four-year-old Michael Schwerner, a white man from Brooklyn, New York, who with his wife Rita had established the Meridian CORE office in January, and CORE worker James Chaney, twenty-one, a black Mississippian. On Sunday the three young men had driven to the town of Lawndale to investigate the burning of a black church there. Around 3 P.M. their blue Ford station wagon was stopped by Deputy Sheriff Cecil Price near the town of Philadelphia, Mississippi. The three were taken to jail in connection with speeding charges, but were released later that night.

Exactly what happened next is not known. But when the men failed to telephone Freedom Summer headquarters, the staff knew they were in trouble. All workers were required to call in at regular intervals, and if they had not done so within fifteen minutes of the appointed time, the project's Jackson office was notified. From there, someone would immediately telephone the local police as well as the FBI and the Justice Department.

Sheriff Lawrence Rainey dismissed the men's disappearance. "If they're missing," he said, "they're just hid somewhere trying to get a lot of publicity out of it, I figure."

The national press now focused its attention on the events in Mississippi. President Johnson met with the parents of Schwerner and Goodman at the White House, but according to the *New York Times* he "did not say what [they] and the parents of other students going to Mississippi that summer wanted to hear—that the federal government would undertake protection of all the students . . . [To do so] would hark all the way back to federal occupation of the South during Reconstruction days, or so officials fear."

Rita Schwerner, wife of the missing Mickey Schwerner, flew to Meridian from Ohio, where she had been training volunteers. "It's tragic," she said, "that white northerners have to be caught up into the machinery of injustice and indifference in the South before the American people register concern. I personally suspect that if Mr. Chaney, who is a [black] native Mississippian, had been alone at the time of the disappearance, that this case, like so many others, . . . would have gone completely unnoticed."

The president sent 200 unarmed sailors to Mississippi to help search for the missing men. They dragged swamps and cut through high grass throughout the countryside. FBI agents also joined in the hunt.

Although the young men's disappearance cast a cloud of fear over Freedom Summer, only a handful of students decided to quit the project. Said one volunteer to a reporter, "Their disappearance, although it might have been calculated to try and drive people out of the state, had just the opposite effect on me and everyone else. Whenever an incident like this happens . . . everyone reacts the same way.

They become more and more determined to stay in this state and fight the evil system that people have to live under here." His words reflected the SNCC philosophy: When beaten down, get right up again; when intimidated, carry on in the face of fear.

Even as the nation's papers carried daily reports on the search for Chaney, Goodman, and Schwerner, racially motivated violence continued in Mississippi. A black church in the town of Clinton was burned after a white minister taught a Bible class there. Four whites shot at a car carrying Freedom Summer volunteers. Police in Columbus arrested seven workers for distributing information on voter registration. Meanwhile, the sailors and federal agents searching for the three missing men found the bodies of other blacks long missing in the state. The discoveries caused no public outcry, even though the nation was collectively wringing its hands over the missing whites. When bodies were found, recalls Dave Dennis, head of CORE's workers in Mississippi, "as soon as it was determined that they were not the three workers, then those deaths were forgotten."

On July 2, 1964, President Lyndon Johnson signed into law the Civil Rights Act initiated by John Kennedy in 1963. But in the Mississippi Delta, the signing meant little to blacks struggling to survive.

Within a week of the disappearances, President Johnson won a major victory in the Senate. Republican senator Everett Dirksen of Illinois agreed to support cloture and thereby end a filibuster against the 1964 Civil Rights Act begun by Southern segregationists. As Dirksen said, quoting Victor Hugo, "Stronger than all the armies is an idea whose time has come." Johnson's political maneuvering had secured passage of the controversial bill without substantial alterations; he signed it into law on July 2, 1964. But its relevance to the lives of black Mississippians, and to the field workers living with them, seemed slight.

About a thousand volunteers were now working throughout the state, setting up freedom schools and canvassing door to door in an attempt to register voters for the new Mississippi Freedom Democratic Party. All summer long doctors came from around the country, most notably the Northeast, to provide free basic health care to blacks in "freedom clinics." Lawyers from such organizations as the NAACP Legal Defense Fund, the National Lawyers Guild, and the American Jewish Committee, aided by law students, worked in legal clinics in an effort to secure basic rights for local blacks.

The establishment of the Mississippi Freedom Democratic Party (MFDP) proved to be the most compelling aspect of Freedom Summer to the nation at large. SNCC's goal in forming the MFDP—an official, legally constituted political party—was to challenge the hegemony of Mississippi's regular Democratic party, which in practice excluded blacks from membership.

By the end of August, 80,000 blacks had joined the MFDP, although in the process more than a thousand people were arrested over three months. In August, Freedom Summer volunteers began to recruit whites for the party, convincing twenty of them in Biloxi to sign MFDP registration forms.

In addition, blacks of all ages flocked to the freedom schools for lessons in traditional academic subjects and in black history, which many were discovering for the first time. The schools rang with music and laughter, despite the fact that teaching in them was an offense punishable by six months in prison.

Segregationists in Mississippi watched the mostly upper-middle-class white volunteers with disdain. "They were met with a feeling of some curiosity, but mostly resentment," recalls William Simmons, spokesman for the white Citizens' Council. "They fanned out across the state, made a great to-do of breaking up our customs, of flaunting [*sic*] social practices that had been respected by people here over the years. That was the time of the hippies just coming, and many had on hippie uniforms and conducted themselves in hippie ways . . . The arrogance they showed in wanting to reform the whole state . . . created resentment. So to say they were not warmly received and welcomed is perhaps an understatement."

Attorney Joseph Rauh

Throughout the summer, Bob Moses and the MFDP geared up to challenge the state's regular Democratic party. Their prime target was the August Democratic National Convention in Atlantic City, where the party would nominate Lyndon Baines Johnson as its presidential candidate. After the Freedom Vote the previous November, Moses and SNCC, with the help of advisers Ella Baker and Bayard Rustin, had begun asking the Democratic leadership in other states to back them if they contested the legitimacy of the all-white Mississippi delegation to the convention. In February 1964, SNCC held a meeting in Atlanta to draw up plans for the confrontation with the Mississippi Democrats. Almost immediately, the California Democratic Council (a liberal faction within the state party) approved a resolution calling for MFDP delegates, rather than those from the regular party, to represent Mississippi at the national convention. At a meeting of liberal Democrats in Washington, Bob Moses convinced Joseph Rauh, head of the D.C. Democratic Party, vice president of the Americans for Democratic Action (ADA), and general counsel to the United Auto Workers, to work with the group. Rauh promised that "if there's anybody at the Democratic convention challenging the seating of the outlaw Mississippi Democrats, I'll make sure that the challengers are seated."

In April, SNCC opened a Washington office for the MFDP, and in Mississippi the party held its inaugural rally in Jackson, attended by 200 delegates from across the state. Despite the widespread black participation in the Freedom Vote, the contest with the well-established Mississippi Democratic party was going to be a mammoth undertaking. President Johnson backed the regular Democrats to avoid losing their political support.

In June, the names of Fannie Lou Hamer and three other MFDP candidates were on the ballot for the Mississippi Democratic primary as delegates to be sent to Atlantic City. All four lost, but the fledgling party had at least demonstrated to Democratic leaders in other states that the MFDP was a functioning political party, ready for battle. In June, the ADA approved a resolution calling for "rejection of the racist Mississippi Democratic delegation" and favoring the acceptance of the "integrated Freedom Democratic Party." Then the Democrats in both Michigan and New York endorsed the MFDP's delegation to the Atlantic City convention.

In late June, the white leaders of the Mississippi Democrats gave ammunition to the MFDP by adopting a platform opposing civil rights and explicitly rejecting the platform of the national party. Earlier that month, the national organization had ruled that all convention delegates would be required to make a pledge of party loyalty. Now the Old Boys in Mississippi were thumbing their noses at the party's national leaders and making it difficult for the president to continue to back them. But Johnson believed he had little choice. The delegations from five other Southern states were threatening to walk out of the convention if the Mississippi segregationists were not seated.

Johnson instructed Senator Hubert Humphrey, a liberal Minnesota Democrat and long-time ally of the civil rights movement, to defuse the MFDP challenge quietly. Humphrey faced no easy task. The Democratic party delegates from nine states had now pledged their support to the upstart MFDP, and twenty-five Democratic congressmen were also backing the newcomers. The press posed an additional problem. The MFDP challenge threatened to steal the headlines at the convention, since President Johnson's nomination was expected to be routine and undramatic. Complicating Humphrey's assignment was the fact that LBJ had already privately promised Mississippi governor Paul Johnson that the MFDP would not be seated at the convention, and that if the all-white Mississippi delegation refused to swear its party loyalty in Atlantic City, at least three of the delegates would be seated anyway.

On August 4, just eighteen days before the start of the Democratic National Convention, the bodies of Chaney, Goodman, and Schwerner were discovered in an earthen dam on a farm a few miles from the town of Philadelphia, Mississippi.

Acting on a tip from an informant reportedly paid $30,000, the FBI had obtained a search warrant and used a bulldozer to rip into the base of the recently built structure. The three young men had been killed with .38-caliber bullets, and the skull of Chaney, the one black victim, had been fractured in a savage beating. The national press corps descended on the state.

Mississippi segregationists were unrepentant. "When people leave any section of the country and go into another section looking for trouble," said Congressman Arthur Winstead, "they usually find it."

As the families and compatriots of the victims mourned their deaths, the parents of the men expressed their wish that the three be buried side by side. That, however, was forbidden by Mississippi's segregation laws. James Chaney was buried alone in a segregated cemetery.

Rev. Edward King and Aaron Henry, the two MFDP delegates the Johnson administration selected to represent the group as delegates-at-large.

It wasn't until December that the FBI made any arrests in connection with the killings. Taken into custody were twenty-one white Mississippians, including Deputy Sheriff Cecil Price, the man who had stopped the three workers for speeding shortly before their disappearance. Although charges against the men were subsequently dropped in state court, six of the accused were later sent to jail for violating federal civil rights laws.

With the national news media focusing on events in Mississippi just before the convention's start, President Johnson worried that delegates from other states would be swayed to support the MFDP. In an attempt to stave off that possibility, he privately warned his party that a chaotic Democratic convention might ultimately benefit the campaign of the conservative Republican nominee, Senator Barry Goldwater.

Meanwhile, the MFDP was preparing to battle the president. On August 6 the young party held its state convention in Jackson, drawing a crowd of 2,500. There they laid out their strategy for the national convention and selected a delegation of sixty-four blacks and four whites. The leaders of the group were Aaron Henry, Fannie Lou Hamer, Victoria Gray, Ed King, and Annie Devine.

"When I got back to Washington . . . , the White House suddenly realized that we had a strategy that was pretty hard to beat," says Washington lawyer Joe Rauh, who had agreed to act as the MFDP's counsel without compensation. The Johnson administration was warning supporters throughout the nation to stay in line, including United Auto Workers president Walter Reuther. Senator Humphrey, who was seeking the vice-presidential nomination, called Joe Rauh. "He'd say, 'Joe, just give me something to tell the president,' Rauh recalls. "I said, 'Why don't you tell him I'm a dirty bastard and completely uncontrollable?' And he

Mississippi Freedom Summer 1964

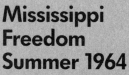

Registering voters was an important part of Freedom Summer. But even more importantly, the volunteers brought a sense of hope and support to black Mississippians. Through the many freedom schools, freedom clinics, freedom theaters, and other efforts, many blacks in Mississippi developed a renewed sense of pride and self-worth.

Tired of Injustice:

An Interview with Dave Dennis

David Dennis headed CORE's Mississippi staff during the 1964 Freedom Summer and served on the steering committee of the Council of Federated Organizations.

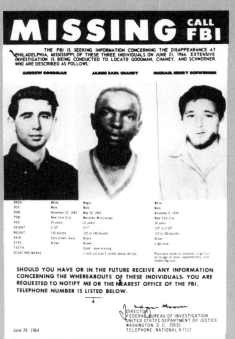

After the bodies of Schwerner, Chaney, and Goodman were found, there was a basic concern about cooling things down because the country was angry . . . I was going to give the eulogy [for James Chaney] at the church in Meridian. I had been approached by my people from the national office of CORE and others to make sure that the speech given was calm. I agreed to do that.

Then, when I got up there and I looked out and saw little Ben Chaney [the slain James' young brother], things just sort of snapped . . . [I couldn't] talk about things getting better, and how we should do it in an easy manner with nonviolence.

You cannot make a man change by speaking a foreign language; he has to understand what you're talking about. This country operated then and still operates on violence. An eye for an eye and a tooth for a tooth—that's what we respect . . . So I just stopped and said what I felt. There was no need to stand in front of that kid, Ben Chaney, and lie to him.

Excerpts from Dave Dennis' eulogy for James Chaney

. . . I feel that he has got his freedom and we are still fighting for it. But what I want to talk about right now is the living dead that we have right among our midst, not only here in the state of Mississippi, but throughout the nation. Those are the people who don't care. [And] those who do care but don't have the guts enough to stand up for it. And those people who are busy up in Washington and other places using my freedom and my life to play politics with. That includes the president on down to the governor of the state of Mississippi . . . as I stand here I not only blame the people who pulled the trigger or did the beating or dug the hole with the shovel. I blame the people in Washington, D.C., and on down in the state of Mississippi for what happened just as much as I blame those who pulled the trigger. Because I feel that, one hundred years ago, if the proper thing had been done by the federal government of this country . . . we wouldn't be here today mourning the death of a brave young man like James Chaney.

. . . You see, I know what is going to happen. I feel it deep in my heart—when they find the people who killed those guys in Neshoba County . . . they [will] come back to the state of Mississippi and have a jury of all their cousins and aunts and uncles. And I know what they are going to say: "Not guilty." Because no one saw them pull the trigger. I'm tired of that! . . . I look at the young kids here, that is something else I grieve about. Little Ben Chaney here and others like him . . .

I don't grieve for James Chaney. He lived a fuller life than many of us will ever live. He's got his freedom, and we're still fighting for ours. I'm sick and tired of going to the funerals of black men who have been murdered by white men . . .

I've got vengeance in my heart tonight, and I ask you to feel angry with me. I'm sick and tired, and I ask you to be sick and tired with me. The white men who murdered James Chaney are never going to be punished. I ask you to be sick and tired of that. I'm tired of the people of this country allowing this thing to continue to happen . . .

I'm tired of that old suggestion that Negroes ought to go back to Africa. I'm ready to go back to Africa the day when all the Jews, the Poles, the Russians, the Germans and the Anglo-Saxons go back where they came from. This land was taken from the Indians, and it belongs just as much to us Negroes as it does to any other group . . .

We've got to stand up. The best way we can remember James Chaney is to demand our rights. Don't just look at me and go back and tell folks you've been to a nice service. Your work is just beginning. If you go back home and sit down and take what these white men in Mississippi are doing to us . . . if you take it and don't do something about it . . . then God damn your souls!

Stand up! Those neighbors who were too afraid to come to this service, pick them up and take them down there to register to vote! Go down there and do it! Don't ask that white man *if* you can register to vote! Just tell him: "Baby, I'm here!" Stand up! Hold your heads up! Don't bow down anymore! We want our freedom NOW!

said, 'Well, the president wouldn't like that . . . ' And I said, 'Well, then you'll have to think of what to tell him yourself, because that's the only thing I can think of telling him . . .'

"I got a lot of pressure right up to the convention time," recalls Rauh, "but what the heck—it was a lot of fun, and I was going to eat whether they pressured me or not, so I went ahead with the fight."

The goal of that fight was to get the MFDP delegation seated at the convention instead of the white Mississippians. To do so, they would first have to convince just eleven of the more than one hundred members on the convention's Credentials Committee to vote for sending the MFDP's request to the convention floor. But once the proposal was raised, a simple voice vote would be too subject to the interpretation of those doing the count, who were allies of the president. To get a fair hearing before the entire convention, the MFDP would have to convince eight state delegations to call for a roll-call vote, not a voice vote, on the MFDP's proposal. This was the "eleven-and-eight" procedure the new party's delegates intended to follow—the strategy that Rauh termed "pretty hard to beat."

Fannie Lou Hamer, a leader of the MFDP.

Rauh helped the MFDP prepare testimony for the convention's Credentials Committee. They would illustrate how Mississippi segregationists kept blacks from voting. "At that time, only six percent of blacks [in Mississippi] were registered to vote," Rauh recalls, "and only about two percent of them actually voted, so this was the perfect case to take to the convention."

Meanwhile, the all-white Mississippi Democratic party launched an attack on the MFDP. At the request of the state's attorney general, a state court banned the new party within the state, saying that it could "cause irreparable damage to the public." Lawrence Guyot, chairman of the MFDP's executive committee, was arrested and sent to jail two days before the start of the convention on a charge dating back to January, when he had been involved in a demonstration. On August 22, the day the convention began in Atlantic City, Mississippi's government labeled the MFDP a "Communist organization."

On the first day of the convention, the MFDP took its case to the national Democratic party's Credentials Committee. Fannie Lou Hamer was the star witness, invoking memories of Medgar Evers' assassination, James Meredith's battle to gain admission to Ole Miss, and the murders of Chaney, Goodman, and Schwerner. "If the Freedom Democratic Party is not seated now, I question America," she said. "Is this America? The land of the free and the home of the brave? Where we have to sleep with our telephones off the hook, because our lives be threatened daily?" She also told of the abuse she had suffered in retaliation for attending a civil rights meeting. "They beat me and they beat me with the long, flat blackjack," said the farm woman. "I screamed to God in pain. My dress worked itself up. I tried to pull it down. They beat my arms 'til I had no feeling in them." Then Hamer broke down and wept, in front of the network television cameras that were providing live national coverage of the testimony. Rita Schwerner, widow of the slain CORE worker, sat next to Hamer while waiting to testify.

President Johnson, watching the proceedings on television, was furious. He had envisioned an untroubled gathering climaxing in his triumphant nomination. Now the order and unity of the Democratic National Convention was being threatened by sixty-eight rural Mississippians, most of them black, most of them poor, and all of them as stubborn as a Dixie mule about what Lawrence Guyot later called "the righteousness of their position." LBJ ordered White House aides to phone the television networks and announce that a presidential press conference would begin immediately.

"Is this America? The land of the free and the home of the brave?"

The cameras stopped rolling in Atlantic City as Johnson's press conference preempted the live convention coverage. The president told the television audience that he predicted a mostly tranquil convention, but that he would oversee a suspenseful contest for the vice-presidential nomination. He did not succeed, however, in blacking out all TV coverage of the testimony. That night, evening news programs ran film footage of Hamer's heartrending appeal to the Credentials Committee. The committee was soon swamped with phone calls and telegrams from angry Americans.

Senator Humphrey asked his protege, Minnesota attorney general Walter Mondale, to head a credentials subcommittee in charge of mediating the MFDP dispute. "They [the MFDP] were pushing on an open door in terms of preventing a future lily-white segregated delegation," Mondale recalls. "The tough question was always, How do we handle it? What should be the best way to resolve this? One theory was you just take the black delegation and seat them, kick the white delegation out . . . Well, that didn't solve any long-term problems. It didn't establish any rule of law for civil rights, and if all it [was] going to be [was] a fight, black against white, one winning, one losing, there was no hope for a healthy political party. So the question was, How to do it?"

Humphrey and Mondale, with White House approval, offered a compromise. The white Mississippi Democrats would be seated if they would swear their loyalty to the ticket, but so would two MFDP delegates, Aaron Henry and Ed King, who would not officially represent Mississippi but would be considered delegates "at-large." The mediators also proposed a resolution calling for southern Democrats to integrate future delegations.

On Monday night, all but three members of the white Mississippi delegation stormed out of the convention; they would not pledge allegiance to a party that consorted with blacks. Nor would the MFDP representatives accept the two-seat compromise; they all wanted to be seated.

On Tuesday, Joe Rauh tried to secure a postponement of the Credentials Committee's vote on the compromise. He wanted time to convince MFDP delegates Bob Moses and Aaron Henry to agree to it. Mondale agreed to the delay, but the credentials panel wanted to act immediately. Joe Rauh remembers the scene. "Have you ever been in a lynch mob?" he says. "Because if you haven't, you haven't seen anything like this. A hundred people shouting, 'Vote! Vote! Vote!' while I'm talking. I finally had to say, 'It's your rudeness that's the problem. I've got a right to speak. I've got the floor. You ought to shut up . . .' 'Vote! Vote! Vote!' It [was] like a machine in there. And it . . . mowed me down." The committee voted to approve the Mondale compromise.

The MFDP still hoped to force its challenge to a roll-call vote before the full convention, but Johnson sent his political allies onto the convention floor to threaten delegates with reprisals if they failed to toe the line on the MFDP. The "eleven-and-eight" strategy had fallen apart; the convention at large voted to endorse the compromise.

Bob Moses and other MFDP leaders were in a hotel room meeting with Humphrey when they saw Mondale and Rauh on television as the deal was approved. "Bob Moses lost his cool," Rauh remembers. "It . . . was like hitting him with a whip—a white man hitting him with a whip. [He felt] everyone had ratted on him . . . So that evening when we were on the news, I said we would continue to fight but I also said this is a great victory which will end up with a new Democratic party, because of the promise that there will never be a lily-white [delegation] again.

"Bob got on [TV] and said you cannot trust the political system—'I will have nothing to do with the political system any longer.'" Fannie Lou Hamer told television reporters that granting only two seats to the MFDP represented "token rights, on the back row, the same as we got in Mississippi. We didn't come all this way for that mess again." Hamer didn't quit. On Tuesday night she led the MFDP contingent, with convention passes borrowed from sympathetic delegates, onto the convention floor. There they took the vacant seats allocated for the Mississippi Democrats, but guards soon arrived to haul the activists away.

An angry Johnson then instructed party officials to remove all but three of the seats in the Mississippi section, and to reserve those seats for the three regular Democrats who had not walked out.

Aaron Henry, who like Rauh now favored acceptance of the compromise, arranged a meeting the next day. Arguments for and against the proposal were voiced, and some civil rights leaders asked the MFDP to approve the plan, arguing that the new party should compromise to reinforce its alliance with white liberals. Martin Luther King, Jr., told the delegates that the choice they were about to make was the greatest decision they would ever have to make. Unswayed by the procompromise arguments, the MFDP delegates rejected the plan.

The MFDP's political tactics could not have been more unconventional. Praying on the convention floor, the delegates fought with the strength of their convictions.

"Those unable to understand why we were not accepting the compromise . . . ," says MFDP delegate Victoria Gray, "didn't realize we would have been betraying those very many people back there in Mississippi whom we represented—not only people who had laid their lives on the line, but many who had given their lives . . . [People] said to us, 'Take this [the compromise], and then next time, you know, there'll be more.' I thought about the many people for whom there was not gonna be a next time . . . It made no sense at all, with all the risk being taken, to accept what we knew for certain to be nothing and go back home to God only knows what . . . You may get home and not have a house. You may get home and a member of your family may be missing . . . So you know, we [were] not going to accept anything less than the real thing."

Wednesday night, the MFDP delegates again marched onto the convention floor with borrowed passes. This time, there were no empty seats, so they stood in the space where the seats had been. Before television cameras, Fannie Lou Hamer vigorously denounced the party for its treatment of her fellow black Mississippians. "Mrs. Hamer [always] spoke from the heart," recalls Bob Moses. "When she spoke at Atlantic City in front of the national TV, she spoke the same way . . . what you felt when she spoke and when she sang was someone who was opening up her soul and really telling you what she felt . . . I think one of the most beautiful things about the movement in Mississippi was that it enabled a person like Mrs. Hamer to emerge." A spiritual leader of the delegation, Hamer led rousing renditions of freedom songs right on the convention floor.

At the convention, one reporter asked Hamer if she was seeking equality with the white man. "No," she said. "What would I look like fighting for equality with the white man? I don't want to go down that low. I want the true democracy that'll raise me and that white man up . . . raise America up."

The fight between the two Mississippi camps had dominated the convention.

From Sharecropper to Lobbyist:

The Political Awakening of Fannie Lou Hamer

. . . My parents were sharecroppers and they had a big family. Twenty children. Fourteen boys and six girls. I'm the twentieth child. All of us worked in the fields, of course, but we never did get anything out of sharecropping. We'd make fifty and sixty bales and end up with nothing.

I was about six years old when I first went to the fields to pick cotton. I can remember very well the landowner telling me one day that if I would pick thirty pounds he would give me something out of the commissary: some Cracker-Jacks, Daddy Wide-Legs, and some sardines. These were things that he knew I loved and never had a chance to have. So I picked thirty pounds that day. Well, the next week I had to pick sixty and by the time I was thirteen I was picking two and three hundred pounds.

. . . Well, after the white man killed off our mules, my parents never did get a chance to get up again. We went back to sharecropping, halving, it's called. You split the cotton half and half with the plantation owner. But the seed, fertilizer, cost of hired hands, everything is paid out of the cropper's half. My parents tried so hard to do what they could to keep us in school, but school didn't last but four months out of the year and most of the time we didn't have clothes to wear. I dropped out of school and cut corn stalks to help the family.

. . . I married in 1944 and stayed on the plantation until 1962, when I went down to the courthouse in Indianola to register to vote. That happened because I went to a mass meeting one night.

Until then I'd never heard of no mass meeting and I didn't know that a Negro could register and vote. Bob Moses, Reggie Robinson, Jim Bevel, and James Forman were some of the SNCC workers who ran that meeting. When they asked for those to raise their hands who'd go down to the courthouse the next day, I raised mine. Had it up high as I could get it. I guess if I'd had any sense I'd a-been a little scared, but what was the point of being scared. The only thing they could do to me was kill me and it seemed like they'd been trying to do that a little bit at a time ever since I could remember.

. . . Well, there was eighteen of us who went down to the courthouse that day and all of us were arrested. Police said the bus was painted the wrong color—said it was too yellow. After I got bailed out I went back to the plantation where Pap and I had lived for eighteen years. My oldest girl met me and told me that Mr. Marlow, the plantation owner, was mad and raising sand. He had heard that I had tried to register. That night he called on us and said, "We're not going to have this in Mississippi and you will have to withdraw. I am looking for your answer, yea or nay?" I just looked. He said, "I will

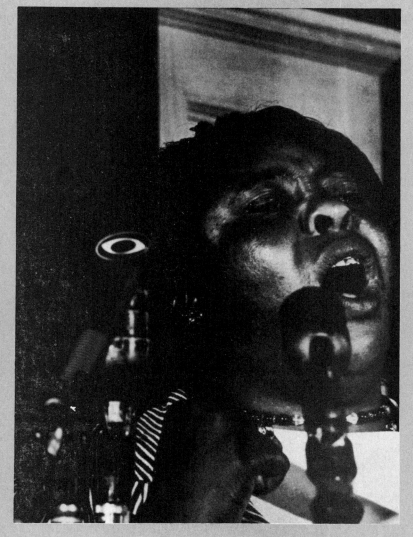

give you until tomorrow morning. And if you don't withdraw, you will have to leave. If you do go withdraw, it's only how I feel, you might still have to leave." So I left that same night. Pap had to stay on till work on the plantation was through. Ten days later they fired into Mrs. Tucker's house where I was staying. They also shot two girls at Mr. Sissel's.

. . . What I really feel is necessary is that the black people in this country will have to upset this applecart. We can no longer ignore the fact that America is NOT the " . . . land of the free and the home of the brave." I used to question this for years—what did our kids actually fight for? They would go in the service and go through all of that and come right out to be drowned in the river in Mississippi.

. . . I've worked on voter registration here ever since I went to that first mass meeting. In 1964, we registered 63,000 black people from Mississippi into the Freedom Democratic Party. We formed our own party because the whites wouldn't even let us register. We decided to challenge the white Mississippi Democratic Party at the National Convention. We followed all the laws the white people themselves made. We tried to attend the precinct meetings and they locked the doors on us or moved the meetings and that's against the law they made for their own selves. So we were the ones that held the real precinct meetings. At all these meetings across the state we elected our representatives to go to the National Democratic Convention in Atlantic City. But we learned the hard way that even though we had all the law and all the righteousness on our side, that white man is not going to give up his power to us.

We have to build our own power. We have to win every single political office we can, where we have a majority of black people . . . The question for black people is not, when is the white man going to give us our rights, or when is he going to give us good education for our children, or when is he going to give us jobs—if the white man gives you anything—just remember when he gets ready he will take it right back. We have to take for ourselves.

. . . I went to Africa in 1964 and I learned that I sure didn't have anything to be ashamed of from being black. Being from the South we never was taught much about our African heritage. The way everybody talked to us, everybody in Africa was savages and really stupid people. But I've seen more savage white folks here in America than I seen in Africa. I saw black men flying the airplanes, driving buses, sitting behind the big desks in the bank and just doing everything that I was used to seeing white people do. I saw, for the first time in my life, a black stewardess walking through the plane and that was quite an inspiration for me.

. . . I was treated much better in Africa than I was treated in America. I often get letters that say, "Go back to Africa." Now I have just as much if not more right to stay in America as whoever wrote those letters . . . It is our right to stay here and we stay and fight for what belongs to us.

This excerpt is from *To Praise Our Bridges*, the autobiography of Fannie Lou Hamer.

Some sources say that Johnson's selection of Hubert Humphrey as his running mate may have depended on how the senator handled the MFDP challenge. Throughout the ensuing presidential campaign, Johnson had to face angry southerners still upset over the convention. Most Mississippi Democrats supported Republican Barry Goldwater, while the overwhelmingly black MFDP campaigned for Johnson. Some Democrats feared that the GOP might take the entire South in the election. In fact, the Republicans won only six states—Alabama, Arizona, Georgia, Louisiana, Mississippi, and South Carolina—while Johnson won the remaining forty-four.

Several months later, the Mississippi Freedom Democratic Party raised the issue of voting rights once again. When Congress reconvened in January, the MFDP went to Washington to challenge the seating of Mississippi's five-member, all-white congressional delegation. The MFDP candidates found some support in the House; 149 members voted to seat them, while 276 backed the old-guard whites. But black Mississippians had begun to open up the Democratic party, paving the way for other minorities and women, who were also under-represented in that organization.

In altered form, many Freedom Summer projects continued after the summer volunteers had left. The Johnson administration provided funding for health clinics and school programs in rural Mississippi. The national preschool enrichment program known as Project Head Start evolved from Freedom Summer, and federal money for nutrition programs and legal aid took up where the Mississippi project left off.

Freedom Summer also presented a chance for black and white movement activists to work side-by-side. But for the first time, a serious rift developed between the white liberals and the black workers. Blacks began to question the motives of the whites who worked with them. Could they be trusted to go all the way, to never compromise their ideals? The racial tension and doubts culminated in the compromise at the Atlantic City Democratic Convention. Many of the black movement people felt that the liberal wing of the Democratic party had let them down.

While the MFDP delegates had struggled at the convention, the federal courts had issued injunctions against white school officials in three Mississippi counties, requiring them to admit black children. In Jackson, forty-three black elementary-school students registered at eight schools formerly open to whites only. In Biloxi, sixteen black youngsters enrolled at four such schools. These pushes toward integration resulted in many new private, segregated white academies.

The MFDP did not win its political challenge in 1964, but the party did reap a new sense of power and dignity. Black people who had never voted not only participated in the political process but took on the most powerful people in the country in front of television cameras and reporters. MFDP members were not savvy politicos trying to redirect Mississippi politics. They were sharecroppers and farm workers trying to direct and improve their own lives. And their efforts were not limited to politics; they organized schools, daycare centers, food banks, and farming cooperatives.

Perhaps the most notable personal metamorphosis of the time was that of Fannie Lou Hamer. The youngest of twenty children in a sharecropping family, her formal education stopped at the third grade. From an early age she worked on a plantation keeping track of other workers' hours. Yet by 1966, *Mississippi* magazine identified her as one of six "women of influence" in the state. Two years after Freedom Summer, Fannie Lou Hamer summed up the changes wrought by those times in this way: "There was no real civil rights movement in the Negro community in Mississippi before the 1964 Summer Project. There were people that wanted change, but they hadn't dared to come out and try to do something, to try to change the way things were. But after the 1964 project when all of the young people came down for the summer—an exciting and remarkable summer— Negro people in the Delta began moving. People who had never before tried, though they had always been anxious to do something, began moving. Now, in 1966, even Negroes who live on the plantations slip off the plantations and go to civil rights meetings. 'We wanted to do this so long,' they say. When some of us get up and blast out at the meetings, these women go back home—these men go back home—and in the next day or two the kids come. They say, 'My mother told us what you talked about last night.' That's great! To see kids, to see these people—to see how far they've come since 1964! To me it's one of the greatest things that ever happened in Mississippi. And it's a direct result of the Summer Project in 1964."

On Sunday, March 21, 1965, 4,000 people left Brown's Chapel in Selma and began the historic march to Montgomery.

Chapter Eight

Selma

The Bridge to Freedom

"I am 65 years old, I own 100 acres of land that is paid for, I am a taxpayer and I have six children. All of them is teachin', workin' . . . If what I done ain't enough to be a registered voter . . . then Lord have mercy on America."

A black man in Selma, Alabama, speaking to the voting registrar

Although the Fifteenth Amendment to the Constitution had in 1870 prohibited racial discrimination in voting, nearly a century later few black southerners had ever been allowed to cast a ballot. In Mississippi, COFO's efforts had helped somewhat—between 1962 and 1964 the number of registered blacks there increased from 5.3 percent to 6.7 percent of the voting-age black population, a small but significant improvement. In Alabama, prospective black voters fared little better. By 1962, some 13.4 percent of voting-age blacks were registered in that state.

Early in 1963, SNCC had only two workers in Selma, Alabama, a town of about 30,000 people in the central part of the state. There was little to indicate that Selma was about to become the center for a major civil rights protest as well as the focus of national attention. Blacks made up approximately half the voting-age population of Dallas County, within which Selma was located, but only one percent of voting-age blacks were registered to vote, in contrast to sixty-five percent of whites. Just 156 of Selma's 15,000 blacks of voting age were on the voting rolls.

Mayor Joseph Smitherman (left) with Sheriff James Clark at a press conference.

In February 1963, two SNCC workers began holding monthly voting clinics, showing people how to fill out the required forms. About forty blacks turned out for the first meeting, but the SNCC workers found that Selma's blacks had reservations about registering and voting. "That's white folks' business," some would say. One elderly woman remarked, "I ain't got enough mind," meaning she could not read or write. Several black preachers, fearing retribution from whites, were loath to host SNCC's voter registration meetings in their churches. At even the smallest of such meetings, police often showed up to harass people. County sheriff James G. Clark, Jr., sent officers to record names; those who attended the clinics were threatened with economic retaliation. When SNCC workers clashed with law officers at the county courthouse, where voter registration was held, they were arrested.

Local officials in Selma made it supremely difficult for those blacks brave enough to attempt to register. The registration office was open only on the first and third Mondays of each month, and the registrars were likely to arrive late, take long lunch hours, and leave early. The few blacks who managed to see the registrar usually "failed" the then-legal literacy tests.

On October 7, 1963, other SNCC workers came to Selma for a "Freedom Day." The workers accompanied black would-be voters to the courthouse to help them register. By 11 A.M., 250 blacks were waiting in line outside the Dallas County Courthouse. But Sheriff Jim Clark was also there, backed by helmeted deputies armed with guns and clubs. Clark had a local photographer take pictures of every person in line and asked the people how their employers might react to the pictures. SNCC workers, carrying signs reading "Register To Vote" and "Register Now for Freedom," were pulled from the steps of the federal government building and shoved into a police car. At 1:55 P.M., SNCC's James Forman told Clark that he would be bringing water and food to the people in line. "If you do, you'll be arrested," said Clark, who forbade the people to get out of line. When two SNCC workers tried to hand sandwiches to the prospective voters, they were pummeled by Sheriff Clark's deputies.

The police also attacked newspeople trying to get close to the action. Nevertheless, news stories and pictures reached Washington, as did reports that the photographs taken of blacks trying to register had been published in newspapers in an attempt to get the blacks fired by white employers. Congressmen also learned from the NAACP's lobbyist in Washington, Clarence Mitchell, about the four-page form that would-be voters had to complete, and about the registrar's irrelevant questions such as, "Does your employer know you are here?"

The Kennedy administration had always hoped to wipe out southern voting-rights discrimination through the courts rather than through Congress. But the administration crippled its own strategy by making mistakes in its appointment of federal judges in the South. In an effort to appease southern politicians, the administration did not carefully monitor the racial attitudes of its judicial nominees. Consequently, several of Kennedy's early appointments turned out to be ardent segregationists with no intention of helping blacks gain access to the ballot. The civil rights bill sent to Congress in 1963 held great promise for ending discrimination in restaurants and other public accommodations, but it offered no comprehensive remedy for discrimination in voting rights. Throughout 1963 and the early part of 1964, Clarence Mitchell lobbied hard but in vain to have voting rights incorporated in a more substantive way into the Civil Rights Act.

After that bill's passage in June 1964, Mitchell and other civil rights leaders asked President Johnson for further legislation securing the right to vote. Johnson asked Attorney General Nicholas Katzenbach to prepare a strategy memo on when and how the bill might be drafted. The Justice Department continued to research the issue, but for the moment, voting rights remained a low-priority issue for the president. Johnson felt the South needed time to adjust to the sudden presence of blacks in hotels and restaurants that had been open only to whites before the Civil Rights Act became law.

In Selma, SNCC responded to the enactment of the Civil Rights Act by trying to integrate all-white theaters and lunch counters. On July 4, when SNCC workers accompanied students to the Thirsty Boy drive-in and the Wilby Theater, they were attacked by whites and arrested for trespassing. The next day, at a voter registration rally at the courthouse, the police jabbed at the demonstrators with cattle prods. Afterwards, Circuit Court Judge James Hare issued an order forbidding blacks to meet publicly in groups of more than three people.

President Lyndon Johnson defeated Senator Barry Goldwater by a wide margin in the November, 1964, election. With the election over, civil rights workers hoped that Johnson would offer new legislation to address the issue of voting rights. For its part, the Justice Department began drafting several versions of a bill for submission to Congress.

Such legislation was badly needed in places like Selma, where blacks attempting to register were sometimes better educated than the registrars who challenged them. Amelia Platts Boynton, a Selma resident, remembers one occasion when an official had trouble reading the questions to a black teacher who wanted to register. "The teacher finally said, 'Those words are "constitutionality" and "interrogatory."'' The registrar turned red with anger," recalls Boynton. "[The teacher] flunked the test and was refused her registration certificate."

As one of the city's few registered blacks, Boynton was called upon to vouch for the character of others trying to register, in accordance with an Alabama law. One day an elderly black man with a shaky hand asked Boynton to help him write his address as he stood before the registrar. "I can't write so good," he explained. The bureaucrat told the man to get out of line if he couldn't write his own address. "Mr. Adkins," the black man told the registrar, "I am 65 years old, I own 100 acres of land that is paid for, I am a taxpayer and I have six children. All of them is teachin', workin' . . . If what I done ain't enough to be a registered voter with all the tax I got to pay, then Lord have mercy on America."

Stories such as these reached the nation's lawmakers through Clarence Mitchell and others. Even to those who did not want to listen, it was becoming obvious that black Americans were not allowed to register to vote in Selma. But neither Congress nor the White House took immediate action on the matter.

Despite Washington's hesitance, SNCC activists worked with the Dallas County Voters League, a local organization founded in the 1930s. They explained to the blacks who dared attend meetings that, through political action, black residents of Selma could get their streets paved, or see that their trash was picked up, or even force the school board to allocate more money to schools that were open only three hours a day and not at all when there was a crop to be planted or harvested. SNCC organizers promised that if blacks in Selma would take the risk of registering and voting, they could challenge the whites-only political system. If the segregationists tried to keep them from exercising their franchise, SNCC assured them, the federal government would step in.

"Our strategy, as usual," SNCC's James Forman later wrote, "was to force the U.S. government to intervene in case there were arrests—and if they did not intervene, that inaction would once again prove the government was not on our side and thus intensify the development of a mass consciousness among blacks. Our slogan for this drive was 'One Man, One Vote.' Who could deny the justice of [that]? [Sheriff] Jim Clark, of course."

In December, Martin Luther King, Jr., traveled to Norway to accept the Nobel Peace Prize, calling himself a "trustee for the twenty-two million Negroes of the United States of America who are engaged in a creative battle to end the night of racial injustice." Birmingham's Bull Connor, upon hearing of the award to his nemesis, said King didn't deserve it and remarked, "Shame on somebody."

Later that month, King announced his plans to go to Selma. "We will probably have demonstrations in the very near future in Alabama and Mississippi based around the right to vote," he said. "We hope that, through this process, we can bring the necessary moral pressure to bear on the federal government to get federal registrars appointed in these areas, as well as to get federal marshals in those places to escort Negroes to the registration places if necessary."

The renowned preacher's planned visit caught the attention of Selma's leaders. Mayor Joseph Smitherman, who had been elected in the fall of 1964, did not want county sheriff Jim Clark to use his violent tactics against King. Though hardly a proponent of integration, Smitherman had been elected on a campaign promise to bring industry to Selma. Pictures of Clark attacking demonstrators on national television would hardly help the industrialization campaign. Smitherman appointed Wilson Baker to the newly created position of public safety director. The commissioner was to enforce the law within the city of Selma, while the sheriff would direct law-enforcement activities within the county. However, Sheriff Clark never really relinquished his role as the highest law-enforcement official in Selma.

Mayor Smitherman sent Baker to see Burke Marshall, head of the Civil Rights Division at the Justice Department. Baker asked Marshall to steer King away from Selma; his arrival, Baker reasoned, would only exacerbate an already tense situation. The lawman offered to ease voter registration requirements for blacks

Clarence Mitchell:

A Profile of the "101st Senator"

Clarence Mitchell sits with Joe Rauh and President Johnson.

Demonstrations in the streets—and their attendant media coverage—did not necessarily bring about civil rights legislation in Congress. In the early 1960s, there were no blacks in the Senate, and only five black representatives. Clarence Mitchell, however, wielded enough power in Washington to be dubbed the 101st senator by Hubert Humphrey. Since 1950, when he became head of the NAACP's Washington Bureau, Mitchell had walked the halls of the Senate with the nation's policymakers, joking and chatting with them but forever arguing that they make the Constitution a reality for blacks. To remind himself of that document's provisions, he carried a copy of it in his wallet. Although blacks were not yet allowed in the smoke-filled rooms, Mitchell was forever knocking on their doors. "When you have a law, you have a law that will work for you permanently," he would tell the senators, not all of whom wanted to listen to the determined NAACP lobbyist. Mississippi's Senator James O. Eastland, who still used the word "nigger" during floor debates, refused to speak to him.

Mitchell was tireless in his crusading. "This guy walks so fast and so far I can't keep up with him," said Joseph Rauh, founder of Americans for Democratic Action, a liberal group that often worked with the NAACP. "Around noon I get hungry; he doesn't eat; late afternoon I want a drink, and he doesn't drink. Not only does he not rest, eat, or drink, but you get called names just for sitting beside him in the galleries."

Nicholas Katzenbach, former United States attorney general, recalls that Mitchell would court votes on key legislation by visiting each senator's office, and if he "wasn't thrown out bodily, he'd mark it down as favorable." As a filibuster stalled action on the 1964 Civil Rights Act, some liberals proposed concessions to accommodate southern conservatives. Mitchell responded with uncharacteristic anger. He said blacks had waited too long for their civil rights to allow the bill to be watered down now. Hubert Humphrey put a hand on Mitchell's knee and said, "Clarence, you're three feet off your chair." Mitchell, nonetheless, prevailed. He reminded the senators that he had met with President Johnson, whom he knew well from Johnson's days as Senate majority leader, and that the president had promised him he would not cave in to the filibuster. The segregationists' deadlock was finally broken, and on June 19, 1964, the bill passed by a vote of seventy-three to twenty-seven. But the act had a major flaw: it did not guarantee blacks the right to vote in local and state elections, which had shut them out for so long.

if King would avoid Selma. The cattle prods and nightsticks, he promised, would also be put away. Baker stated that he wanted to avoid violence—that it was Sheriff Clark who was responsible for the brutality. Baker couldn't promise he would be able to keep the sheriff in check if Martin Luther King came to town. With Baker waiting, Marshall telephoned King to try to convince him to shun Selma. King's response was brief. Hanging up the phone, Marshall turned to Baker and said, "They're coming to Selma . . . They've already put too much work in on the project to turn back now."

On January 2, 1965, King spoke from the pulpit of Brown's Chapel African Methodist Episcopal Church, in Selma. The Nobel Peace Prize winner drew an overflow crowd of 700. "We will seek to arouse the federal government by marching by the thousands [to] the places of registration," he said. "When we get the right to vote, we will send to the statehouse not men who will stand in the doorways of universities to keep Negroes out, but men who will uphold the cause of Justice. Give us the ballot." King planned to stage mass marches to the courthouse on the two registration days per month.

With King's arrival, Selma became national news, as did the overall southern pattern of denying blacks the right to register and vote. In his State of the Union Address, President Johnson articulated the goal of eliminating "every remaining obstacle to the right and the opportunity to vote," but voting rights came seventh on his list of domestic priorities.

In Selma, public safety director Baker asked Sheriff Clark not to allow any police brutality that could become national news. King's speech also caused concern to SNCC workers in the city. Although the Dallas County Voters League had invited King to town, SNCC feared its voter registration project would be overshadowed by King and the television cameras that trailed him endlessly.

The national press was now anticipating a confrontation in Selma over voting rights. When reporters asked white officials there why so few blacks were registered, Sheriff Clark said it was "largely because of their mental I.Q." Judge Hare, the man who had enjoined more than three blacks at a time from gathering publicly, told one reporter, "You see, most of your Selma Negroes are descended from the Ebo and Angola tribes of Africa. You could never teach or trust an Ebo back in slave days, and even today I can spot their tribal characteristics. They have protruding heels, for instance."

In Washington, the Justice Department began a two-pronged attack on Selma's voter registration practices. On January 11, 1965, the department reported to the president that its Civil Rights Division was drafting legislation to outlaw the use of literacy tests in voter registration and allow federal personnel to register voters where necessary. The second part of the strategy was a suit against the state of Alabama, charging that the statewide voter registration test should be amended because it amounted to a purposeful obstruction of the civil rights of blacks.

On January 18, King and the SCLC began their Selma campaign. They had arranged protest marches and planned to show the nation the violence that blacks met when attempting to register to vote. Commissioner Baker knew of the plan and intended to steer clear of confrontation. King accompanied a group of Selma blacks to an all-white restaurant without incident. He then led them in a march to the courthouse, defying the court order against congregating. As per Baker's orders, there were no arrests, but Sheriff Clark herded those waiting to register into an alley behind the building, and no blacks registered that day.

The SCLC feared that, with no violence to cover, journalists from the national press would drift away, taking Washington's attention with them. The activists staged another march on the courthouse the next day. This time, the demonstrators refused to obey Clark's orders to wait in the alley.

"Clark had a big club in his hand," Amelia Boynton, the veteran Selma activist, later recalled, "and he yelled to me, 'Where are you going? . . . You all got to get in this line [in the alley] . . . ' Before I could gather my wits, he had left the steps and jumped behind me, grabbed me by my coat, propelled me around and started shoving me down the street. I was stunned. I saw cameramen and newspaper reporters around and . . . I said, 'I hope the newspapers see you acting this role.' He said, 'Dammit, I hope they do.'"

Stirred by the sheriff's dramatic arrest of Boynton, about sixty people surged through the front door of the courthouse and refused to heed Clark's order to leave. They, too, were arrested. The next day's editions of the *New York Times* and the *Washington Post* ran photographs of Clark violently pushing Boynton down the street with his billy club. Baker's strategy had crumbled quickly.

With speaking engagements elsewhere, King had to leave town for a while. But the movement did not falter. That Wednesday, January 20, three groups of would-be voters marched to the front door of the courthouse and refused to move. Clark arrested them for obstructing the sidewalk. Two days later, more than a hundred of Selma's black schoolteachers descended upon the courthouse to protest Boynton's arrest. An elite group among the city's blacks, teachers typically steered clear of civil rights activity for fear of being fired by the white school board. Their action was a welcome surprise to the movement.

"This courthouse is a serious place of business," said Sheriff Clark, "and you seem to think you can take it just to be Disneyland on parade. Do you have business in this courthouse?"

"The only business we have is to come to the Board of Registrars to register . . . ," replied Rev. Frederick Reese, president of both the Dallas County Voters League and the Selma Teachers Association.

"The Board of Registrars is not in session . . . ," retorted Clark. "You came down here to make a mockery out of this courthouse and we're not going to have it."

The sheriff prodded the teachers with his nightstick, forcing them off the courthouse steps. The teachers regrouped and then, in dignified silence, began to march away. They headed for Brown's Chapel, where they held a rally.

After returning from his speaking engagements, King began to see the realization of the SCLC's goals for Selma—that nonviolent demonstrations would arouse violence on the part of the racists and, as King later wrote, "Americans of conscience in the name of decency [would] demand federal intervention and legislation."

Andrew Young of the SCLC called the teachers' march "the most significant thing that has happened in the racial movement since Birmingham." The triumphant greeting among the organization's workers became, "Brother, we got a *movement* going on in Selma." Even the city's schoolchildren were now involved, having witnessed their teachers marching. Other middle-class blacks also responded to the call. "The undertakers got a group, and they marched," recalls Rev. Reese. "The beauticians got a group; they marched. Everybody marched after the teachers marched . . . "

During one march, a fifty-three-year-old demonstrator named Annie Lee Cooper chose to resist Sheriff Clark's strongarm tactics. Seeing Cooper step out of the line of marchers, Clark jabbed her with his elbow and ordered her to step back in line. Instead, Cooper turned and punched the lawman in the face. As Clark began to fall, Cooper slugged him again. Two deputies tried to wrestle her to the ground, but she broke loose, ran to Clark, and again punched him. Finally, three deputies managed to pin Cooper down, and the sheriff whacked her in the head with his club. The next day, photographs of the sheriff raising his stick over the woman's head as his deputies held her down appeared in leading newspapers. Although Cooper had struck first, and repeatedly, the movement had salvaged a victory from the incident.

Mayor Smitherman and Wilson Baker were losing patience. They had tried to keep the reins on Clark, but the repeated demonstrations and King's presence were provoking the sheriff. At a press conference, the mayor expressed his anger at the civil rights leader.

On Monday, February 1, the SCLC's strategy called for King to get himself arrested. His letter from a Birmingham jail two years earlier had caught the nation's attention, and the SCLC hoped for a similar coup in Selma. This time, however, King would enter jail with the letter already written.

On Monday morning, King addressed the marchers he was about to lead to the courthouse. He cautioned them not to be distracted by national publicity or the confrontations with Sheriff Clark, but to focus on their objective—the right to vote. "If Negroes could vote, there would be no Jim Clarks," said King. "Our children would not be crippled by segregated schools . . . " The minister then led 250 marchers from the church. They walked in an uninterrupted line, ignoring the city ordinance that demanded they break into small clusters. Commissioner Baker got out of his car and, in a voice rasping from a sore throat, said, "This is a deliberate attempt to violate the parade ordinance which you have obeyed for three weeks. If you don't break the line up into small groups, I'll have to arrest you." The people kept going, and Baker got back into his car and caught up with King two blocks later. Baker told the demonstrators they were under arrest.

Spurred by news of King's arrest, 500 of Selma's schoolchildren marched to the courthouse, violating the court order, and were arrested. The city's jails were getting crowded. The next day, leading newspapers including the *New York Times* displayed page-one photos of King praying just before his arrest. Wednesday brought the arrests of more than a hundred additional marchers, followed by the arrests of 300 more schoolchildren. Each evening, the television news covered the mass arrests and showed children being led off to jail. Tales of brutality within the jails abounded—that there were no toilets, only buckets, and that in one improvised "prison camp" captives were forced to stand in single file and if a man stepped out of line, a guard would strike him.

Senator Jacob Javits, a New York Republican, termed the mass arrests "shocking" and contacted the Justice Department. He later told reporters that department officials were monitoring Selma to determine whether new legislation might be necessary or if the administration should authorize federal officials to register voters. King, meanwhile, had sent telegrams to several congressmen saying that "events of the past month here in Selma have raised serious questions as to the adequacy of present voting rights legislation." A congressional delegation of fifteen traveled to Selma to investigate.

"Brother, we got a *movement* going on in Selma."

Congressman Charles Diggs of Detroit, a black man, was a member of that team. "I think it's a general consensus of the delegation—which was bipartisan . . . [and] made up of Negro and white congressmen from various parts of the country—that new legislation is going to be necessary if Negroes are going to be able to exercise the franchise as freely in the South . . . as they can in Detroit, New York, California, and places like that," Diggs commented.

Andrew Young called the White House to ask that an emissary be sent to Selma to report back to the president. He also requested that Johnson make a statement in support of voting rights and prepare legislation to ensure those rights. Young was told that the president was monitoring the situation, that he had already spoken out in favor of voting rights in his State of the Union message, and that the Justice Department was studying the legislation question.

To keep the voting rights issue at the top of the presidential and congressional agendas, the SCLC needed to hold the nation's attention. The activists soon got some help from an unexpected source. On February 4, the militant Black Muslim minister Malcolm X came to speak in Selma at the invitation of SNCC. At first, King's colleagues feared that the controversial leader might incite the local people and jeopardize King's control of the movement. King was still in jail when Malcolm X told a capacity crowd at Brown's Chapel that "the white people should thank Dr. King for holding people in check, for there are other [black leaders] who do not believe in these [nonviolent] measures." Andrew Young hurried Coretta Scott King into the church, hoping she would dilute the impact of Malcolm X's presence. Mrs. King remembers the Black Muslim saying, "If the white people realize what the alternative is, perhaps they will be more willing to hear Dr. King." It would be one of Malcolm X's final speeches; three weeks later the radical leader was shot to death in Harlem.

On the day of Malcolm X's speech, President Johnson held a press conference to deliver a statement in support of voting rights. It was his first direct response to Selma and a welcome surprise to the activists. "I should like to say that all Americans should be indignant when one American is denied the right to vote," said Johnson. "The loss of that right to a single citizen undermines the freedom of every citizen. That is why all of us should be concerned with the efforts of our fellow Americans to register to vote in Alabama . . . I intend to see that that right is secured for all our citizens." The same day, a federal judge issued an order requiring the registrar in Selma to process at least 100 applications per day.

On Friday, February 5, King's final day in jail, his "Letter From A Selma Jail" appeared as an advertisement in the *New York Times*. "When the King of Norway

When Amelia Boynton was violently arrested by Sheriff James Clark, the media captured the moment for the nation.

Radical black nationalist Malcolm X offered himself as an alternative to people who declined to cooperate with Martin Luther King and the SCLC.

More than 300 youngsters were arrested by Clark and his deputies when they protested at the Dallas County Courthouse.

participated in awarding the Nobel Peace Prize to me, he surely did not think that in less than 60 days I would be in jail. He, and almost all world opinion, will be shocked because they are little aware of the unfinished business in the South . . . when the Civil Rights Act of 1964 was passed, many decent Americans were lulled into complacency because they thought the days of difficult struggle were over. Why are we in jail? Have you ever been required to answer 100 questions on government, some abstruse even to a political science specialist, merely to vote? Have you ever stood in line with over a hundred others and after waiting an entire day seen less than ten given the qualifying test? This is Selma, Alabama, where there are more Negroes in jail with me than there are on the voting rolls."

The following day, presidential press secretary George Reedy announced Johnson's intention to send a "proposal" on voting rights to Congress, but he did not give specifics or say when the action would be taken. King went to Washington, hoping to meet with the president, but was told that Johnson was preoccupied with Vietnam. The civil rights leader left for Birmingham, where he met with another disappointment: A planned march of "thousands" drew barely 200 people. But on February 8, word came that Johnson would now see King. The two met for fifteen minutes, and though nothing specific was agreed upon, the minister had at least made his case directly to the president.

On Tuesday, February 16, SCLC executive staff member C. T. Vivian led twenty-five demonstrators through the rainy streets of Selma to the county courthouse to protest a new voter registration policy. Officials had announced that blacks wishing to register could sign a ledger, and those who did so would be served first on the two days per month when the registrar's office was open. To Vivian, the new rule gave a false impression that concessions were being made to Selma's blacks. He walked up the courthouse steps and began to lecture Sheriff Clark, who was blocking the doorway with a group of armed deputies.

"We want you to know, gentlemen, that—every one of you—we know your badge numbers, we know your names . . . " Vivian scolded. "There are those who followed Hitler like you blindly follow this Sheriff Clark. They didn't think their day would come. But they also were pulled into the courtroom and they were also given their death sentences . . . You're racists in the same way Hitler was a racist . . . You can't keep anyone in the U.S. from voting without hurting the rights of all other citizens. Democracy's built on this. This is why every man has the right to vote . . . And this is what we're trying to say to you. These people have the right to stand inside this courthouse. If you'd had your basic civics courses, you'd know this, gentlemen."

Sheriff Clark remembers, "[Vivian] started shouting at me that I was Hitler, I was a brute, that I was a Nazi. I don't remember all . . . and I lost my temper then." Clark ordered the television cameramen to turn off their lights, and when they did he suddenly struck Vivian in the mouth, sending him sprawling onto the stone steps. "You can arrest us, Sheriff Clark," said Vivian, putting a hand to his bleeding lip. "You don't have to beat us . . . You beat people bloody in order that they will not have the privilege to vote." Clark said later he didn't recall hitting Vivian, but did say, "I went to the doctor and got an X ray and found out I had a linear fracture in a finger on my left hand."

"This is Selma, Alabama, where there are more Negroes in jail with me than there are on the voting rolls."

The scene provided gripping footage on the news that evening. Mayor Smitherman and Wilson Baker tried to tell reporters that Clark alone was to blame for the incident, but Martin Luther King rejoined, "I'm here to tell you that the businessmen, the mayor of this city, and everybody in the white power structure of this city must take responsibility for everything that Jim Clark does in this community."

Vivian was invited to speak in the nearby town of Marion on February 18 about his confrontation with Clark. The meeting culminated in a nighttime march, a tactic the activists knew was dangerous. The area was surrounded by auxiliary police, state troopers, and angry white civilians.

Just before the attack, the streetlights went out. Newspeople were threatened and harassed; panicked demonstrators scurried to flee the ruffians. Eighty-two-year-old Cager Lee had been beaten and was bleeding. His grandson, twenty-six-year-old Jimmy Lee Jackson, rushed him into a cafe to escape further abuse, but several troopers followed them in. One officer hit Jackson's mother, and the young man struck back. Another trooper hit Jackson in the face with a stick, and according to later testimony, yet another pulled a gun and shot him in the stomach. He died seven days later. Dozens of other people, including NBC reporter Richard Valeriani, were badly beaten.

The next day, the story of the police brutality hit the front pages of the nation's newspapers. Valeriani appeared on television from his hospital bed, his speech slurred and his head bandaged.

The constant violence had begun to take an emotional toll on the movement. The entire nation now understood the reign of terror by which southern bigots kept blacks from voting. Still the violence continued, and on February 22 the Justice Department phoned King to warn him of a possible plot on his life.

There was no word yet from the president on the new voter registration proposal. On Tuesday, February 23, a group of Republican congressmen in Washington

One of the many confrontations between C. T. Vivian and Sheriff Clark.

The funeral of Jimmy Lee Jackson.

Not all whites living in Selma approved of the violence against black people. Here, demonstrators show their support publicly.

issued a statement: "How long will Congress and the American people be asked to wait while this administration studies and restudies Dr. King's request for new federal legislation? The need is apparent. The time is now."

That Sunday, two days after the death of Jimmy Lee Jackson, the SCLC's James Bevel suggested in a sermon that the civil rights marchers take their case straight to Governor George Wallace in Montgomery. He proposed to march the entire distance from Marion, the site of Jackson's shooting, to the state capital.

On Tuesday, March 2, President Johnson met with Roy Wilkins and Clarence Mitchell of the NAACP to discuss legislation creating federal voter registration. Meanwhile, King told reporters that Johnson had a "mandate from the American people—he must go out this time and get a voting rights bill that will end the necessity for any more voting rights bills."

At Jimmy Lee Jackson's funeral, held the next day, mourners draped a large white banner over the entrance to Brown's Chapel bearing the words, "Racism Killed Our Brother." King, speaking at the memorial service, said Jackson had been murdered by those who beat people "in the name of the law"; by politicians who fed their constituents "the stale bread of hatred and the spoiled meat of racism"; by a federal government that was eager to spend money on a war in Vietnam while refusing to "protect the lives of its own citizens seeking the right to vote"; and by "every Negro who passively accepts the evils of segregation and stands on the sidelines in the struggle for justice. Jimmy Lee Jackson's death says we must work unrelentingly to make the American dream a reality."

"We was infuriated to the point that we wanted to carry Jimmy's body to George Wallace and dump it on the steps of the Capitol," said Albert Turner, a local civil rights leader in Marion. "We had decided that we were going to get killed or we was going to be free."

King declared his support for the fifty-mile march, beginning the following Sunday across the Edmund Pettus bridge in Selma and continuing along Route 80 to the state capital in Montgomery. For some, the mood was somber. There had been, as SNCC's John Lewis put it, "too many funerals . . . people with courage and dignity gave the supreme sacrifice, really, paid the supreme price. It was troublesome and it was a very low moment for many of us, a very dark and lonely hour, because, in a real sense, we felt a great sense of responsibility."

Governor Wallace wanted no part of a march that would cast him in the role of murderer. At a press conference, he announced that the state would not permit the march because it would tie up traffic on the highway. Wallace put the highway patrol on alert.

SNCC, the civil rights group with the longest history in Selma, tried to talk the SCLC out of staging the march. In a letter to King, John Lewis wrote, "We strongly believe that the objectives of the march do not justify the dangers . . . consequently the Student Nonviolent Coordinating Committee will [only] live up to those minimal commitments . . . to provide radios and cars, doctors and nurses, and nothing beyond that."

The SCLC was undeterred. The march would begin as scheduled on March 7. It would take at least four days, providing plenty of time for dialogue with the nation's news reporters.

On Friday, March 5, King visited Johnson and the two conferred for over an hour. Afterwards King told reporters he had asked the president to include federal registrars in the voting rights bill and abolish all use of literacy tests. The two leaders did not know that the Justice Department had created a proposal that compromised on the literacy test question: If, in a state or county that employed the test, fewer than fifty percent of those of voting age were either not registered or not voting, the literacy test would be banned. The proposal also allowed the use of federal registrars in any state or county where literacy tests were suspended. The proposal was on its way to the White House as King left.

The next day, some seventy sympathetic whites held their own march on Selma's Dallas County Courthouse. They were led by Rev. Joseph Ellwanger, chairman of the Concerned White Citizens of Alabama. Standing on the steps where C. T. Vivian had been beaten, Ellwanger read a statement saying they had "come to Selma today to tell the nation that there are white people in Alabama who will speak out against the events which have recently occurred in this and neighboring counties and towns. We consider it a shocking injustice that there are still counties in Alabama where there are no Negroes registered to vote and where Negroes have reason to fear hostility and harassment by public officials when they do try to register . . . We are horrified at the brutal way in which the police at times have attempted to break up peaceful assemblies and demonstrations by American citizens who are exercising their constitutional right to protest injustice . . . "

As Ellwanger spoke, a group of segregationists began a counter rally, singing "Dixie" in an effort to drown out the speech. Ellwanger raised his voice, and the contingent of supportive whites struck up a rendition of "America the Beautiful." Blacks, too, had been drawn to the scene, and they chimed in with "We Shall Overcome." Wilson Baker rushed to the courthouse and urged Ellwanger to leave before a riot broke out. Ellwanger and his group left, as did the black bystanders, but a SNCC photographer was attacked by the segregationists. When the man managed to lock himself in a parked car, the mob hoisted the vehicle off the ground, but Baker persuaded them to put it down and let the photographer go.

King did not return to Selma after his White House meeting. He had frequently been away from his church in Atlanta and, although he had promised to lead the march, he now said he needed to be in his own pulpit that day. He would join the march to Montgomery later.

Although SNCC did not approve of the march, the executive committee agreed to let SNCC members participate as individuals. On the morning of the march, SCLC workers Hosea Williams, Andy Young, and James Bevel met at Brown's Chapel and flipped a coin to decide who would lead the march in King's absence. It fell to Hosea Williams to lead the demonstrators; SNCC chairman John Lewis would walk beside him. Six hundred people, standing two by two, lined up behind them. To everyone's surprise, there were no police in sight as Williams and Lewis led the marchers six blocks to Broad Street and began to cross the Edmund Pettus Bridge spanning the Alabama River in East Selma.

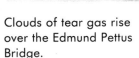

Clouds of tear gas rise over the Edmund Pettus Bridge.

"When we arrived at the apex of the Edmund Pettus Bridge," recalls Lewis, "we saw a sea of blue[-clad] Alabama state troopers." Gas masks hung from the belts of the troopers, who were slapping billy clubs against their hands. Williams asked Lewis if he could swim. Lewis looked down at the cold river and answered, "No."

As the marchers approached the far side of the bridge, Major John Cloud ordered them to turn back. "It would be detrimental to your safety to continue this march," he said. "You are ordered to disperse, go home or to your church. This march will not continue. You have two minutes . . . "

Williams asked, "May we have a word with you, Major?" Cloud replied that there was nothing to talk about. He waited, then commanded, "Troopers, advance." Fifty policemen moved forward, knocking the first ten to twenty demonstrators off their feet. People screamed and struggled to break free as their packs and bags were scattered across the pavement. Tear gas was fired, and then lawmen on horseback charged into the stumbling protesters.

"The horses . . . were more humane than the troopers; they stepped over fallen victims," recalls Amelia Boynton. "As I stepped aside from a trooper's club, I felt a blow on my arm . . . Another blow by a trooper, as I was gasping for breath, knocked me to the ground and there I lay, unconscious . . . "

"All I could see was the outburst of tear gas," said Sheyann Webb, then eight years old. "I saw people being beaten and I tried to run home as fast as I could.

The Media and the Movement:

An Interview With Richard Valeriani

Richard Valeriani joined NBC in 1962 and covered the civil rights protests in Albany, Birmingham, and Selma for the network. He later spent twenty years in Washington, where he reported on the State Department, White House, and Pentagon. Valeriani currently works for NBC News in New York.

I think that television helped accelerate the progress of a movement whose time had come. The wires, newspapers, and magazines would eventually have had a similar impact. But it would not have been nearly so immediate. The other thing that television did, and I think this is overlooked, is that it forced the print media to be more honest than it had ever been in covering these events. In the old days, the wire service guy would sit there in Birmingham and call up the local sheriff . . . He would write the sheriff's point of view entirely. Television forced [print journalists] to go there and see what was happening, and then they could not distort it.

. . . A lot of people identified the press with the movement. We were in the middle. I used to get complaints all the time. The local whites said that we were helping outside agitators and that if we went away, they would go away. They said that in effect we were part of the movement, instigating the movement, encouraging them to do these things. On the other hand, we'd get complaints from blacks that we were not encouraging the movement, that we were not doing enough to propagandize their cause. The best you could do was to juxtapose something that Bull Connor said with something that Martin Luther King said or with something that Jim Clark said. But we were constantly caught.

One night, when Chuck Quinn and I were covering the Selma events together, there was to be a nighttime march in Marion, Alabama. Nighttime marches were always dangerous . . . we knew there was going to be trouble right away because local folks threatened us, sprayed our cameras with black paint so we couldn't shoot, ordered us to put the cameras down, and harassed us. It was a very tense situation. When the march started, the cops went in and broke it up, very violent. They killed Jimmie Lee Jackson that night. The passions that were aroused led somebody to walk up behind me and hit me in the back of the head with an ax handle. Now luckily for me, he hit me with a roundhouse swing instead of coming overhead and hitting me on the top of the skull. I staggered and was stunned, and a state trooper came up to this guy who hit me. He took the ax handle away, threw it on the steps of city hall, and said, "I guess you've done enough damage with that tonight." But the policeman did not arrest him. Then another white man walked up to me and said, "Are you hurt? Do you need a doctor?" I put my hand to the back of my head and then looked at it and it was full of blood. I said, "Yeah, I think I do. I'm bleeding." And then he thrust his face right up against mine and said, "Well, we don't have doctors for people like you." But my crew got me off to the hospital. The next day the mayor visited me at the hospital and apologized, and they finally did arrest the guy after it had caused something of a national uproar.

The Invasion of Selma:

An Interview with Joseph Smitherman

Joseph Smitherman operated an appliance store until 1960, when he was elected to the Selma City Council. Four years later, he became mayor of Selma. Except for a one-year hiatus, Smitherman has held that office ever since, and is now serving his sixth term. Smitherman reports that in the fourth- and fifth-term elections, he won seventy and eighty percent of the black vote, respectively.

They picked Selma just like a movie producer would pick a set. You had the right ingredients. Clark, in his day, had a helmet liner like General Patton, an Eisenhower jacket, and a swagger stick. Baker was very impressive. And I guess I was the least of all—I was 145 pounds and had a crew cut and big ears. So you had a young mayor with no background or experience, and you had this dynamic figure, Wilson Baker, a professional law enforcement officer, a moderate, if you please. And you had Sheriff Clark, who was a military figure.

. . . I was not there [on Bloody Sunday]. I stayed away, at city hall. I did not understand how big it was until I saw it on television. I was only about three blocks from it, but I didn't go out on the streets. I would stand on city hall because being around Dr. King was a political no-no.

. . . We became the march capital of the world. Kids would come in, students, to get their spurs in Selma. I remember I had a phone call from the University of Minnesota and some young girl said, "We're coming to your city tomorrow." I don't know what I told her really, but I didn't care for it. She chartered an airplane and brought a group of students to Montgomery Airport. Landed, rented a bus, came over here, marched two hours, got in the bus, went back up in the plane.

. . . Even then you knew [racial discrimination] was wrong but you would always rationalize: "Why were they pushing this and why were they trying to tear up the society by coming on this strong with demonstrations? Why didn't these outside agitators leave us alone to work out our own problems?" That was generally the attitude. Of course we knew it was wrong to shoot fire hoses and turn dogs loose; we never did that here. But we all shared the blame.

And as I began to run home, I saw horses behind me . . . Hosea Williams picked me up and I told him to put me down, he wasn't running fast enough."

"The police were riding along on horseback beating people," remembers Andrew Young. "The tear gas was so thick you couldn't get to where the people were who needed help . . . there were people who came back to the church and started talking about going to get their guns. And you had to talk them down . . . 'What kind of gun you got? .32, .38? You know how that's going to hold up against the automatic rifles and . . . shotguns that they've got? And how many you got? They [the police] had at least 200 shotguns out there with buckshot in them. You ever see buckshot? You ever see what buckshot does to a deer?' . . . You make people think about the specifics of violence, and then they realize how suicidal and nonsensical it is."

Television coverage of the police assault interrupted the networks' regular programming; ABC broke into its broadcast of the film *Judgment at Nuremberg*. "When that beating happened at the foot of the bridge, it looked like war," recalls Mayor Smitherman. "That went all over the country. And the people, the wrath of the nation came down on us."

From Atlanta, Martin Luther King sent telegrams to prominent clergymen across the nation, saying, "In the vicious maltreatment of defenseless citizens of Selma, where old women and young children were gassed and clubbed at random, we have witnessed an eruption of the disease of racism which seeks to destroy all America. No American is without responsibility . . . Join me in Selma for a ministers' march to Montgomery on Tuesday morning, March 9."

In Alabama's capital, Governor Wallace declared that "Those folks in Selma have made this a seven-day-a-week job, but we can't give one inch. We're going to enforce state law." Selma's mayor tried to discredit King, saying the incident should make it "evident to the Negro people . . . that King and the other leaders who ask them to break the law are always absent from the violence as he was today."

On the day after "Bloody Sunday," as it was soon dubbed, the SCLC asked U.S. District Court Judge Frank M. Johnson to forbid Governor Wallace from interfering with Tuesday's march. The judge did not comply, but said he would hold a Thursday hearing on the matter. On Tuesday morning, he enjoined the protesters from marching until after the hearing. King and the SCLC now had to decide whether to defy the federal courts, which had been a primary ally of the movement since the 1954 *Brown* decision. In fact, civil rights leaders generally felt that this particular judge had been fair to them over the years. But the activists did not want to back off. King had called for the march, and hundreds of people from all over the country had come to participate. The march could not be cancelled.

The Justice Department asked King to reconsider, but he refused. He then received an emergency visit from former Florida governor LeRoy Collins, head of the Justice Department's Community Relations Service, which had been specifically created to deal with racial conflicts. King was adamant. He said later, "I would rather die on the highway in Alabama than make a butchery of conscience by compromising with evil." At a subsequent meeting, however, Collins told King that, if the marchers turned back when they reached the line of police, there would be no violence. King, according to several accounts, responded noncommittally.

Before the march, King told a capacity crowd at Brown's Chapel they had "no alternative but to keep moving . . . We've gone too far now to turn back. And, in a real sense, we are moving and we cannot afford to stop, because Alabama and our nation have a date with destiny . . . "

On "Turnaround Tuesday," Rev. Ralph Abernathy led the marchers in prayer before they turned and headed back to the church.

The minister led 1500 people out of the church and across the Pettus Bridge. Again, state troopers were waiting. Fifty miles away in Montgomery, Governor Wallace listened on the telephone as an aide reported every step of the march. In Washington, the Justice Department monitored its own telephone report. As on Sunday, Major John Cloud told the marchers, "You are ordered to stop. Stand where you are. This march will not continue." Gently swaying from side to side, the phalanx of marchers sang "We Shall Overcome." Afterwards, King knelt and asked Rev. Ralph Abernathy to lead the demonstrators in prayer. Then, to most everyone's surprise, King rose and conducted the marchers back to the church. Many of King's followers were confused and upset. "All of a sudden I realized that the people in front were turning around and coming back," recalls Orloff Miller, a Unitarian minister from Boston, "and I was aghast. What is going on? Are we not going through with this confrontation? What's happening?"

Many movement activists felt King had betrayed them. Some even suspected he had made a secret deal with the federal government, and SNCC accused him of selling out.

King later explained that he had promised to proceed with the march only until police violence was imminent. "We would disengage then," King wrote later, "having made our point, revealing the continued presence of violence and showing clearly who are the oppressed and who are the oppressors, hoping, finally, that the national administration in Washington would feel and respond . . . "

King asked those who had come to Selma for the march to stay on for a few more days, and many did. Later that night, Rev. Miller and two other white Unitarian ministers, Clark Olsen and James Reeb, were attacked as they left a soul-food restaurant in Selma. Reeb was struck on the head with a club; he died two days later. The death of the thirty-eight-year-old clergyman provoked a national outcry and demonstrations in many cities. The president issued a statement, saying, "The best legal talent in the federal government is engaged in preparing legislation which will secure [the] right [to vote] for every American."

As white America vented its anger, some blacks felt bitter that the killing of the white minister had stirred a nation unmoved by the death of Jimmie Lee Jackson. "It seemed to me that the movement itself was playing into the hands of racism," said Stokely Carmichael, looking back. "What you want is the nation to be upset when anybody is killed . . . but it almost [seems that] for this to be recognized, a white person must be killed."

In Selma, tensions were at a peak. Police cordoned off the area around Brown's Chapel to pen in the demonstrators and keep hostile whites out. On the fourth day, a small group of demonstrators broke through the ropes—which the protesters had dubbed the "Berlin Wall"—and had a verbal confrontation with some of Sheriff Clark's men. But there was no violence, and Wilson Baker escorted the demonstrators back to the church. Realizing the futility of the barricade, Baker ordered it removed.

On Friday, March 12, King traveled to Montgomery for the hearing before Judge Johnson. The preacher defended the SCLC's request that the demonstrators be allowed to march to Montgomery without state interference. Sheriff Clark asked that King be held in contempt of the court's order not to march on the previous Tuesday. The judge responded, "Any contempt proceeding will be a matter between the court and the contempter, and is not any business of James Clark." King told Johnson he had never intended to lead the marchers all the way to Montgomery on Tuesday, but only to confront the state troopers and demonstrate the activists' resolve. The judge handed down no decision that day.

On Saturday, Alabama governor George Wallace flew to Washington, D.C., in the state's powder-blue airplane, which had a Confederate flag emblazoned on its side. The governor met with President Johnson, who tried to convince Wallace to assist with the march. Justice Department staffer Burke Marshall was at the meeting. He recalls, "Governor Wallace didn't quite grovel, but he was [very] pliant by the end of the two hours, with President Johnson putting his arm around him and squeezing him and telling him it's a moment of history, and how do we

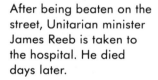

After being beaten on the street, Unitarian minister James Reeb is taken to the hospital. He died days later.

Ministers and the March:

An Interview with Orloff Miller

Boston-born Orloff Miller was one of the hundreds of clergy who heeded Martin Luther King's call to join the Selma march. Miller represented the Unitarian Universalist Church, which emphasizes freedom in religious belief and toleration of dissenting opinions. A Unitarian minister for twenty-five years, Miller currently lives in San Francisco.

. . . When the telegram came from Martin Luther King asking ministers of all faiths to come to Selma, I had been back two months from Mississippi. We had visited the projects sponsored by the Council of Federated Organizations, and much to my delight, I found Unitarian Universalist students very much involved in the Mississippi Freedom effort. And so I was ready for that telegram when it arrived. . . . I immediately got on the phone and called ministers who were connected with our programs all across the United States and Canada.

. . . Most of us went to Selma without even a toothbrush because we thought it was a one-day event. Nevertheless, when Dr. King asked if we could remain a few days, a number of us decided to stay, I among them.

. . . Jim Reeb, Clark Olsen, and I decided to have dinner together. We had been told that we should not try to eat in the white community downtown, but in some of the black restaurants. Jim had been associate minister at All Souls Unitarian Church in Washington, D.C., until he went to Boston six months before the march. While he was in Washington, he had been our minister liaison with student groups at American University and George Washington University and the other schools around Washington. Clark was minister of the Unitarian Fellowship in Berkeley at the time.

. . . We double-checked at the SCLC office for directions to the restaurant. We went to Walker's Cafe and found a lot of our colleagues there. The restaurant was hard-pressed to find enough food. I remember I ordered steak and I got chicken . . . After dinner, as we started walking across the street, there appeared four or five white men and they yelled at us, "Hey, you niggers." We did not look across at them, but we quickened our pace . . . One of them was carrying a club, and Clark said he turned around and saw the club just as it was swung. Jim Reeb, who was closest to the curb, caught the full impact of that blow on the side of his head . . .

We took Jim by ambulance to University Hospital in Birmingham, sixty-five miles away. We had to stop first at the SCLC office, because the hospital would not accept Jim for care without some kind of a deposit. Diane Nash made out a check for $150 . . . We got a few miles out of town and the ambulance had a flat tire. A sheriff's car came along, they flashed their flashlights inside the ambulance, and they asked us all kinds of questions. "Who is that there? What happened?" We explained and asked for an escort. They refused. "You won't need an escort, you don't need anybody to help," they said . . . We actually hit 110 miles [per hour] at one point heading for Birmingham . . .

It's a terrible thing to have to say, but for some reason it took the death of a white clergyman to turn things around. Tuesday was the "Turnaround Day"—not only of the march, but also of how America saw the civil rights struggle. Because when Jim Reeb, a white clergyman from the North, was killed in Selma, people suddenly sat up and took notice and from then on things changed in the movement. People came from all over the country to Selma. Selma became a flood of demonstrators. People went to Washington and they [put pressure] on President Johnson. When ministers went to the White House, Johnson rightly said, "Where have you been all these years?" And where had we been? We finally woke up and it was Jim's death that woke us up.

want to be remembered in history? Do we want to be remembered as petty little men, or do we want to be remembered as great figures that faced up to our moments of crisis?" The president then escorted the governor out, hoping, Marshall says, "that Governor Wallace, who was by that time like a rubber band, would act like a responsible governor."

After Wallace left the White House, the president held a news conference in the Rose Garden. "What happened in Selma was an American tragedy," said Johnson, his face solemn. "The blows that were received, the blood that was shed, the life of the good man that was lost, must strengthen the determination of each of us to bring full equality and equal justice to all of our people. This is not just the policy of your government or your president. It is in the heart and the purpose and the meaning of America itself." This time, the president backed his words with action. He announced that on Monday he would send a bill to Congress to "strike down all restrictions used to deny the people the right to vote."

That Monday night, seventy million people watched on television as Johnson stood before Congress to announce the voting rights legislation. He spoke not only to the politicians but to his fellow Americans, asking them to support the blacks' quest for true suffrage. "Their cause," Johnson said, "must be our cause, too. Because it's not just Negroes, but it's really all of us who must overcome the crippling legacy of bigotry and injustice. And," he concluded, "we *shall* overcome."

The president had used the movement's most powerful theme. C. T. Vivian remembers the moment well. "We were all sitting around together . . . and when LBJ said, 'And we shall overcome,' we all cheered. And I looked over . . . and Martin was very quietly sitting in the chair, and a tear ran down his cheek. It was a victory like none other. It was an affirmation of the movement."

Selma's Mayor Smitherman also noticed the president's choice of words. "President Johnson came on and said, 'We shall overcome,' and it was like you'd been struck by a dagger in your heart . . . I mean, you know, what's the guy doing?"

In Montgomery, SNCC's chairman James Forman was less impressed, calling the president's use of the movement's phrase a "tinkling empty symbol." The day after Johnson's speech, Forman led a march in Montgomery to the capitol building. Some of the activists were attacked by mounted city police brandishing cattle prods. Deputies with ropes and whips lashed the demonstrators. Forman and the young blacks with him were enraged that such brutality continued after the president's speech.

In an address to a joint session of Congress on March 15, 1965, President Lyndon Johnson presented his proposal for a Voting Rights Act. The president concluded his speech with the words, "We shall overcome."

Speaking in a church later that night, Forman said, "I want to know, did President Johnson mean what he said? See, that's what I want to know, because there's only one man in the country that can stop George Wallace and those posses . . . these problems will not be solved until [the man] in that shaggedy old place called the White House begins to shake and gets on the phone and says, 'Now listen, George, we're coming down there and throw you in jail if you don't stop that mess' . . . I said it today and I will say it again: If we can't sit at the table, let's knock the fuckin' legs off, excuse me."

Martin Luther King, Jr., rose to speak next. Showing uncharacteristic ire, he intoned, "I'm not satisfied as long as the Negro sees life as a long and empty corridor with a 'No Exit' sign at the end. The cup of endurance has run over." The speeches inflamed the crowd. King tried to calm the people, reminding them that the Montgomery bus boycott eleven years earlier had endured its darkest moments just before the United States Supreme Court ruled that the buses must be integrated. But the angry crowd was not in the mood for a history lesson. Then Andrew Young approached King, who listened briefly to his SCLC aide before announcing triumphantly, "Judge Johnson has just ruled that we have a legal and constitutional right to march from Selma to Montgomery." The crowd roared its approval.

The ruling cleared the way for the march to take place, but Governor Wallace still had not agreed to provide the marchers with police protection. He called the protesters "Communist-trained anarchists" and said that the state could not afford to pay state troopers to protect them. President Johnson responded by federalizing the Alabama National Guard and ordering its 1,800 members to watch over the march. Johnson also dispatched 2,000 Army troops, 100 FBI agents, and another 100 federal marshals. On Sunday, March 21, the Selma-to-Montgomery march finally got underway.

Four thousand people, black and white, gathered at Brown's Chapel for the fifty-four-mile journey. Some who had never marched before joined those who had been demonstrating for ten years. King was in the lead, walking with Ralph Bunche, a fellow Nobel Peace Prize winner, and Rabbi Abraham Heschel of the Jewish Theological Seminary. Belligerent segregationists lined the route, taunting the demonstrators and holding signs such as "Yankee Trash Go Home," but there were no attacks.

"As far as the marchers were concerned, everything went off smoothly," remembers Amelia Boynton, "but the troopers and organized marshals were kept busy beating the bushes for possible snipers."

The March from Selma to Montgomery

At night the marchers slept in tents they pitched along the route, and a team of volunteers shuttled food and supplies to them from march headquarters in Selma. Veterans and novices alike were sustained by a spirit of history in the making. "You didn't get tired, you really didn't get weary," recalls John Lewis, whose group had originally opposed the march. "You had to go—it was more than an ordinary march. To me, there was never a march like this one before, there hasn't been one since . . . It was the sense of community moving there, and as you walked you saw people coming, waving, bringing you food or bringing you something to drink."

"My feets is tired, but

my soul is rested."

"The teenagers were a great inspiration," says Boynton. "I was much impressed with a fifteen-year-old Selma boy, [Leroy] Moton. His face beamed with pride as he carried the American flag . . . Every now and then he would burst into song and we would join him, often singing 'The Star-Spangled Banner.'"

Major John Cloud, who had ordered the attack on the first march, rode in his patrol car at the head of the march for part of the way, as did Sheriff Clark. Reporters asked Clark if he had any feelings about the event. "No," he replied. "I'm glad to get rid of the ones that are leaving [Selma], but I wish they'd come back and get the rest of them . . . "

By the final leg of the march, some 25,000 people were striding toward Alabama's capital city. Near the end of the five days' walk, the SCLC learned of a possible plot to assassinate King as the throng entered Montgomery. Andrew Young knew that King would not leave the march; the question was how to preserve both the triumphant finale and King's life.

"Martin always wore the good-preacher blue suit," says Young. "And I figured since we couldn't stop him from marching, we just had to kind of believe that it was true when white folks said we all look alike. So everybody that was about Martin's size and had a blue suit, I put in front of the line with him . . . There were some very important people who felt as though they were being pushed back, but all of the preachers loved the chance to get up in the front of the line with Martin Luther King. I don't think to this day most of them know why they were up there."

As the march made front-page news throughout the nation, the Voting Rights Act was before Congress. In the House Judiciary Committee, Congressman Emanuel Celler said, "Recent events in Alabama, involving murder, savage brutality, and violence by local police, state troopers, and posses, have so aroused the nation as to make action by this Congress necessary and speedy . . . the climate of public opinion throughout the nation has so changed because of the

Alabama outrages, as to make assured the passage of this solid bill—a bill that would have been inconceivable a year ago."

On Thursday, March 25, the march reached Montgomery, passing the Dexter Avenue Baptist Church, King's congregation during the Montgomery bus boycott. "It was a great moment to go back to Montgomery," recalls Coretta Scott King, "because, you see, for us it was returning to Montgomery after ten years. And I kept thinking about ten years earlier, how we were . . . just blacks [in the movement] . . . " By contrast, the Selma-to-Montgomery march "had Catholic priests, and nuns, and you had other clergy, and you had a lot of white people. It was really a beautiful thing to pass Dexter Avenue Church and go toward the capitol marching together."

The national television networks provided live coverage as Martin Luther King marched up to the capitol with many of the movement's heroes by his side. There was Rosa Parks, the woman whose refusal to move to the back of the bus had triggered the Montgomery boycott; Roy Wilkins of the NAACP; Whitney Young of the National Urban League; A. Philip Randolph of the Brotherhood of Sleeping Car Porters; and John Lewis of SNCC. King walked up the capitol steps and faced his fellow marchers. "Last Sunday," he said, "more than eight thousand of us started on a mighty walk from Selma, Alabama. We have walked on meandering highways and rested our bodies on rocky byways . . . Sister Pollard, . . . who lived in this community during the [bus] boycott, . . . was asked if she didn't want a ride, and when she answered 'no,' the person said, 'Well, aren't you tired?' And with ungrammatical profundity she said, 'My feets is tired, but my soul is rested.'"

Rosa Parks was one of the honored guests at the Montgomery ceremonies. The Montgomery bus boycott ten years before was seen by many activists as the beginning of the movement.

Behind the civil rights leader, the capitol building was flying the Confederate flag. Governor Wallace occasionally looked out at the crowd from behind venetian blinds. King told his audience that, using the vote, black Americans could join whites as equals in a "society at peace with itself, a society that can live with its conscience." But he predicted that getting blacks registered would be hard work, even if the Voting Rights Act were approved. "The road ahead is not altogether a smooth one. There are no broad highways to lead us easily and inevitably to quick solutions. We are still in for a season of suffering." Then he continued triumphantly, "However difficult the moment, however frustrating the hour, it will not be long, because truth crushed to the earth will rise again. How long? Not long. Because you shall reap what you sow. How long? Not long . . . because the arc of the moral universe is long, but it bends towards justice. How long? Not long. Because mine eyes have seen the glory of the coming of the Lord."

Ending with a recitation of "The Battle Hymn of the Republic," King stressed the song's final lines: "Be jubilant, my feet, our God is marching on . . . His truth is marching on."

After the speech, eight march leaders were chosen to enter the capitol and present a petition to Governor Wallace, asking him to remove all obstacles to black voter registration in the state of Alabama. Amelia Boynton, one of the eight, recalls that when the group approached the capitol, they "encountered state troopers standing shoulder-to-shoulder in a solid line . . . and a second row of city officers with riot guns and bayonets. The officers moved toward us in formation, and someone asked, 'What do you want?' We told them we wanted to see the governor and were told he was not in. This was only minutes after our spokesman, SCLC secretary Rev. Joseph E. Lowery of Birmingham, had been told by Governor Wallace's personal secretary that the governor was in his office." When the eight activists persisted, the governor's executive secretary agreed to take the petition from them.

The marchers had been advised to leave the Montgomery area as quickly as possible after the demonstration. The previous evening, Governor Wallace had appealed on television for those not participating in the march to avoid the capitol area, but the activists knew that violence was a real possibility. People had volunteered to drive the marchers back to Selma, where many of them lived or had lodgings. One such volunteer was Viola Liuzzo, a white homemaker from Detroit. After dropping off one group of marchers at Brown's Chapel that evening, she headed back toward Montgomery, accompanied by Leroy Moton, the teenager who had carried an American flag during the march. Her Michigan license plates must have made her Oldsmobile an easy mark for the four Ku Klux Klansmen who chased her on Route 80. As their car pulled alongside Liuzzo's, one of the four shot her twice in the face, killing her. Liuzzo's car ran into a ditch. When the murderers came to look inside, Moton saved himself by pretending to be dead.

After the Klansmen had gone, the young man managed to flag down another demonstrator who was driving by. Within hours, the FBI discovered that one of its undercover informants had been in the car with the Klansmen. At noon the next day, President Johnson announced on television that the FBI had arrested the four. "My father," said the president, "fought them [the Klan] many long years ago in Texas, and I have fought them all my life, because I believe them to threaten the peace of every community where they exist."

In Montgomery, more than 25,000 people listened to speakers in front of the state capitol building. Alabama's state flag flies with the Confederate flag on the government building.

Governor Wallace, appearing on the "Today" show, was defensive. "Of course I regret the incident," he said, "but I would like to point out that people are assaulted in every state in the union . . . With 25,000 marching in the streets and chanting and maligning and slandering and libeling the people of this state, as they did for several hours on this network and the other networks, I think the people of our state were greatly restrained."

Support for the Voting Rights Act increased in the wake of the violence. A dispute over whether to ban the use of poll taxes was the one factor that delayed the bill's speedy passage. Such taxes had long been used to prevent blacks from voting in several southern states, but the Johnson administration feared that striking them down by federal statute alone might be unconstitutional. To resolve the issue, Johnson asked the attorney general to file suit against the four states where poll taxes were still employed—Alabama, Mississippi, Texas, and Virginia.

Senator Harry Byrd of Virginia told an aide, "You know, you can't stop this bill. We can't deny the Negroes a basic constitutional right to vote." On May 26, the Senate passed the bill by a vote of seventy-seven to nineteen. In the House, the bill withstood five weeks of debate before winning approval on July 9.

On August 6, President Johnson sat in the President's Room off the Capitol Rotunda in Washington, preparing to make the Voting Rights Act the law of the land. President Abraham Lincoln had signed the Emancipation Proclamation one hundred and four years earlier in that same room. Rosa Parks, Martin Luther King, Jr., and other civil rights luminaries stood by Johnson as he signed the bill.

"The vote is the most powerful instrument ever devised by man for breaking down injustice and destroying the terrible walls which imprison men because they are different from other men . . . ," said the president. "[The Voting Rights Act] is one of the most monumental laws in the entire history of American freedom."

Securing the Voting Rights Act was a major victory for the civil rights movement. But it was only one part of the larger struggle for dignity, equality, and justice. Segregation lingered in many spheres, black unemployment remained disproportionately high, and violence still flared against black men, women, and children. But with the passage of the Voting Rights Act, black citizens had at last gained access to one of the most potent tools of democracy. Black voters throughout the nation began to elect people of color to such public offices as mayor, state legislator, and congressional representative. Those officials began to serve constituencies that finally included people of all races.

By the summer following the bill's passage, 9,000 blacks in Dallas County, Alabama, had registered to vote. Sheriff Jim Clark was voted out of office. Over the next decade, as more black people throughout the South began to register and vote, segregationists lost seats of local power. At the state level, progress was much slower. Governors Orval Faubus of Arkansas and George Wallace of Alabama remained in office for several more terms. Nationally, senators James Eastland of Mississippi and Strom Thurmond of South Carolina held their posts for many years. But even these once-ardent segregationists eventually found it politically prudent to soften their rhetoric and seek black support. Joseph Smitherman, still Selma's mayor at this writing, was elected to six consecutive terms of office. He says that in the last election he gained as much as eighty percent of the black vote.

The voting power of blacks also affected federal appointments. President Kennedy named Thurgood Marshall to a United States circuit court of appeals in 1961. In 1965 President Johnson selected Marshall as his solicitor general and two years later asked him to serve as the nation's first black justice of the Supreme Court. In 1966 Johnson appointed the nation's first black cabinet member, Robert Weaver, to the position of secretary of the Department of Housing and Urban Development. President Jimmy Carter appointed Andrew Young to the position of United Nations ambassador. Young went on to become the mayor of Atlanta, while Unita Blackwell became mayor of Mayersville, Mississippi—a state with more black elected officials than any other. By 1984, black mayors had been elected in 255 cities.

The North was also affected by the increased participation of blacks in the electoral process. In 1966, Edward W. Brooke of Massachusetts became the first black elected to the United States Senate. The next year, Carl B. Stokes became the first black mayor of a major city when he won that office in Cleveland. Tom Bradley won Los Angeles' mayoral seat in 1973, and former SNCC worker Marion Barry was elected mayor of Washington, D.C., in 1979. In 1983, Harold Washington became Chicago's chief executive.

Few people in the movement believed that morality could be controlled by legislation. But expecting things to change without the force of law would be treating freedom like a gift subject to the generosity of the giver, and not a right due each American citizen. Securing legislation was a crucial step in making the country more democratic. Voting, access to public accommodations, and an equal education were no longer matters of local largess; they were matters of law.

Over a period of ten years, the civil rights movement not only dramatically altered the nation, but also transformed a race. Black people who had lived under oppression for 300 years gained a new sense of dignity and power and a truer sense of citizenship. White people were changed as well—after an unquestioned acceptance of a segregated society, many examined how they treated their black neighbors and went on to accept civil rights as human rights. But changing the hearts and minds of most white people would take more than legislation. After the Selma march, the assassination of Malcolm X, and the signing of the Voting Rights Act, a new sense of injustice began to burn in northern cities.

The movement's emphasis shifted from the moral imperatives that had garnered support from the nation's moderates—issues such as the right to vote and the right to a decent education—to issues whose moral rightness was not as readily apparent: job and housing discrimination, Johnson's war on poverty, and affirmative action. The movement tackled these varied issues in many different ways, from black nationalism, black power and even a call for full-scale revolution to a continuation of marches, protests, court battles, and sit-ins. Nonviolence was no longer the only tool for change; many blacks had seen too many murders, too many betrayals. The built-up anger expressed itself in the 1965 riots in Watts and Harlem, and later in Chicago, Detroit, and many other cities. Violence fractured the movement's widespread moral support. The split in the coalition between white liberals and black activists, seen in an early stage at the 1964 Democratic Convention, widened dramatically.

But the violent events of later years and the many new directions of the civil rights movement cannot obscure the remarkable accomplishments wrought by the men and women, black and white, who in ten short years rewove the fabric of American society. The decade spanning the *Brown* decision of 1954 and the Voting Rights Act of 1965 saw more social change, more court decisions, and more legislation in the name of civil rights than any decade in our nation's history. Those changes were forced by millions of Americans who, with a sense of service and justice, kept their eyes on the prize of freedom.

"I know one thing we did right
was the day we started to fight.
Keep your eyes on the prize,
hold on, hold on."

Epilogue
Where Have They Gone?

The civil rights movement involved thousands of people, black and white, young and old, who fought to make America live up to its promise of equality. The lives of these people in the years following 1965 reflect both changes in the country and changes in the movement itself. Many turned their attention to the Vietnam war; others participated in the Black Power movement; some went into politics and law. Others simply carried on with their lives, deciding, as E. D. Nixon said after the successful Montgomery bus boycott, "I wanna enjoy some of this stuff myself."

The following list is by no means comprehensive, but it presents biographical information that indicates the changed direction of the movement and the country. Names are listed in order of their first significant appearance within the text.

CHAPTER ONE

James Nabrit, who joined the Howard University faculty during Charles Houston's time, became president of Howard in 1960. In 1965 he was appointed United States deputy representative to the United Nations Security Council. After returning to Howard University in 1968, he retired from the presidency in 1969. He died in 1997 at the age of ninety-seven.

Thurgood Marshall, who in 1938 succeeded Charles Houston as special counsel to the NAACP, was appointed by President Kennedy to the United States Court of Appeals for the Second Judicial Circuit in 1961. After four years on that appellate court, Marshall was named United States solicitor-general and, in 1967, President Johnson appointed him an associate justice of the United States Supreme Court. He died in 1993. As one obituary noted, "We make

movies about Malcolm X, we get a holiday in honor of Dr. Martin Luther King, but every day we live with the legacy of Justice Thurgood Marshall."

Spottswood W. Robinson III, who was the special counsel for the southeast region of the NAACP, served as dean of the Howard University School of Law. In 1966 Robinson became the first black appointed to the United States Court of Appeals for the District of Columbia Circuit and served as chief judge from 1981 to 1986. He assumed senior status in 1989 and died in 1998.

Robert Carter, an attorney with the Legal Defense Fund, became the director of a local chapter of the American Civil Liberties Union and was then appointed a United States District court judge for the Southern District of New York. He died in 2012.

Linda Brown, of *Brown v. Board of Education*, lives in Topeka, Kansas, where she teaches music. She has two grown children. Her school, Monroe Elementary, was designated a U.S. National Historic Site unit of the National Park Service in 1992.

Oliver Brown, Linda Brown's father, left Topeka four years after the 1954 decision and became a pastor at a Methodist church in Springfield, Missouri. He died in 1961 at the age of forty-two. His participation in the *Brown* case inspired his younger daughter, Cheryl Brown Henderson, to cofound the Brown Foundation for Educational Equity, Excellence and Research in 1988.

Jack Greenberg served as director-counsel of the NAACP Legal Defense Fund from 1961 to 1984 and now teaches at Columbia Law School where he is a full-time faculty member.

CHAPTER TWO

James O. Eastland retired in 1978 after thirty-five years as a Mississippi senator. Eastland chaired the Senate Judiciary Committee from 1956 until 1978. He died in 1986.

Mose Wright gave lectures for the NAACP on the Emmett Till case before moving to Argo, Illinois, where he farmed until his death in 1973.

Curtis Jones, who visited Money, Mississippi, with his cousin Emmett Till in 1955, was a Chicago policeman for thirty years. When he died in 2000 he had never fired his weapon.

Roy Bryant sold his confession to *Look* magazine in 1956 and was ostracized by the local community. He moved to another town to begin a new general store, but that business failed as well due to boycotts from black customers. He died in 1994.

Charles Diggs, Jr., the black United States congressman from Michigan, held his congressional seat through twelve succeeding terms and was the first chair of the Congressional Black Caucus. He was convicted in 1978 of padding his congressional office payroll. He left federal prison in 1981 and in 1983 earned a bachelor's degree from Howard University and became an undertaker in Maryland. He died in 1998.

Mamie Till (Bradley) Mobley, mother of Emmett Till, taught in the Chicago public schools for twenty-five years and received a master's degree in administration in 1976. She died in 2003 at the age of eighty-one. In the same year, her autobiography, *Death of Innocence: The Story of the Hate Crime that Changed America*, was published.

CHAPTER THREE

Jo Ann Robinson, the English professor who helped plan and launch the Montgomery bus boycott, resigned from Alabama State in 1960 because of the school's objections to faculty participation in civil rights protests. She later moved to Los Angeles, where she taught in the public schools until her retirement in 1976. Her memoir, *The Montgomery Bus Boycott and the Women Who Started It*, was published in 1987. She died in 1992.

E. D. Nixon, a key organizer of the Montgomery bus boycott and longtime activist in A. Philip Randolph's Brotherhood of Sleeping Car Porters, served as director of a housing project recreation program in Montgomery. He retired as president of the Alabama NAACP in 1977 and died in Montgomery in 1987. The Montgomery County public school system recognized his civil rights work by naming an elementary school after him in 2001.

Rosa Parks, whose refusal to surrender her seat on a segregated bus launched the Montgomery boycott, was fired from her job as a seamstress shortly after her arrest. She remained without a steady job for over a year. She eventually moved to Detroit, where for more than twenty years she was a secretary and receptionist in the Michigan office of United States congressman John Conyers. She started a foundation, the Rosa and Raymond Parks Institute for Self-Development, and wrote two memoirs. Starting in 1956, Parks appeared regularly as an honored guest at many civil rights functions. She received the NAACP's Spingarn Medal in 1979, the Presidential Medal of Freedom, and the Congressional Gold Medal. When she died in 2005, she became the first woman to lie in repose in the United States Capitol

Rotunda. A U.S. postage stamp, a statue in the Capitol Rotunda, and many events marked the one hundredth anniversary of her birth in 2013.

Clifford Durr, the white lawyer who supported the Montgomery boycott, continued to work on civil and human rights cases. In 1966 he received the Civil Liberties Award from the New York Civil Liberties Union. Durr died in 1975.

Virginia Durr remained a supporter of civil rights causes and in 1985 published her autobiography, *Outside the Magic Circle*. President Bill Clinton praised her after her death in 1999: "Her courage, outspokenness, and steely conviction in the early days of the civil rights movement helped change this nation forever." In 2003 a collection of her civil rights correspondence was published and in 2006 she was inducted into the Alabama Women's Hall of Fame.

Fred Gray, the black attorney who represented Rosa Parks in Montgomery, has remained an active civil rights lawyer in Alabama. In 1970 he was elected to the Alabama state legislature and served until 1974. Gray obtained a $10 million settlement in 1974 from the United States government on behalf of the black men who had unknowingly participated in the Tuskegee Syphilis Study, a forty-year clinical trial to study the effects of untreated syphilis. He was named president of the National Bar Association in 1985 and in 2002 became the first black president of the Alabama Bar Association. He is the author of two books, *Bus Ride to Justice*, first published in 1995, and *The Tuskegee Syphilis Study*, published in 1998.

Martin Luther King, Jr., continued as a leader of the civil rights movement until he was assassinated on April 4, 1968, in Memphis, Tennessee. His birthday, January 15, is now a federal holiday.

Ralph Abernathy headed the SCLC from 1968 to 1977, when he resigned to run for Congress. Abernathy lost the election, but continued to serve as pastor of Atlanta's West Hunter Street Baptist Church. Abernathy's autobiography, *And the Walls Came Tumbling Down*, was published in 1989. He died in 1990, five weeks before his sixty-fourth birthday.

CHAPTER FOUR

Daisy Bates, president of the Arkansas chapter of the NAACP in 1957, shared the NAACP's Spingarn Medal the following year with the nine students who first integrated Little Rock's Central High School. In 1972, Bates led an attack on President Nixon's decision to cut funds for economic opportunity programs in Mitchellville, Arkansas. Bates revived the Arkansas State Press in 1984 and sold it in 1987. Her memoir, *The Long Shadow of Little Rock*, first published in 1962 and reprinted in 1986, became the first reprinted book to win an American Book Award. She died in Little Rock in 1999. Arkansas designated the third Monday in February as a state holiday to honor Daisy Gatson Bates.

Orval Faubus, a Democrat, became governor of Arkansas in 1955 and was reelected five times, serving until 1967. Faubus ran for governor in 1970, 1974, and 1986, but lost each time. He died in 1994.

Wiley Branton, after serving as chief counsel for the Little Rock Nine, became director of the Southern Regional Council's Voter Education Project. From 1965 to 1967 he served as special assistant to United

States attorneys general Nicholas Katzenbach and Ramsey Clark. At the time of his death in 1988, he was a partner in a Washington, D.C., law firm.

Ernest Green graduated from Central High School in 1958. After earning both bachelor's and master's degrees in sociology from Michigan State University, Green worked in New York with the A. Philip Randolph Institute, attempting to get more blacks into apprenticeships in the building trades. President Jimmy Carter appointed Green assistant secretary of labor for employment and training. In 1999, President Bill Clinton awarded the Little Rock Nine the Congressional Gold Medal. Green retired in 2009 as managing director for municipal finance at Barclays Capital (formerly Lehman Brothers) in Washington, D.C.

Melba Patillo Beals, one of the Little Rock Nine, graduated from San Francisco State University. She received a master's degree in journalism from Columbia University then worked for six years as a news reporter for NBC in San Francisco. She is the author of two memoirs, *Warriors Don't Cry*, based on her diaries at Central High, and *White Is a State of Mind*. She received a doctorate degree in education from the University of San Francisco and is Chair Emeritus of Communications and Media Studies at Dominican University of California.

Winthrop Rockefeller, a Republican who worked with Arkansas governor Orval Faubus and tried to resolve the Little Rock crisis before it escalated, was himself elected governor of Arkansas in 1967. He served until 1971. Rockefeller died in 1973.

CHAPTER FIVE

James Lawson, who led the Nashville workshops on nonviolence, went on a fact-finding mission to Vietnam in 1965. He participated in many antiwar protests. In 1968 he was chairman of the Memphis sanitation strike. Remaining active in the SCLC, in 1986 he hosted Bishop Desmond Tutu of South Africa on his visit to Los Angeles. Lawson was president of the Los Angeles chapter of the SCLC from 1979 to 1993. He served as pastor of the Holman United Methodist Church for twenty-five years until his retirement in 1999. After being expelled from Nashville's Vanderbilt University for his civil rights work in 1960, Lawson joined the faculty as distinguished visiting professor from 2006 to 2009. He donated his civil rights papers to Vanderbilt in 2013.

John Lewis, chairman of SNCC from 1963 to 1966, resigned from that organization in 1966 because of its increasing militancy. (He was replaced by Stokely Carmichael.) He later served as director of community organization projects for the Southern Regional Council. In 1970 Lewis was named director of the Voter Education Project. He first ran for Congress in 1986 and in the Democratic primary he unexpectedly defeated his closest rival—another former SNCC worker, Julian Bond. He continues to represent Georgia's 5th District in Congress. In 2013 Congressman Lewis and Vice President Joe Biden walked with more than five thousand people across Selma, Alabama's Edmund Pettus Bridge to commemorate the forty-eighth anniversary of "Bloody Sunday" and the march from Selma to Montgomery.

Diane Nash, a leader of the sit-in movement, moved to Chicago shortly after the Selma to Montgomery march. She became active in the antiwar movement and traveled to Hanoi as a guest of Vietnam's women's union in 1967. She was formerly married to fellow civil rights worker James Bevel. Nash continues to lecture on civil and human rights issues.

Ezell Blair, Jr., one of the first sit-in participants, was among thirteen founders of the National Conference on Black Power. He remained active in the civil rights movement, lecturing and working in a variety of positions. In 1970 he changed his name to Jibreel A-A. K-A. Khazan. He has worked with developmentally disabled people in New Bedford, Massachusetts, where he has lived since 1965. North Carolina A&T State University, his alma mater, holds an annual breakfast to commemorate the sit-in. Part of the Woolworth's lunch counter is now at the Smithsonian Museum of American History.

Ella Baker remained a key SNCC adviser and sat on the board of the Southern Conference Education Fund (SCEF). She was the subject of a documentary called *Fundi: The Story of Ella Baker*, which aired on PBS. In 1980 New York City held a tribute to Baker, who continued to live in Harlem until her death in 1986. SNCC Freedom Singer Bernice Johnson Reagon composed "Ella's Song" in her memory. The lyrics include Ella's own words: "We who believe in freedom cannot rest."

Harris Wofford was assistant director of the Peace Corps from 1964 to 1966. He served as president of Bryn Mawr College from 1970 to 1978 and practiced law in Philadelphia for seven years. He rejoined government as Pennsylvania's Secretary of Labor and Industry from 1987 to 1991, as a United States Senator from 1991 to 1994, and as chief executive officer of the federal agency that oversees domestic volunteer programs such as AmeriCorps from 1995

to 2001. Since his retirement in 2001, he has taught at the University of Maryland and volunteered for various charitable and service organizations. He received the 2012 Presidential Citizens Medal from President Obama.

Z. Alexander Looby, the attorney for the Nashville sit-in protestors whose home was bombed in 1961, became a Nashville city councilman. Looby died in 1972.

Ben West was Nashville's mayor from 1951 to 1963. He later served on several transportation boards, including the National Safety Council, and was a member of the President's Commission on Traffic Safety. West died in 1974.

James Farmer, who founded CORE in 1941 and served as its national director from 1961 to 1966, worked for a short time as assistant secretary for administration for the Department of Health, Education and Welfare during the Nixon administration. In 1975 he cofounded the Fund for an Open Society. His autobiography, *Lay Bare the Heart*, was published in 1985. He taught at Mary Washington College from 1984 to 1999. In 1998 he received the Presidential Medal of Freedom from President Bill Clinton. Farmer died in 1999 in Fredericksburg, Virginia.

Bull Connor, the Birmingham police commissioner, was forced out of office in 1963. In 1966, he suffered a stroke that left him confined to a wheelchair. He died in 1973.

James Peck filed suit against the FBI for failing to prevent the beating he received during the 1961 Freedom Ride. In 1975 Gary Thomas Rowe, Jr. testified to a Senate committee that while he was working as an undercover FBI informant, he participated in the beating and informed the FBI in advance that the local police were going to allow the beating to occur. A Federal judge granted Peck a settlement of $25,000 in 1983. That same year Peck suffered a stroke, which left him paralyzed on one side of his body. He died ten years later in a nursing home in Minneapolis.

John Seigenthaler began working for *The Tennessean* as a reporter in 1949. He left in 1961 to serve as administrative assistant to attorney general Robert F. Kennedy. Seigenthaler returned to the newspaper as editor in 1962 and later served as publisher and president until his retirement in 1991. From 1982 to 1991 he also served as founding editorial director of *USA Today*. The John Seigenthaler Center at Vanderbilt University houses the First Amendment Center, which he founded in 1991. He is currently host of the Nashville public television series *A Word on Words*.

CHAPTER SIX

Bernice Johnson Reagon, one of the original Freedom Singers from Albany, Georgia, was formerly married to fellow singer Cordell Reagon. They had two children, Toshi and Kwan. After their divorce, Reagon finished her undergraduate degree at Spelman College and earned a doctorate in history at Howard University. She was founder and artistic director of the a cappella group Sweet Honey in the Rock from 1973 to 2004. In 1974, she began working at the Smithsonian Institution, where she founded the program in Black American Culture at the National Museum of American History and served as curator of the Division of Community Life until 1993. While at the Smithsonian, she organized

national conferences on the music of the civil rights movement and produced the three-volume recording *Voices of the Civil Rights Movement*. She earned a Peabody Award for her work on the National Public Radio series *Wade in the Water: African American Sacred Music Traditions* and composed the score for the Peabody Award–winning television series *Africans in America*. Reagon is professor emeritus at American University. She and her daughter Toshi performed at the White House for President Obama in 2010 as part of a program on the music of the civil rights movement. Reagon continues to speak about the intersection of her work as an activist, scholar, performer, and composer.

Charles Sherrod, who helped organize the Albany community in 1961, left SNCC and Georgia to obtain a master's degree in sacred theology from Union Theological Seminary in New York City. He returned to Georgia and, with his wife Shirley, cofounded the Southwest Georgia Project for Community Education and a land trust for black farmers. From 1976 to 1990, he was a member of Albany's Board of City Commissioners. He also served as a prison chaplain and taught at Albany State University, which had banned him from campus during his days as a SNCC organizer. Sherrod currently is on the board of the Albany Civil Rights Institute.

Laurie Pritchett, the chief of police in Albany, Georgia, left that city in 1966 to become the police chief in High Point, North Carolina. He retired in 1974 and died in 2000.

Asa Kelley served as a judge in the Superior Court of Dougherty County, Georgia, from 1968 until his death in 1997. He was an advocate for prisoner rehabilitation and alternative sentencing for nonviolent criminals that included treatment for substance abuse and community service.

Andrew Young, executive vice president of the SCLC from 1967 to 1970, became a member of the Georgia delegation to the United States House of Representatives in 1972. He served as United States ambassador to the United Nations during the Carter administration. In 1981 he was elected mayor of Atlanta and was reelected for a second term in 1985. He lost in the Democratic primary for governor of Georgia in 1990. Young cochaired the committee that brought the Olympics to Atlanta in 1996. He has written two books, started the Andrew Young Foundation, and cofounded Why Tuesday, an organization that is proposing to move voting from Tuesday to the weekend to increase voter participation.

Wyatt T. Walker was chief of staff of the SCLC from 1960 to 1964. In 1964 he served as vice president of Educational Heritage, Inc., a publishing company. He has also been vice president of the Greater New York YMCA and special assistant to New York governor Nelson Rockefeller. Walker retired as pastor of the Canaan Baptist Church in Harlem in 2004 after thirty-seven years. He currently lives in Virginia.

Tom Hayden, who worked with SNCC, was one of the founders of Students for a Democratic Society (SDS), a California state assemblyman for ten years and a state senator for eight years. He has written or edited nineteen books and lectures frequently on a broad range of political issues. Hayden is currently director of the Peace and Justice Resource Center in Culver City, California.

Casey Hayden, a former SNCC staff worker in Mississippi, worked as a city administrator while Andrew Young was mayor of Atlanta. Her 1965 paper, written with fellow SNCC worker Mary King, "Sex and Caste: A King of Memo" influenced white feminists. Two memoirs of her work with SNCC have been included in the anthologies *Deep in Our Hearts* and *Hands on the Freedom Plow.* Formerly married to Tom Hayden, she now uses her birth name Sandra Cason and lives with her husband Paul Buckwalter in Tuscon, Arizona.

Bob Zellner, one of the first white Southerners to join SNCC, became an organizer for the Southern Conference Educational Fund as well as a union organizer in New Orleans. While finishing his PhD dissertation on the Southern civil rights movement, he taught at colleges in Pennsylvania and Long Island. His memoir *The Wrong Side of Murder Creek: A White Southerner in the Freedom Movement* is the basis of the 2013 Spike Lee film *Son of the South.* Zellner now lives in Southampton, New York.

Burke Marshall, former assistant attorney general, edited a book, *The Supreme Court and Human Rights* in 1982. At the time of his death in 2003, he was professor emeritus at Yale Law School, where he had taught since 1970.

Fred Shuttlesworth, founder of the Alabama Christian Movement for Human Rights and a cofounder of the SCLC, served as pastor of the Greater New Light Baptist Church in Cincinnati, Ohio, for forty years until he retired in 2006. He returned to live in Birmingham in 2008 for stroke treatment and died there in 2011. The Shuttlesworth Archive is based in the Cincinnati church he founded. The Birmingham-Shuttlesworth International Airport was renamed in his honor.

A. G. Gaston, the grandson of slaves, was one of the most successful black businessmen in the United States. His business enterprises included real estate, insurance, banking, and communications. He continued to be involved in his string of businesses until his death in 1996 at the age of 103.

James Bevel, an early Nashville student activist and a key SCLC worker in charge of direct action, became involved with the antiwar movement and influenced Dr. King's decision to come out against the war. After King's death, he was forced to leave the SCLC. He was Lyndon LaRouche's running mate in the 1992 presidential election and helped plan the Million Man March in 1995. Bevel was convicted of incest in 2008 and died the same year of pancreatic cancer.

The March on Washington

A. Philip Randolph, after the March on Washington in 1963, continued as president of the Negro American Labor Council. He was a founder and the first president of the A. Philip Randolph Institute of New York City, an organization that sponsors educational projects and fights for jobs in the skilled trades for blacks. Randolph died in 1979 at the age of ninety.

Bayard Rustin, an important early adviser to Martin Luther King, Jr., was a founder of the SCLC and deputy director of the March on Washington. Rustin cofounded and directed the AFL-CIO's A. Philip Randolph Institute and was co-chairman at the time of his death in 1987. He chaired the executive committee of the Leadership Conference on Civil Rights, was an active leader in the socialist party and its successor Social Democrats USA, and participated in election monitoring overseas for Freedom House. Throughout his life, he kept a low public profile because he was openly gay at a time of hostility toward gays and lesbians.

CHAPTER SEVEN

Myrlie Evers worked as a secretary for the NAACP with her husband Medgar. After Medgar's assassination, she continued to press for justice until Byron De La Beckwith's conviction thirty-one years later in 1994. Her book on Medgar, *For Us, the Living*, was produced as a television movie in 1982. Evers worked as vice president for an advertising firm in New York and then served as director of community relations for ARCO in Los Angeles. She remarried and, after her second husband died, became chairperson of the NAACP. During her tenure, she raised the funds to restore the NAACP's financial stability. She founded the Medgar Evers Institute in Jackson, Mississippi. In 2013 Myrlie Evers Williams became the first woman to deliver the invocation prayer at a presidential inauguration.

James Meredith, after graduating from Ole Miss in 1963, spent the next year at the University of Ibadan in Nigeria, West Africa. When he returned to this country, he enrolled at Columbia Law School. In 1966, before completing his studies, he led a March Against Fear in Mississippi. He was shot during the march. Civil rights leaders came to take his place but when Meredith recovered, he completed the march alongside them. He graduated from Columbia Law School, ran two unsuccessful campaigns for Congress as a Republican, and worked for U.S. Senator Jesse Helms. Meredith has written two books, *Three*

Years in Mississippi and *A Mission from God: A Memoir and Challenge for America*. He is currently a tree farmer in Jackson, Mississippi.

Amzie Moore remained an important and active leader in the Mississippi NAACP until his death in 1979, at age sixty-nine.

Robert Moses was a SNCC field organizer who coordinated voter registration in Mississippi during Freedom Summer in 1964. After leaving SNCC in 1966, he temporarily began using his middle name Parris instead of Moses. He spent two years in Canada to avoid the draft during the Vietnam War, taught math in Tanzania, and returned to the United States in 1976. While finishing his PhD dissertation in philosophy at Harvard, he began to teach algebra at his oldest daughter's school in Cambridge, Massachusetts. With funds from a 1982 MacArthur Fellowship, he started The Algebra Project to improve math literacy in the public schools and continues to serve as its president. He coauthored the book *Radical Equations: Civil Rights From Mississippi to the Algebra Project* and coedited *Quality Education as a Constitutional Right*. He has been a visiting professor at Cornell and at Princeton. His wife, Dr. Janet Moses, MD, is also a SNCC veteran.

Marion Barry was mayor of Washington, D.C., from 1979 to 1991. He served six months in prison after being convicted of crack cocaine possession. He was reelected as mayor in 1994. He is currently serving an eight-year term on the city council.

Constance Baker Motley, who represented James Meredith on behalf of the NAACP Legal Defense Fund, was elected to the New York State Senate in 1964. President Johnson named her a judge of the United States District Court for the Southern District of New York in 1967 and she continued to serve on that court until her death in 2005.

Unita Blackwell, active in the Mississippi Freedom Democratic Party (MFDP), became the first black woman to be elected mayor in Mississippi. She served as mayor of Mayersville from 1976 to 2001. During her time as mayor, she attended President Carter's Energy Summit at Camp David, earned a master's degree in regional planning from the University of Massachusetts–Amherst, and in 1990 was the first woman elected president of the National Conference of Black Mayors. She received a MacArthur Genius Fellowship in 1992. Her memoir, *Barefootin'*, was published in 2006. Blackwell was diagnosed with dementia in 2008.

Nicholas Katzenbach, who worked in the Justice Department for more than five years as assistant, deputy, acting, and then attorney general, was appointed United States under secretary of state in 1966. He joined IBM in 1969 and remained there until 1986, when he retired as senior vice president for law and external relations. Katzenbach then became a partner in a major law firm based in New Jersey. He died in 2012 at the age of ninety.

John Doar served as first assistant and then assistant attorney general in the Justice Department's Civil Rights Division from 1960 to 1967, the critical years of the civil rights movement. He would later serve as special counsel to the House of Representatives Judiciary Committee, which investigated Watergate and prepared articles of impeachment against President Nixon. He was awarded the Presidential Medal of Freedom in 2012. He still practices law in New York City.

John Salter has been engaged in activist-oriented community organization in the Pacific Northwest, Chicago, upstate New York, and the Navajo Nation, among other places. He retired in 1994 as professor of American Indian studies at the University of North Dakota and is author of *Jackson, Mississippi, An American Chronicle of Struggle and Schism*. He changed his name to John Hunter Gray and then to Hunter Gray to reflect his father's Native American ancestral name before his father's adoption by a white family named Salter. He is also known as Hunter Bear and lives in Idaho with his wife Eldri.

Charles Evers assumed the post of field director of the Mississippi NAACP after his brother Medgar was assassinated. He was mayor of Fayette, Mississippi, from 1969 to 1981 and from 1985 to 1989. He was the first black man since Reconstruction to be elected to any office in Mississippi. He was unsuccessful in campaigns for governor and for the United States Senate. *Have No Fear*, his autobiography written with Andrew Szanton, was published in 1997.

William Simmons was active in organizing the Jackson Citizens' Council and devoted much of his time to promoting the Citizens' Council movement, appearing on television and speaking before audiences through the United States. For many years he worked to establish independent schools through the South and served as president of the Southern Independent School Association. In later years he established The Fairview Inn, an award-winning bed and breakfast inn in his childhood family home in Jackson, which he operated until shortly before his death in 2007.

Allard Lowenstein was elected to the 91st Congress as a representative from the Fifth District of New York. He was a member of the Democratic National Committee from 1972 to 1976, an adviser to California governor Jerry Brown in 1975, and the United States representative to the United Nations Commission on Human Rights in 1977. Lowenstein was murdered in 1980.

Stokely Carmichael became chairman of SNCC in 1966 and was an advocate of black power. He left SNCC the following year and briefly joined the Black Panther Party. He changed his name to Kwame Toure to pay homage to African leaders Kwame Nkrumah and Ahmed Sekou Toure. In lectures across the world, he described himself as a pan-Africanist, believing Africa is home to all black people. He was arrested in his adopted homeland of Guinea in 1986 for allegedly advocating revolution against the military dictatorship of the West African country. He was released from jail after three days and continued to live in Guinea until his death in 1998 at the age of fifty-seven.

Fannie Lou Hamer, vice chairman of the MFDP, continued to work for civil rights in Mississippi. In addition, she started a pig cooperative and day-care center, remained active in state politics, and spoke on feminist and antiwar issues throughout the country. She died in 1977.

Joe Rauh, the counsel for the MFDP in Atlantic City, remained active in liberal politics throughout his life. He was counsel for the Leadership Conference on Civil Rights and worked with Clarence Mitchell in lobbying for the Voting Rights Acts of 1965, 1970, and 1975, the Fair Housing Act of 1968, and other civil rights legislation. In 1986, Rauh led the opposition to the nomination of Justice William Rehnquist for the position of chief justice of the Supreme Court. A year after his death in 1992, President Clinton awarded him the Presidential Medal of Freedom.

Lawrence Guyot, chairman of the MFDP, graduated from Rutgers University School of Law in 1972 and served on the Lawyers' Committee for Civil Rights Under Law from 1972 to 1974. In 1982 and 1986, he helped organize the Afro-American Cultural, Technological, and Scientific Olympics (ACTSO). Guyot retired from his work for the city of Washington, D.C., in 2005. He continued to speak out about voting rights and the civil rights movement until his death in 2012, a few weeks after the reelection of President Obama.

CHAPTER EIGHT

Clarence Mitchell, the "101st Senator," was legislative chairman of the Leadership Council on Civil Rights. In recognition of his pivotal role as a lobbyist for the Civil Rights Act of 1968, he was awarded the NAACP Spingarn Medal. He died in 1984.

Sheriff Jim Clark, after losing his bid for reelection in Selma, left that city and wrote a book entitled *I Saw Selma Raped.* He ran a mobile home dealership in Alexandria, Alabama, until he was arrested for smuggling marijuana and served nine months of a two-year sentence in federal prison. He died in 2007 in an Elba, Alabama, nursing home.

Joseph Smitherman, mayor of Selma during the Selma march, was mayor of that city for thirty-six years. After he renounced segregation, he gained some black support, but in 2000 lost his last race to a black computer consultant. He died in 2005.

Amelia Boynton (Robinson), a local leader of the Selma campaign, continued to work in the Alabama civil rights movement. She spent many years helping black farmers and people with housing difficulties resolve their problems. *Bridge Across the Jordan,* her autobiography, was published in 1991. She attended the Democratic National Convention in 2012 in a wheelchair at the age of 101. She now lives in Tuskegee, Alabama.

Roy Wilkins was executive secretary of the NAACP from 1955 until his retirement in 1977. He died in 1981.

Joseph Ellwanger was pastor of the Cross Lutheran Church in Milwaukee for thirty-four years until he retired in 2001. He was involved in the sanctuary movement for Guatemalan refugees. He wrote *Let My People Go,* a book on black history. Reverend Ellwanger and his wife Joyce received a Lifetime Achievement Award from the Wisconsin Network for Peace and Justice in 2012.

Sheyann Webb, who at age eight marched in Selma, coauthored a book, *Selma, Lord, Selma,* which was made into an ABC television movie in 1999. She started the K.E.E.P. Productions Youth Development Program in 1982. Sheyann Webb Christburg continues to speak across the country about her experiences during the Selma march. She is currently coordinator of student activities for Alabama State University.

Hosea Williams was national executive director of the SCLC from 1969 to 1971 and again from 1977 to 1979. In 1971 he founded the service organization Hosea Feed the Hungry and Homeless, which he ran for almost thirty years. In 1972 he became pastor of the Martin Luther King, Jr. People's Church of Love; *The Atlanta Constitution* reported that it had no sanctuary but did have a large bingo operation. In 1974, Williams was elected to the Georgia legislature and was a member until 1985. He later served on the Atlanta City Council and the DeKalb County Commission. In later years, he was arrested for traffic violations and served time in prison for leaving the scene of two accidents. Before he died in 2000, an Atlanta street was renamed Hosea L. Williams Drive.

George Wallace was reelected governor of Alabama in 1970, 1974, and 1982, the last with support from black voters. He survived an attempted assassination in 1972 but was paralyzed for life. He ran for president of the United States four times without success. He died in Montgomery, Alabama in 1998.

Orloff Miller, the Unitarian minister who traveled with James Reeb in Selma, created a ministry for AIDS patients in San Francisco as a field secretary for the AIDS Interfaith Network. There he met a German woman who became his wife. After his retirement as a Unitarian minister in 1991, Miller and his wife moved to southwestern Germany, where he served as minister at large for European Unitarians from 1993 to 2000. He currently lives in Ludwigshafen, Germany.

Notes

The primary sources used to compile this account of the American civil rights movement appear below. The interviews have been separated into two sections—those original to this project, and those from other oral-history collections. The chronologically shifting emphasis from books to interviews to magazine and newspaper coverage reflects the increased attention the media paid to the movement.

Some books were consulted for several chapters. These include *Before the Mayflower*, by Lerone Bennett, Jr.; *In Struggle*, by Clayborne Carson; *Encyclopedia of Black America*, edited by W. Augustus Low and Virgil A. Clift; *The Origins of the Civil Rights Movement*, by Aldon D. Morris; *Let the Trumpet Sound*, by Stephen B. Oates; *My Soul Is Rested*, by Howell Raines; and *Fire in the Streets*, by Milton Viorst. Although used for general reference throughout this project, these books appear only in the chapter(s) for which they were a primary reference.

Chapter One

Books: *Unlikely Heroes*, by Jack Bass; *Before the Mayflower*, by Lerone Bennett, Jr.; *Eisenhower and Black Civil Rights*, by Robert Frederick Burk; *The Southern Case for School Segregation*, by James Kilpatrick; *Portrait of a Decade*, by Anthony Lewis; *Groundwork*, by Genna Rae McNeil; *Inside the Warren Court*, by Bernard Schwartz; *They Closed Their Schools*, by Bob Smith; *Standing Fast: The Autobiography of Roy Wilkins*, by Roy Wilkins.

We would specifically like to note Richard Kluger's book, *Simple Justice*, a masterful work without which we could not have written this chapter.

Articles: "The South Will Go Along," by Harold Fleming in *The New Republic*, May 31, 1954; "Attitudes Toward Desegregation," by Herbert Hyman and Paul Sheatsley, in *Scientific American*, December, 1956; "The Climax of an Era," by Carey McWilliams, in *The Nation*, May 29, 1954; "Segregation and the Supreme Court," by Arthur Sutherland, in *The Atlantic Monthly*, July, 1954.

Newspapers: *Birmingham Post Herald*, May 19, 1954; *New York Times*, May 18, 1954; *Washington Post*, May 19, 1954.

Interviews: From the Ralph J. Bunche Oral History Collection, housed at the Moorland-Spingarn Research Center, Howard University, we drew interviews with Wiley Branton, Dr. Kenneth Clark, William Coleman, Charles Duncan, Arthur Fletcher, George Hayes, Thurgood Marshall, James Nabrit, Herbert Reed, Frank Reeves, and June Schagaloff.

Eyes on the Prize Interviews: We spoke with James Bash, Eliza Briggs, Harry Briggs, Jr., Harry Briggs, Sr., Herbert Brownell, Robert Carter, Dr. Kenneth Clark, William

Coleman, Linda Brown Smith, Vanessa Venable, Thomas R. Waring, Robert Williams, Paul E. Wilson, and Judge John Minor Wisdom.

Chapter Two

Books: *Time Bomb*, by Olive Arnold Adams; *Wolfwhistle*, by William Bradford Huie; *Coming of Age in Mississippi*, by Anne Moody.

Articles: "Shocking Story of Approved Killing in Mississippi," by William Bradford Huie, in *Look*, January 24, 1956; "What Happened to the Emmett Till Killers?" by William Bradford Huie, in *Look*, January 22, 1957; "Reflections on a Murder: The Emmett Till Case," by William M. Simpson, in *Southern Miscellany: Essays on History in Honor of Glover Moore*.

Newspapers: *Chicago Defender*, July 2, 9, 1955; August 13, 20, 27, 1955; September 7, 10, 17, 24, 1955; *Cleveland Call and Post*, September 24, 1955; October 1, 8, 15, 22, 1955; *Greenville Delta Democrat-Times*, September 21, 1955; *Greenwood Commonwealth*, September 21, 22, 1955; *Pittsburg Courier*, August 20, 27, 1955; September 10, 17, 1955; October 1, 8, 1955.

Eyes on the Prize Interviews: Charles Diggs, Myrlie Evers, James L. Hicks, William B. Huie, Curtis Jones.

Chapter Three

Books: *Outside the Magic Circle*, by Virginia Foster Durr; *Stride Toward Freedom*, by Martin Luther King, Jr.; *King: A Critical Biography*, by David Lewis; *The Origins of the Civil Rights Movement*, by Aldon D. Morris; *Let the Trumpet Sound*, by Stephen B. Oates; *My Soul is Rested*, by Howell Raines; *Odyssey: Journey Through Black America*, by Earl and Miriam Selby.

Articles: "Origins of the Montgomery Bus Boycott," by David J. Garrow, in *Southern Changes*, October-December, 1985; "Challenge and Response in the Montgomery Bus Boycott of 1955-1956," by J. Mills Thornton, in *Alabama History Review*, July 1980; "The Walking City, A History of the Montgomery Boycott," a series by Norman W. Walton, in *The Negro History Bulletin*, October 6, 1956, November 20, 1956, February 20, 1957, April 20, 1957, and January 21, 1958.

Newspapers: *Montgomery Advertiser*, December 1955 through April 1956.

Eyes on the Prize Interviews: Rev. Ralph Abernathy, Joseph Azbell, Virginia Durr, Georgia Gilmore, Donie Jones, Coretta Scott King, Rufus A. Lewis, E. D. Nixon, Rosa Parks, Jo Ann Robinson.

Chapter Four

Books: *The Long Shadow of Little Rock*, by Daisy Bates; *Crisis in the South: A Selection of Editorials from the Arkansas Gazette; Growing Up Southern*, edited by Chris Mayfield; *The Little Rock Crisis*, by Tony Freyer; *Crisis at Central High*, by Elizabeth Huckaby; *Little Rock U.S.A.: Materials for Analysis*, by Wilson Record and Jane Cassels Record.

Articles: *Time*, September 23, 1957 and October 7, 1957.

Newspapers: *Arkansas Democrat*, September 23, 1957; *New York Times*, September 23-26, 1957; *Washington Post*, September 22, 1957; *Washington Star*, September 25, 26, 1957.

Interviews: From the Ralph J. Bunche Oral History Collection, Moorland-Spingarn Research Center: Wiley Branton, Luther Hodges.

Eyes on the Prize **Interviews:** Harold Engstrom, Orval Faubus, Ernest Green, Marcia Webb Lecky, Melba Pattillo Beals, Craig Rains, Arthur Shores.

Chapter Five

Books: *Transformation of Southern Politics*, by Jack Bass and Walter De Vries; *John F. Kennedy and the Second Reconstruction*, by Carl Brauer; *In Struggle*, by Clayborne Carson; *Nashville Since the 1920s*, by Don H. Doyle; *Lay Bare the Heart*, by James Farmer; *Black Protest*, edited by Joanne Grant; *Black Ballots*, by Steven F. Lawson; *The New Negro*, edited by LeRoy Locke; *CORE*, by August Meier and Elliott Rudwick; *Kennedy Justice*, by Victor Navasky; *Freedom Ride*, by James Peck; *My Soul Is Rested*, by Howell Raines; *A Thousand Days*, by Arthur Schlesinger, Jr.; *Robert Kennedy and His Times*, by Arthur Schlesinger, Jr.; *Negroes With Guns*, by Robert F. Williams; *Of Kennedys and Kings*, by Harris Wofford.

Articles: "Bigger Than a Hamburger," by Ella J. Baker, in *The Southern Patriot*, June 1960; "A Conference on the Sit-ins," by Ted Dienstfrey, in *Commentary*, June 29, 1960; "Southern Students Take Over," by Helen Fuller, in *The New Republic*, May 2, 1960; "We Are All So Very Happy," by Helen Fuller, in *The New Republic*, April 25, 1960; "The Negro Revolt Against 'The Negro Leaders,'" by Louis E. Lomax, in *Harper's Magazine*, June 1960; "Evolution of Non-Violence," by Carleton Mabee, in *The Nation*, August 12, 1961; "In Pursuit of Freedom," by William Mahoney in *Liberation*, September 1961; "Sit-Ins: The Students Report," edited by Jim Peck, published May 1960 by The Congress of Racial Equality, New York, New York; *Report of the Raleigh Conference*, by the Student Nonviolent Coordinating Committee; "The Montgomery Freedom Rider Riots of 1961," by J. Mills Thornton III (paper delivered at the annual meeting of the Alabama Historical Association in Florence, Alabama, April 28, 1984).

Newspapers: *The Afro American*, April 23, 30, 1960; *Atlanta Constitution*, February 1956; March 9, 1960; May 18, 22, 24-26, 1960; May 5, 6, 9, 10, 15-20, 22-25, 27, 29, 30, 1961; *Chicago Defender*, March 26, 1960; April 2, 9, 16, 23, 30, 1960; May 7, 14, 21, 28, 1960; June 4, 11, 1960; *Christian Science Monitor*, August 31, 1960; October 20, 24, 29, 1960; January 1, 1961; February 9, 1961; *Cincinnati Post & Times Star*, April 30, 1960; *CORE-LATOR* (CORE monthly newspaper), September 1960; *The Evening Star*, October 13, 24, 1960; February 2, 7, 26, 1961; March 2, 3, 7, 8, 11, 17, 20, 1961; August 20, 1961; November 18, 1961; February 2, 1980; *Jackson Star-Times*, March 27, 1961; *Montgomery Advertiser*, May 22-24, 1960; *New York Times*, February 14, 15, 1960; January 29, 1961; February 6, 19, 1961; March 7, 17, 20, 1961; *Philadelphia Tribune*, March 1, 1960; *Southern School Reporting Service*, April 1960; *Washington Daily News*, March 7, 1961; *Washington Post*, March 22, 1960; April 23, 1960; November 26, 27, 29, 1960; December 24, 1960; February 7, 13, 23, 24, 1961; March 28, 1961; May 25, 1961; August 21, 24, 1961.

Interviews: From the oral history collection of the John F. Kennedy library: conversations between Robert F. Kennedy and Burke Marshall; an interview with Burke Marshall. From The Civil Rights Documentation Project: Ella Baker.

Eyes on the Prize **Interviews:** Will D. Campbell, Gordon Carey, James Farmer, Nicholas Katzenbach, James M. Lawson, Jr., Fred Leonard, John Lewis, Leo Lillard, Diane Nash, James Peck, Bernie Schweid, John Seigenthaler, Rev. C. T. Vivian, Harris Wofford.

Chapter Six

Books: *The Making of Black Revolutionaries*, by James Forman; *The FBI and Martin Luther King, Jr.*, by David Garrow; *King: A Critical Biography*, by David Lewis; *Let the Trumpet Sound*, by Stephen B. Oates; *Southern Businessmen and Desegregation*, edited by Elizabeth Jacoway and David Colburn; *Down to Now*, by Pat Watters.

Articles: Bains, Lee. "Birmingham, 1963: Confrontation Over Civil Rights." Senior thesis, Harvard College, 1977. From *The Journal of Southwest Georgia History*, Fall, 1984: "SNCC and the Albany Movement," by Clayborne Carson; "The Albany Movement: A Chapter in the Life of Martin Luther King, Jr.," by Stephen B. Oates; "'De Lawd' Descends and Is Crucified: Martin Luther King, Jr. in Albany, Georgia," by John A. Ricks III.

Newspapers: *Pittsburg Courier*, December 23, 30, 1961; January 6, 13, 20, 1962; February 24, 1962; March 3, 10, 31, 1962; April 21, 1962; May 12, 1962; August 4, 11, 18, 1962; September 22, 29, 1962.

Interviews: From the oral history collection of the John F. Kennedy Library: Robert F. Kennedy, Burke Marshall.

Eyes on the Prize Interviews: Dr. William G. Anderson, James Armstrong, Mel Bailey, Rev. James C. Bevel, Rev. Joseph Ellwanger, Don Evans, A. G. Gaston, Patricia Harris, Bernice Johnson, Rudolf Lee, Laurie Pritchett, Charles Sherrod, Rev. Fred Shuttlesworth, David J. Vann, Rev. Wyatt T. Walker.

March On Washington

Books: *The Making of Black Revolutionaries*, by James Forman; *Fire in the Streets*, by Milton Viorst.

Eyes on the Prize Interviews: Rev. Ralph Abernathy, James Forman, Corretta Scott King, Bayard Rustin.

Chapter Seven

Books: *Integration at Ole Miss*, by Russell Barrett; *The Rise of Massive Resistance*, by Newman Bartley; *Unlikely Hereos*, by Jack Bass; *Freedom Summer*, by Sally Belfrage; *For Us, The Living*, by Myrlie Evers; *The Making of Black Revolutionaries*, by James Forman; *The Summer That Didn't End*, by Len Holt; *The Past That Would Not Die*, by Walter Lord; *Mississippi: The Long Hot Summer*, by William McCord; *The Martyrs*, by Jack Mendelsohn; *Three Years in Mississippi*, by James Meredith; *Kennedy Justice*, by Victor Navasky; *Mississippi: The Closed Society*, by James Silver; *Stranger at the Gates*, by Tracy Sugarman; *Mississippi Notebook*, by Nicholas Von Hoffman; *Letters From Mississippi*, edited by Elizabeth Sutherland; *Climbing Jacob's Ladder*, by Pat Watters and Reese Cleghorn; *Attack on Terror: The FBI Against the Ku Klux Klan*, by Don Whitehead.

Newspapers: *New York Times*, June 28-July 9, 1964.

Articles: "Congressional Committee Report on What Happened When Schools Were Integrated in Washington, D.C.," a pamphlet published by the Citizens' Council of Greenwood, Mississippi; "Why I Live in Mississippi," by Medgar Evers, in *Ebony,* September 1963; "How a Secret Prevented a Massacre at Ole Miss," by George B. Leonard, T. George Harris, and Christopher S. Wren, in *Look*, December 31, 1962.

Eyes on the Prize Interviews: Unita Blackwell, Hodding Carter III, Dave Dennis, John Doar, Darrell Evers, Myrlie Evers, James Forman, Victoria Gray-Adams, Lawrence Guyot, Casey Hayden, Tom Hayden, Erle Johnston, Nicholas Katzenbach, John Lewis, Walter Mondale, Amzie Moore, Robert Moses, Peter Orris, Joseph Rauh, William J. Simmons, Kwame Toure (Stokely Carmichael), and Hollis Watkins.

Chapter Eight

Books: *Bridge Across Jordan*, by Amelia Platts Boynton; *Selma 1965*, by Charles Fager; *The Making of Black Revolutionaries*, by James Forman; *Protest at Selma*, by David Garrow; *Lyndon*, by Merle Miller; *Selma, Lord, Selma*, by Sheyann Webb and Rachel West Nelson with Frank Sikora; *The Longest Debate*, by Charles and Barbara Whalen.

Newspapers: *Atlanta Constitution*, February 1965; March 1, 2, 7, 9-14, 1965; *Baltimore Sun*, March 10, 1965; *New York Times*, February 1, 5, 8, 12, 19, 25, 1965; March 1, 2, 7, 9-14, 1965.

Articles: "How a Movement Begins," by Alvin Adams, in *Jet*, March 18, 1965; "Malcolm X," by Alvin Adams, in *Jet*, March 18, 1965; "Young Man Tries to Register To Vote Five Times Before Death," by Alvin Adams, in *Jet*, March 18, 1965; "Against Great Odds . . . Southern Negroes Try," by James Austin, in *Community*, December 1963; "The Untold Story of the March to Montgomery," by Simeon Booker, in *Jet*, April 8, 1965; "To Witness," by V. Rev. Msgr. Daniel M. Cantwell, in *Community*, May 1965; "The Voter Registration Drive in Selma, Alabama," by John R. Fry, in *Presbyterian Life*, October 1963; "Beyond the Bridge," by Paul Good, in *The Reporter*, April 8, 1965; "Behind the Selma March," by Martin Luther King, Jr., in *The Saturday Review*, April 3, 1965; "New Radicals in Dixie," by Andrew Kopkind, in *The New Republic*, April 10, 1965; "Midnight Plane to Alabama," by George B. Leonard, in *The Nation*, May 10, 1965; "Enforcing Civil Rights," a letter from Burke Marshall, in *The New Republic*, November 16, 1963; "Tension, Not Split, in the Negro Ranks," by Arlie Schardt, in *The Christian Century*, May 12, 1965; "Southern Editors and Selma," by Donald R. Shanor, in *Journalism Quarterly*, Spring 1967; tributes to Clarence Mitchell by Gloster B. Current and Sen. Daniel Patrick Moynihan, in *The Crisis*, March 1984; "Registrations in Alabama," by Howard Zinn, in *The New Republic*, October 26, 1963.

Eyes on the Prize Interviews: Rev. James C. Bevel, Sheyann Webb Christburg, Jim Clark, Rev. Joseph Ellwanger, Rev. Dana Greeley, Rev. Orloff W. Miller, Rachel West Nelson, Rev. Frederick D. Reese, Amelia Boynton Robinson, Normareen Shaw, Joseph Smitherman, Albert Turner, Richard Valeriani, C. T. Vivian, George C. Wallace, Ralph W. Yarborough, and Andrew Young.

Selected Bibliography

Adams, Olive Arnold. Time Bomb: *Mississippi Exposed and the Full Story of Emmett Till*. The Mississippi Regional Council of Negro Leadership, 1956.

Bains, Lee, Jr. "Birmingham, 1963: Confrontation Over Civil Rights." Senior thesis, Harvard College, 1977.

Barrett, Russell. *Integration at Ole Miss*. Chicago: Quadrangle Books, 1965.

Bartley, Numan. *The Rise of Massive Resistance*. Baton Rouge: Louisiana State University Press, 1969.

Bass, Jack. *Unlikely Heroes*. New York: Simon and Schuster, 1981.

Bass, Jack, and Walter De Vries. *Transformation of Southern Politics: Social Change and Political Consequence Since 1945*. New York: Basic Books, 1976.

Bates, Daisy. *The Long Shadow of Little Rock: A Memoir*. New York: David McKay, 1962.

Belfrage, Sally. *Freedom Summer*. New York: Viking, 1965.

Bennett, Lerone, Jr. *Before the Mayflower: A History of Black America* (fifth edition). New York: Penguin, 1984.

Brauer, Carl M. *John F. Kennedy and the Second Reconstruction*. New York: Columbia University Press, 1977.

Burk, Robert Frederick. *The Eisenhower Administration and Black Civil Rights*. Knoxville: University of Tennessee Press, 1984.

Carson, Clayborne. *In Struggle: SNCC and the Black Awakening of the 1960s*. Cambridge: Harvard University Press, 1981.

Crisis in the South: A Selection of Editorials from the Arkansas Gazette. Little Rock, 1958.

Doyle, Don. *Nashville Since the 1920s*. Knoxville: University of Tennessee Press, 1985.

Evers, Myrlie. *For Us, The Living*. Garden City, New York: Doubleday, 1967.

Fager, Charles E. *Selma 1965* (second edition). Boston: Beacon Press, 1985.

Farmer, James. *Lay Bare the Heart: An Autobiography of the Civil Rights Movement*. New York: Arbor House, 1985.

Forman, James. *The Making of Black Revolutionaries*. New York: Macmillan, 1972.Washington, D.C.: Open Hand, 1985.

Franklin, John Hope. *From Slavery to Freedom: A History of Negro Americans* (third edition). New York: Vintage Books, 1967.

Freyer, Tony. *The Little Rock Crisis: A Constitutional Interpretation*. Westport, Connecticut: Greenwood Press, 1984.

Garrow, David J. *The FBI and Martin Luther King, Jr*. New York: W. W. Norton, 1981.

———. *Protest at Selma*. New Haven: Yale University Press, 1978.

Grant, Joanne, ed. *Black Protest: History, Documents, and Analyses, 1619 to the Present*. New York: Fawcett World Library, 1968.

Hamer, Fannie Lou. *To Praise Our Bridges: An Autobiography*. Jackson: KIPCO, 1967.

Harding, Vincent. *The Other American Revolution*. Los Angeles: Center for Afro-American Studies, 1980.

———. *There Is A River: The Black Struggle for Freedom in America*. New York: Harcourt, Brace, Jovanovich, 1981.

Hentoff, Nat. *Peace Agitator: The Story of A. J. Muste*. New York: Macmillan, 1963.

Holt, Len. *The Summer That Didn't End*. New York: Morrow, 1965.

Huckaby, Elizabeth. *The Crisis at Central High: Little Rock, 1957-58*. Baton Rouge: Louisiana State University Press, 1980.

Jacoway, Elizabeth, and David R. Colburn, eds. *Southern Businessmen and Desegregation*. Baton Rouge: Louisiana State University Press, 1982.

Kilpatrick, James. *The Southern Case for School Segregation*. New York: Crown-Collier, 1962.

King, Martin Luther, Jr. *Stride Toward Freedom: The Montgomery Story*. New York: Harper, 1958.

———. *Why We Can't Wait*. New York: Harper and Row, 1964.

Kluger, Richard. *Simple Justice*. New York: Alfred A. Knopf, 1975.

Lawson, Steven F. *Black Ballots: Voting Rights in the South*. New York: Columbia University Press, 1976.

Lewis, Anthony, and the *New York Times*. *Portrait of a Decade: The Second American Revolution*. New York: Random House, 1964.

Lewis, David. *King: A Critical Biography*. New York: Prager, 1970.

Locke, Alain LeRoy, ed. *The New Negro*. New York: Atheneum, 1975.

Loewen, James W., and Charles Sallis, eds. *Mississippi: Conflict and Change*. New York: Pantheon, 1980.

Lord, Walter. *The Past That Would Not Die*. New York: Harper and Row, 1965.

Low, W. Augustus, and Virgil A. Clift, eds. *Encyclopedia of Black America*. New York: McGraw-Hill, 1981.

Mayfield, Chris, ed. *Growing Up Southern: Southern Exposure Looks at Childhood, Then and Now*. New York: Pantheon, 1981.

McCord, William. *Mississippi: The Long Hot Summer*. New York: Norton, 1965.

McNeil, Genna Rae. *Groundwork: Charles Hamilton Houston and the Struggle for Civil Rights*. Philadelphia: University of Pennsylvania Press, 1983.

Meier, August, and Elliott Rudwick. *CORE: A Study in the Civil Rights Movement 1942-1968*. Urbana: University of Illinois Press, 1975.

Mendelsohn, Jack. *The Martyrs: Sixteen Who Gave Their Lives For Racial Justice*. New York: Harper, 1966.

Meredith, James Howard. *Three Years in Mississippi*. Bloomington: Indiana University Press, 1966.

Miller, Merle. *Lyndon, an Oral Biography*. New York: G. P. Putnam's Sons, 1980.

Moody, Anne. *Coming of Age in Mississippi*. New York: Dial Press, 1968.

Morris, Aldon D. *The Origins of the Civil Rights Movement*. New York: The Free Press, 1984.

Navasky, Victor S. *Kennedy Justice*. New York: Atheneum, 1971.

The Negro Handbook. Chicago: Johnson Publishing Company, 1966.

Oates, Stephen B. *Let the Trumpet Sound: The Life of Martin Luther King, Jr.* New York: Harper and Row, 1982.

Peck, James. *Freedom Ride*. New York: Simon and Schuster, 1962.

Raines, Howell. *My Soul is Rested*. New York, G. P. Putnam's Sons, 1977.

Record, Wilson, and Jane Cassels Record, eds. *Little Rock, U.S.A.: Materials for Analysis*. San Francisco: Chandler, 1960.

Schlesinger, Arthur, Jr. *A Thousand Days: John F. Kennedy in the White House*. Boston: Houghton Mifflin, 1965.

———. *Robert Kennedy and His Times*. Boston: Houghton Mifflin, 1978.

Schwartz, Bernard, with Steven Lesher. *Inside the Warren Court*. Garden City, New York: Doubleday, 1983.

Selby, Earl, and Miriam Selby. *Odyssey: Journey Through Black America*. New York: G. P. Putnam's Sons, 1971.

Silver, James. *Mississippi: The Closed Society*. New York: Harcourt, Brace and World, 1966.

Simpson, William M. "Reflections on a Murder: The Emmett Till Case." In *Southern Miscellany: Essays on History in Honor of Glover Moore*, edited by Frank Allen Dennis. Jackson: University Press of Mississippi, 1981.

Smith, Bob. *They Closed Their Schools: Prince Edward County, Virginia, 1951-1964*. Chapel Hill: University of North Carolina Press, 1965.

Sugarman, Tracy. *Stranger at the Gates: A Summer in Mississippi*. New York: Hill and Wang, 1966.

Sutherland, Elizabeth, ed. *Letters from Mississippi*. New York: McGraw, 1965.

Viorst, Milton. *Fire in the Streets: America in the 1960s*. New York: Simon and Schuster, 1979.

Von Hoffmann, Nicholas. *Mississippi Notebook*. New York: D. White, 1964.

Watters, Pat. *Down to Now: Reflections on the Southern Civil Rights Movement*. New York: Pantheon, 1971.

Watters, Pat, and Reese Cleghorn. *Climbing Jacob's Ladder: The Arrival of Negroes in Southern Politics*. New York: Harcourt, Brace and World, 1967.

Webb, Sheyann, and Rachel West Nelson, with Frank Sikora. *Selma, Lord, Selma: Girlhood Memories of the Civil-Rights Days*. University of Alabama Press, 1980.

Whalen, Charles, and Barbara Whalen. *The Longest Debate*. New York: Mentor, 1985.

Whitehead, Don. *Attack on Terror: The FBI Against the Ku Klux Klan in Mississippi*. New York: Funk and Wagnalls, 1970.

Williams, Robert F. *Negroes With Guns*. Edited by Marc Schleifer. Chicago: Third World Press, 1973.

Wilkins, Roy, with Tom Mathews. *Standing Fast: The Autobiography of Roy Wilkins*. New York: Viking, 1982.

Wofford, Harris. *Of Kennedys and Kings: Making Sense of the Sixties*. New York: Farrar, Straus, Giroux, 1980.

Credits

Chapter One

Page 1: AP/Wide World; page 3: Moorland-Spingarn Research Center; page 4: Moorland-Spingarn Research Center; page 6: all from NAACP; page 8: Smithsonian Institute: page 12: all from Library of Congress; page 13 (top): Elliott Erwitt/ Magnum Photos, Inc.; (bottom left and right): Leonard Freed/ Magnum Photos, Inc.; page 14: Moorland-Spingarn Research Center, Howard University; page 22: courtesy Life Picture Service, *Life Magazine*, © 1954, Time, Inc. Photos by Robert W. Kelley, Robert Phillips/Black Star, Hank Walker, Carl Iwasaki, and George Skadding; (bottom center): also courtesy of the Brown Family Collection; page 25: NAACP; page 26 (top): NAACP; (bottom): George Tames/The *New York Times*; page 34: AP/Wide World.

Chapter Two

Page 36: Library of Congress/Ben Shahn; page 38: AP/Wide World; page 39; Dan Weiner, Courtesy of Sandra Weiner; page 40 (left): AP/Wide World; (top right and bottom): Ed Clark, *Life Magazine*, © 1955, Time, Inc.; page 43: The *Chicago Defender*; page 44: AP/Wide World; page 45: all from Ed Clark, *Life Magazine*, © 1955, Time, Inc.; page 47: AP/Wide World; page 50: Ernest C. Withers, Sr.; page 53: all from UPI/Bettmann Newsphotos.

Chapter Three

Page 58: Tommy Giles; page 60: Dan Weiner, Courtesy of Sandra Weiner; page 63: Tommy Giles; page 64: Highlander Research and Education Center Archives; page 68 (top): Courtesy of Jo Ann Robinson; (bottom): Arthur L. Freeman; page 71: AP/Wide World; page 74: AP/Wide World; page 75 (top): Dan Weiner, Courtesy of Sandra Weiner; (bottom): AP/Wide World; page 76: Dan Weiner, Courtesy of Sandra Weiner; page 80: all from Dan Weiner, Courtesy of Sandra Weiner; page 83: AP/Wide World; page 84: all from Dan Weiner, Courtesy of Sandra Weiner; page 86 (top): AP/Wide World; (bottom left): Dan Weiner, Courtesy of Sandra Weiner; (bottom right): Don Cravens; page 88: Courtesy of T.M. Alexander.

Chapter Four

Page 90: UPI/Bettmann Newsphotos; page 92: The *New York Times*; page 93: UPI/Bettmann Newsphotos; page 94: UPI/ Bettmann Newsphotos; page 95: AP/Wide World; page 98 (top): UPI/Bettmann Newsphotos; (bottom): *Arkansas Gazette*; page 101: UPI/Bettmann Newsphotos; page 102: *Arkansas Gazette*; page 103: UPI/Bettmann Newsphotos; page 105: AP/ Wide World; page 111 (top): Thomas McAvoy, *Life Magazine*, © Time, Inc.; (center): Burt Glinn/Magnum Photos, Inc.; (bottom left): AP/Wide World; page 113: UPI/Bettmann Newsphotos; page 117: Courtesy of Louisianna University Press; page 118: AP/Wide World.

Chapter Five

Page 120: Bruce Davidson/Magnum Photos, Inc.; page 123: *The Southern Patriot*, Courtesy of Anne Braden; page 124: Courtesy of the Fellowship of Reconciliation; page 128 (top): courtesy of Diane Nash; (bottom): photo by Jack Moebes/ Greensboro News and Record; page 131: The *Tennessean*; page 134: all from AP/Wide World; page 137: *The Southern Patriot*, Courtesy of Anne Braden; page 138: George Tames/The *New York Times*; page 141 (top): UPI/Bettmann Newsphotos; (bottom): *Greenville News-Piedmont Co.*/James G. Wilson; page 144: A Philip Randolph Institute; page 146: AP/ Wide World; page 149: National Archives (306-PS- #819-63- 4063); page 150: all from UPI/Bettmann Newsphotos; page 152: Tommy Giles; page 154: UPI/Bettmann Newsphotos; page 155: The *Tennessean*; page 156 (top): UPI/Bettmann Newsphotos; (bottom): AP/Wide World.

Chapter Six

Page 162: Bruce Davidson/Magnum Photos, Inc.; page 166 (top): Library of Congress; (bottom): Danny Lyon/Magnum Photos, Inc.; page 169: UPI/Bettmann Newsphotos; page 174: AP/Wide World; page 175: UPI/Bettmann Newsphotos; page 176: Joe Alper; page 180 (bottom): Danny Lyon/Magnum Photos, Inc.; (top): The *Birmingham News*; page 185: all from Charles Moore/Black Star; page 191: Charles Moore/Black Star; page 192 (top): Charles Moore/Black Star; (bottom): UPI/ Bettmann Newsphotos; page 195: *Birmingham Post-Herald*.

March On Washington Interlude

Page 196: Fred Ward/Black Star; page 198: A. Philip Randolph Institute; page 199: UPI/Bettmann Newsphotos; page 200: all from Library of Congress; page 201: Danny Lyons/Magnum Photos, Inc.; page 202: Ken Thompson; page 203: Bob Adelman/Magnum Photos, Inc.

Chapter Seven

Page 206: Tamio Wakayama; page 210: NAACP; page 214: UPI/ Bettmann Newsphotos; page 217: Dan J. McCoy/Black Star; page 223: UPI/Bettmann Newsphotos; page 225: UPI/ Bettmann Newsphotos; page 226: photo no. AR 8255-3K John F. Kennedy Library; page 227 (top): Courtesy of Mary Lee Moore; (bottom): Ken Thompson; page 232: Lyndon B. Johnson Library; page 233: AP/Wide World; page 235: © 1978 Matt Herron; page 236 (top left): © 1978 Matt Herron; (top center): Bob Fletcher/SNCC Photo; (bottom left): Danny Lyon/ Magnum Photos, Inc.; (bottom right): © 1978 Matt Herron; page 237 (top left): Tamio Wakayama; (top right): Charles Moore/Black Star; (bottom left): © 1978 Matt Herron; (bottom right): Ken Thompson; page 238: Courtesy of the F.B.I.; page 239: © 1978 Matt Herron; page 241: UPI/Bettmann Newsphotos; page 244: UPI/Bettmann Newsphotos; page 246: © 1978 Matt Herron.

Chapter Eight

Staff

Eyes on the Prize: America's Civil Rights Years

A Production of Blackside, Inc.
Boston, Massachusetts

Executive Producer:
Henry Hampton

Book Staff:

Writer:
Juan Williams

Editorial Director:
Robert Lavelle

Picture Editor:
Frances Norris

Assistant Editor:
Bennett Singer

Senior Researcher:
Laurie Kahn-Leavitt

Manuscript Editor:
Hannah Benoit

Art Director:
Lisa DeFrancis

Reviewers:
Prudence Arndt
Orlando Bagwell
Ruth Batson
Callie Crossley
James A. DeVinney
Steve Fayer
Judy Richardson
Llewellyn Smith
Judith Vecchione

Adviser:
David Garrow
    Associate Professor of
    Political Science at the City
    College of New York and
    the City University Graduate
    Center

Additional Reviewers:
John Dittmer
    Associate Professor of
    History
    DePauw University
Steven Lawson
    Professor of History
    University of South Florida

Book Production:
Pond Press

Film Staff:

Executive Producer:
Henry Hampton

Series Senior Producer:
Judith Vecchione

Series Producer:
Jon Else

Series Consulting Executive Producer:
Michael Ambrosino

Producers:
Orlando Bagwell
Callie Crossley
James A. DeVinney
Judith Vecchione

Associate Producers:
Prudence Arndt
Llewellyn Smith

Series Writer:
Steve Fayer

Senior Researcher:
Laurie Kahn-Leavitt

Series Research Consultant:
Judy Richardson

Editors:
Daniel Eisenberg
Jeanne Jordan
Charles Scott

Assistant Editors:
Ann Bartholomew
MJ Doherty
Victoria Garvin

Stock Footage Coordinator:
Kenn Rabin

Production Manager:
Jo Ann Mathieu

Production Assistant:
Peter Montgomery

Editing Room Assistants:
Elizabeth Carver
Eliza Gagnon
Meredith Woods

Production Interns:
Renee Bovelle
Charisse Chavious
Gordon Eriksen
Theresa Garofalo
Rosiland Jordan
Ismael Ramirez
Joseph Rogers
Ruth Shupp
Lisa Silvera
Dawne Simon
Alfonzo Smith
Matthew Sucherman
Peter Vrooman

Series Academic Advisers:

Clayborne Carson
David Garrow
Vincent Harding
Darlene Clark Hine

Additional Academic Advisers:

Wiley Branton
John Dittmer
Tony Freyer
Paul Gaston
Steve Lawson
Genna Rae McNeil
Aldon Morris
J. Mills Thornton
Howard Zinn

Additional Staff:

Business Manager:
J. Benjamin Harris

Accountant:
Lorraine Flynn

Project Administrator:
Inez Robinson

Production Secretaries:
Sara Chazen
Karen Chase

Additional Publishing Staff

Director of Publishing:
Robert Lavelle

Telecourse Director/ Managing Editor:
Toby Kleban Levine

Educational Consultant and Editor of the School Reader:
Steven Cohen

Educational Consultant and Editor of the Community Guide:
Robert C. Hayden

National Advisory Board:

Reginald Alleyne, Esq.
Ruth M. Batson, co-chairperson
Mary Francis Berry
The Hon. Julian Bond
Joseph Breiteneicher, co-chairperson
Geoffrey Cowan, Esq
Edwin Dorn
Peter B. Edelman, Esq
Paul Fishman
Marion Fishman
Faith Griefen
Adelaide C. Gulliver
Charles V. Hamilton
Robert Hohler
Stephen Horn
Eliot Hubbard
Ellen Jackson
Willard R. Johnson
The Rev. Lawrence N. Jones
Vernon E. Jordan, Jr.
H. Peter Karoff
Melvin King
Thomas C. Layton
The Hon. John Lewis
The Rev. Jack Mendelsohn
The Hon. Parren Mitchell
Woodrow A. Myers, Jr., M.D.
Eleanor Holmes Norton
Alvin Poussaint, M.D.
Anne Poussaint
Kathryn C. Preyer
Robert O. Preyer
Ann E. Raynolds
Judy Sapers
Carl Sapers, Esq.
Muriel Snowden
Otto Snowden
Wallace Terry
Sue Bailey Thurman
Rutledge A. Waker
Laya Wiesner
Loretta J. Williams

Funders:

Eyes on the Prize is funded by public television stations, the Corporation for Public Broadcasting, and by major grants from the Ford Foundation, Lotus Development Corporation, and the Lilly Endowment. Additional funding has been provided by the Abelard Foundation, the Alabama Humanities Foundation, the Ruth Batson Educational Foundation, Bay Packaging and Converting Co., Inc., the Bird Companies Charitable Foundation, the Boston Foundation, the Boston Globe Foundation, the Columbia Foundation, Cummins Engine Corporation, the Maurice Falk Medical Fund, the Freed Foundation, Freedom House, the Charles Friedman Family Foundation, the Georgia Council on the Humanities, the Wallace Alexander Gerbode Foundation, the Richard and Rhoda Goldman Fund, the Irving I. Goldstein Foundation, the Edward W. Hazen Foundation, Hillsdale Fund, Inc., the Charles Evans Hughes Foundation, the Hyams Trust, Joint Foundation Support, Inc., the Kraft Foundation, the Metropolitan Foundation of Atlanta, the Mississippi Council on the Humanities, the Model Fund, the New York Community Trust, the PBS Program Fund, the Philadelphia Foundation, the Polaroid Foundation, the Mary Norris Preyer Fund, Raytheon Company, the Rockefeller Foundation, the San Francisco Foundation, the Sapelo Island Research Center, Sun Company, the Tides Foundation, and the Villers Foundation.

Special thanks to the Charles H. Revson Foundation, for their support of *Eyes on the Prize*.

Index

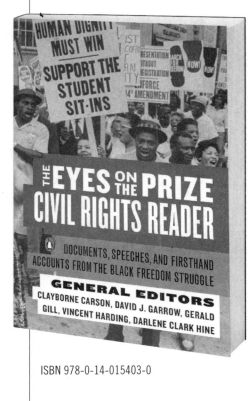